L C

Lincoln Christian College

£4.24

D1257455

LETTERS OF
ST. PAULINUS OF NOLA

ANCIENT CHRISTIAN WRITERS

THE WORKS OF THE FATHERS IN TRANSLATION

EDITED BY

JOHANNES QUASTEN   WALTER J. BURGHARDT

THOMAS COMERFORD LAWLER

No. 36

WESTMINSTER, MARYLAND
THE NEWMAN PRESS

LONDON
LONGMANS, GREEN AND CO.
1968

LETTERS OF
ST. PAULINUS OF NOLA

TRANSLATED AND ANNOTATED

BY

P. G. WALSH
Department of Humanity
University of Edinburgh

VOLUME II

Letters 23–51

WESTMINSTER, MARYLAND
THE NEWMAN PRESS

LONDON
LONGMANS, GREEN AND CO.
1968

THE NEWMAN PRESS
WESTMINSTER, MD., U.S.A.

LONGMANS, GREEN AND CO. LTD
48 GROSVENOR STREET, LONDON W 1

*Associated companies, branches and representatives
throughout the world*

First published in U.S.A. 1967
First published in Great Britain 1968

LIBRARY OF CONGRESS CARD NUMBER: 66–28933

De Licentia Superioris S.J.
Nihil obstat: J. QUASTEN, cens. dep.

Imprimatur: PATRICIUS A. O'BOYLE, D.D., Archiep. Washingtonen.
d. 19 Maii 1966

© 1967 BY REV. JOHANNES QUASTEN,
REV. WALTER J. BURGHARDT, S.J., AND
THOMAS COMERFORD LAWLER

PRINTED IN THE UNITED STATES OF AMERICA

CONTENTS

270.20924
P 32
V. 2.

LETTERS OF
ST. PAULINUS OF NOLA

LETTER 23

To Severus[1]

Paulinus greets his brother Severus.

1. Why do you seek to exact more love from me?[2] Totality does not allow of increase. If the sea can overflow its barriers, if all that is naturally full can experience a short-lived increase, then my love for you can be enhanced. I maintain that love in its fulness within its proper limit, for I love you as myself, and just as I cannot add a cubit to my stature,[3] so I cannot increase my love for you.

Yet I place no limit on my longing. You think that you do enough for me by that constant honour and devotion by which you try, with such regular letters, to compensate me for your absence. But instead you awake the gluttony of my love. Your failure to satisfy me with the pleasure of your letters is all the greater because by the very diligence and kindness of your words you awake in me a greater desire for seeing you in the flesh. For you are my brother in Christ, joined to me in such unique brotherhood.

Indeed, what greater attendance can be devoted to God or to one's neighbour than you show to Christ in my person? In Him are fulfilled both God's commands, for by the majesty of His nature He is our God, and by assuming our nature He became our neighbour. Therefore, as this care develops in you, your charity is perfected, boundless in its perfection because it is bounded in Christ, *of whose greatness there is no end.*[4]

I

But may our end be in Him, that we may live through Him without end, since Christ is the universal source (for all things are through Him)[5] and in particular the apex (since He is the head of the body of which we are members). *The Lord is sweet and righteous;*[6] He is sweet to me through your person. You are as great to me as is *the multitude of His sweetness.*[7] All of you, mind and tongue, I long for. Your savour is for me the sweetness of Christ, like a garden or *the smell of a plentiful field,*[8] a fragrance you have gained by hastening after the fragrance of His ointments.[9] You are His field as He in turn is ours, for in Him we sow and from Him we reap.

But the field which you are does not bristle with thorns, nor is it dry with sand, or rough and bare with rocky places, where the seed that falls is choked, left uncovered, or scorched. No, you are the field which God blessed *with the dew of heaven and fertility of the earth.*[10] So your tongue is bedewed with the word of God, and your heart, which God finds fertile, receives the seed and multiplies it in spiritual harvest, so that with your fruits *the Reaper fills His hand, and He that gathereth sheaves, His bosom.*[11] It is God Himself who is referred to here, for He is both sower and reaper of the word in us. He is also the hand, the right hand of God, which we fill with good works; He is also the bosom of Abraham in which we find rest[12] as reward for our works.

2. So it is God who now fills me with the blessings of your love. He blesses and visits, feeds and enlightens me by your letters and your couriers, through both of which He reveals to me the goodly treasure of your heart. For *out of the abundance of the heart the mouth speaketh,* and *every animal,* as Scripture says, *consorts with the like to*

itself.[13] So God has blessed you, *because the innocent and upright have adhered to you, and because you have not sat with the wicked.*[14] You hate wickedness and love your own soul,[15] which you surrendered to Christ so that it might be lost to this life but preserved for eternity. By losing itself, it enriches itself, if only it holds itself cheap through love for Christ. Through such love you hold your soul cheap, but God holds it dear, and I scent its sweetness; I scent it through the honeycombs of your lips which breathe forth Christ, and I bless the Lord, the Word of God, Himself God.

Like man whom He created, God Himself attains stages of physical development in our minds; He is born, He grows, He reaches the flower of manhood, He comes to old age. But we must beg Him not to remain too long or continually in us as One small and weak and poor. In you, however, I can boast (for your blessings are my boast) that I have experienced His development, and recognise that He is full-grown in goodness and a child in wickedness,[16] old in wisdom, strong in faith, poor in the spirit of holy humility, rich in love.

For you excelled all others in your earlier kindnesses to my poor self; as I have often attested, you were the most devoted of friends, the most conscientious of neighbours, the most loving of brothers. But now that your mode of visiting me is changed, you have transcended even yourself in surpassing kindness. It would have been enough for me to deserve a letter from you and see your couriers on one journey a year.[17] In their faces I would obtain not only a substitute for your presence, but also the image of your faith.[18] But it was not enough for you to perform punctiliously the established norm; your abundant love regarded my silence over a winter's delay as too long. *Your heart grew hot within you, and in the meditation* of your duty, *a* sacred *fire* of righteous impatience *flamed out* from you.[19] And it was not enough to hasten to me by composing a letter; you had also to increase the joy of your words by choosing its bearer from amongst your holy comrades.

3. *Blessed is he whom thou hast chosen and taken to thee*[20] for this task. Through him you make a loan to God. For though in the true confession of self-knowledge I am a sinner, the mistaken belief of your ingenuous heart considers me, in your own words, a holy man, and you love me not with a man's love but with Christ's. Therefore *you will receive the reward of a prophet,*[21] because you receive even those who are not prophets with the honour due to prophets by reason of Christ's name.

But I am not owed a like grace for welcoming brother Victor[22] with deep regard and great gratitude when he came to me in God's name to represent you. As *an unprofitable servant* I did only *what I ought to have done,*[23] for the transparent truth forced me to welcome and venerate in him the spotless sheep. Not only his sheepskin, but also the spirit of meekness and the gentleness of Christ explicit in his speech and silence showed that he was a sheep of the fold. I truly recognised in him the pattern of the blessed Martin and Clarus,[24] and shortly afterward I discovered from your letter that he has become a follower of the illustrious master.

Victor, *the son of peace,*[25] has himself told me that he is the son of Martin in his new life, and was the companion of Clarus on his journey to that life. He is truly, as you have written, a man of God, *humble of heart*[26] but not lowly in grace, the vessel of mercy and the abode of the

Highest, whom he welcomes and delights with the peaceful lodging of a fearful soul. Victor has not merely conferred on me the twin blessings of letter[27] and cloaks which he brought from you; he has also added others from the riches of his mind. He is not merely most welcome to me because of our spiritual comradeship, but also diligent in bodily service. For I dare to mention this matter of the burden I bear[28] so that none of his kindnesses may go unmentioned. I am sure that these services are your joy, because the good your servant does is your portion.

4. He attended me, then. Yes, he attended me, and wretch that I am, I allowed it. He who was not a slave to sin ministered to this sinner; this unworthy person was tended by the servant of righteousness. But I hope that my great burden is somewhat lightened because I did not claim the attendance of my holy brother through pride, but rather allowed it out of fear of hurting his love and confident myself of receiving a blessing. His holy service in God's name and his fostering love in the spirit of freedom were a blessing for me. For this reason I acceded to his voluntary kindness for my own advantage, for I assumed that his power of supplication for me would be the more powerful as the merit won from his holy acts was greater. By his prayers he will certainly ensure that my role in adding to his rewards will not thereby increase my burdens.

I confess that I loved the blessing of his service, since I feared that if I rejected it, it would withdraw from me. I thought of the words of Scripture: *He would not have blessing, and it shall be far from him.*[29] Therefore I surrendered myself wholly to his hands and loving heart, since it was through the bowels of his charity that he applied his ministering hands to anoint my limbs and wash my feet. He was thoroughly genteel in disposition, yet he was quick to be first in performing menial tasks, so that he would scarcely allow me to pour water on his hands. For I have come to love this gesture of service mentioned in your book,[30] so that I savoured at least this tiny part of the holy actions of Martin. Victor himself desired every day not only to wash my feet but also to clean my sandals, had I allowed it. He was greedy to control his spirit and therefore was active in bodily slavery.

5. But I confess that once (and once only) I followed the example of the apostles in the washing of feet. I have read that they offered their feet to be washed by the Lord who attended them.[31] Indeed, they would not have obtained their portion of the inheritance save by such menial service on His part; for the good Lord, Teacher of the way to salvation, bestowed the reward of ruling upon the office of the servant. In this way He set an example of human humility for those for whom He prepared a share in God's high estate. So once they had understood the mystery of this great gift and realised the greatness of the blessing, those who had hesitated to proffer their feet when He first prepared to minister to them finally asked that not only their feet but their whole bodies be washed from head to foot.[32]

I, too, revered the Lord Jesus in my brother Victor, for every faithful soul is of God, and he who is humble of heart is the heart of Christ; and I confess that to heal my weakness I begged my fellow servant, a better man than me, to rub me with oil or water. I did not fail to obtain the anticipated help, for the oil, as if invested with healing properties by his holy hands, seeped into my marrow all the more smoothly because of the gentleness of the application,[33] and *the bones that had been humbled rejoiced; my soul blessed the Lord, and all that is within me blessed His holy name.*[34] For this exercise, more loving than physical, aided the invigoration of my feelings. By it my good brother restored my frail limbs with his shaping hands, and by refreshing my bones lent keenness to my mind. Undoubtedly his faith assisted his hands, for whilst his loving hand rubbed my feeble flesh, the grace of his faith washed my soul as it suffered with my body, and the external oil which brought health became for me the inner *oil of gladness.*[35]

6. Hear now of another way in which Victor tended my bodily needs. He showed concern not only for my recovery but also for thrift, and he taught me how to take an easily prepared meal of simple food by cooking gruel with a drop of oil and plenty of water. But he seasoned it with such salt of grace and such sweetness of love that we needed neither cooks nor expert preparation; his simplicity combined with love mingled the purity of water with the oil of sweetness which no persistent flies could befoul.[36]

He is truly a spiritual cook, more accomplished at feeding the inner man. To remove the fare which leads to gluttony, he made the gruel not with wheat flour but with meal or millet. And even so he was anxious not to appear to treat me in too refined a manner, for he was preparing to school me for the frugal appetite of monks. He pounded beans in with the millet, so that I might more quickly lay aside the fastidious taste of the senator.[37] But the blessing from his sweet soul provided my luxury, and I rejoiced that my brother showed spiritual awareness even in such bodily attendance and was feeding me with the food of the prophets.

With this hotch-potch he emulated the loaves of affliction which the prophet Ezechiel was ordered to make for himself from various kinds of vegetables and cereal to represent the confusion of the Jews, who were unmindful of God and *changed their glory into the likeness of a calf that eateth grass.*[38] The prophet was ordered to bake the loaves on the dung of oxen and, when they had been baked, to eat them by measure under the foul ashes amidst the tears of captivity.[39] This was so that they might foresee the punishment which was to befall their wickedness, physically designated in the prophet, and that they might even then return to the Lord, if the anger of the offended God, not merely proclaimed in words but also stamped on the bodies of His prophets, could recall them to repentance.

7. Therefore my brother Victor desired me to learn to humble my soul not only by fasting but also by my eating, and sadly to consume the bread of grief in recollection of my former sins and realisation of my present ones. Yet he spared me to some extent by mixing in only beans with the meal and millet, though this perhaps was owing to his forgetfulness rather than his restraint. For with the circumspection of his faith the holy man would have feared to withhold from me anything stipulated by Holy Scripture. To complete the baking of the prophet's loaf wholly according to the divine word, he would have mixed into the porridge lentils, barley, and vetch as well. The pot would have given a loud crack and broken because these different vegetables were boiling and spilling over its edges, for the concoction would have fought a civil war.

Nonetheless, however, he filled a large pot with the fewer kinds of produce, and brought in to me steaming bowls emitting a strong smell, smoking out with the stinking vapour not only the surroundings of my modest board but also the whole area of my little room. To increase the blessing conferred on me, he bestowed on my table the meal of another prophet as well, for he brought to me the pot of Eliseus[40] into which he had put some meal. No poisonous herb had he boiled in it, but the seasoning of salvation, carrying out each of his actions in the name of the Lord; hence I felt safe and untroubled, and I did not cry out to him: *Death is in the pot, O man of God.*[41]

For now our life is in the pot, since the Lord Jesus, the Word of God, *became flesh and dwelt amongst us.*[42] He took to Himself the earthenware vessels of our bodies, which had slipped from His hands through the slippery nature of our voluntary wickedness and were worn out through our daily sins; now the Potter Himself sought to refashion us for a better purpose. He, too, became from the slime of our bodies *as a vessel that is destroyed,*[43] as Scripture says; in other words, *in the likeness of sinful flesh, that He might condemn sin by sin.*[44] And so He says: *Moab is the pot of My hope,*[45] for He took His body not merely from Juda, but also from Moab, not merely from the fount of saints, but also from that of sinners. He boiled off in a pot, so to speak, the rawness of our flesh, and He sanctified His own flesh as food for us forever. As He Himself says, His flesh is truly the food of life.[46]

His flesh is also that cauldron which, according to Jeremias,[47] burns sins and destroys them on that fire of which He says: *I am come to cast fire on the earth.*[48] Let us pray that it is kindled in us also, so that we may be cooked in the cauldron of the Lord's body, which is the Church, and our faults burnt away. Thus purified, we may become as silver *tried by the fire, tested in the earth, refined seven times,*[49] so that now not as faggots to be burnt but rather as fruitful vineshoots we may remain in the same Lord, who is the true Vine. May the same Lord also become for our food the sweet grape, which was hung for us on the lever of the cross,[50] showing us and allowing us to taste the fruit from the promised land, so that we may no longer seek after the poor growth of the uncultivated fields, amongst which we risk plucking also the noxious clusters of wild vines. This certainly happened to me when my soul, whose culture is the word of God,[51] was rough with the thorns of worldly cares. I yearned for this present life, so short in years and barren of good, and amongst my meaningless actions I gathered harmful sins like poisonous plants amongst wild grass, and so I admitted death to the cauldron of my body or my heart. But thanks be to God, who *has delivered me from the body of this death through Jesus Christ our Lord.*[52] As He mingled the strength of His spirit with my weakness, my bitter wickedness and barren uselessness were transformed to sweetness and fertility, for the word of God poured into my heart like the transforming sprinkling of salt which brings salvation or life.

8. But let me hasten back to brother Victor. He also made the meal in my jar abundant because of the blessing it received through his using it in God's name. Thus he gave me something from the jug of Elias, which the divine prophet by holy words filled so that there was unfailingly enough, and with which during three years' famine he fed the holy widow of Sarephta and her sons.[53]

I believe that in this account of the widow told through the prophet, Christ was feeding the Church with the bread not of corn but of the word. Of the widow He says: *Blessing, I will bless her widow.*[54] He means the widow who Paul says is free for the marriage she desires once her husband is dead;[55] for when the Law came to an end (and Christ is its end), the Church passed on to the freedom of grace and married Christ, since she had been widowed of the Law. The oil of grace and the meal of blessing now contained in this vessel did not fail during the famine of all the Gentiles outside Israel, whose wretched fasting from the food of life and from faith in the Trinity was suitably prefigured by that three-year famine of old.[56]

But to finish what I was saying, our store of meal so experienced God's grace through the hand of Victor that where before there was scarcely sufficient for loaves there is now more than enough for gruel as well. When the brotherhood of monks comes eager for the evening meal after the day's fasting, the meal does double service, filling them with baked loaves or with liquid gruel.

9. But though Victor was keen to introduce my stomach to coarser fare, my dear brother also tended my weakness, because he remedied the failings of my faith when I took that porridge. He carried out this manual labour on my behalf and made this dish with a single helper. This latter man I had taken in from the countryside and was nursing back to health. In years he is old but in mind a child, for in his failing days he has been reborn to grace, and his aged flesh has blossomed forth to new life. The cooking of brother Victor has made him fat, for as a rustic he is used to such food and it suits his toothless gums. *This poor man cried out, and the Lord heard him; He*

brought him out of the darkness and the shadow of death.[57] Now he is *sprinkled with hyssop and cleansed*, and *in the voice of joy and praise* he feasts and cries out: *I have gone astray like a sheep that was lost. I will bless the Lord at all times.*[58] He gave me understanding and *brought me out of the mire of dregs, and He put a new canticle into my mouth.*[59] I was young, and have grown old, *but my days have not been consumed in vanity, because He that is mighty has done great things to me.*[60] *He has made me to drink with the torrent of his pleasure, and my flesh has flourished again.*[61] *He sent me provisions in abundance,*[62] and gave plenty to my empty soul. And now *my old age is in the mercy of abundance* till *I sleep and rest in peace for the length of my days.*[63]

10. I come now to the greater service which brother Victor did for me. He deigned to cut my hair with his own hands, but desired me to be obliged to you for this kindness, for he said that it was at your command that he showed his skill. Accordingly I asked him that you should both do with earnest prayer what he had done with practised hand; that you should both entreat the Lord that my sins, which *are multiplied above the hairs of my head*[64] and because of which my soul is unkempt, may not be shorn by cutting them halfway, but rather may be cut to the flesh as though a razor shaved them.

The razor, however, sometimes cuts in a way healthy for me, but sometimes harmfully. Christ God is the Razor which heals and beautifies me, for He circumcises my heart, shaves off my sins, makes smooth my soul's head, and tends my mind's face. He cleanses me like the captive woman in the Law[65] and frees me of the bristling hair of wretched slavery, so that like the woman who was to

marry the Israelite I may be stripped of the crimes of my
flesh, my rough hairs, so to say, before I must meet the
Lord. Then I may shine with heart revitalised as with new-
grown hair, and nurturing my life like the hair of the
Nazarite[66] I can consecrate it to God in chastity and thrift.

11. We must be watchful, however, lest the opposite
and hostile razor, which shaved the head of the human race
in the persons of our first parents who were beguiled by
baneful deceit, mount our head, that is, the faith by which
Christ becomes our Head. We must be watchful lest it
strip us of spiritual grace as though the grace were the hair
of the Nazarite.

The hero in the book of Judges, who was consecrated
by prophecy, is a proof of the immensity of the blessing
that comes to those who keep their hair, and of the ruin
that befalls the careless ones who are shorn of it.[67] He was
invincible while he kept his hair, captured when it was cut
off, and reinvigorated when it grew afresh. Would that he
had been as wise at taking precautions against the woman
as he was strong at throttling the lion![68] But after prevail-
ing by spiritual grace, he was overcome by the enticements
of the flesh; after overcoming the strong, he was defeated
by weakness.

Such a fate is inevitable for those who do not subdue
their female element, the flesh, to the male, which is the
spirit, in obedience to the laws of God; these men like
malleable husbands with effeminate spirit accede as it were
to the evil designs of a wife. They fall below the standards
of the master, who once he had acknowledged Christ prevailed in the great struggle at the very outset of the war-
fare and *condescended not to flesh and blood.*[69]

12. We should accordingly examine all of Samson's

sufferings after he was seduced by a faithless wife, for the spiritual plight which we sinners shall suffer is commensurate with the bodily suffering of Samson, which is described for our instruction. The enemy will mock us if we are robbed of the grace of Christ as Samson was shorn of his hair. The enemy will gouge out our eyes, imprison us, and allot us to the asses' task of turning millstones.[70] So the Lord warns us through His prophet not to condemn our necks to the ass's millstone by refusing to submit them to Christ's yoke: *Do not become like the horse and the mule who have no understanding.*[71]

As the same prophet says elsewhere,[72] a man who does not understand his own high status (the natural distinction which controls by reason all other living things upon the earth) though endowed with reason to be able to understand and worship his Creator, is through his wanton sinning compared with beasts and made like them if he fails to make use of this great gift of the Creator. This was clearly fulfilled, as we see, in the case of the king of Babylon,[73] who was stripped of human feeling and endured such a fate in his bestial heart as punishment for wicked idiocy and crazy pride. Once a man falls into sin and slips from righteousness, he is like Samson rightly deprived of the strength of both wisdom and grace. He is punished by blindness and the millstone, for he deserves beasts' work who deprives himself of the light of reason, and who makes himself like to wild animals by being a slave to his body.

13. Think of the life of men of this kind, so that you may fully visualise the appearance of the beast turning the millstone. Just as the eyes of Samson were sewn up with rags, so the mental eyes of such men are sewn up with the

foulness of their lives, and because of the waywardness of
their senses they live a miserable life of drudgery as if they
were walking round millstones. They do nothing for their
own benefit, but have to work hard for that of another.
They stand *in the way of sinners*,[74] shackled with the
chains of their desires. Their very prison is oppressed with
the darkness of their sins and thick with the filth of their
guilt. They suffer the prison of the mill within themselves,
and they turn like a millstone the rock that is their heart,
hardened by obstinate wickedness; they grind flour for
their enemies from the mouldy meal of their souls. For, as
Scripture says, the sinner makes haste to lose his life,[75] and
in the same way he who commits sin grinds his enemy's
wheat with the mill of his life, in order to feed the devil.
The soul which starves itself is the devil's bread. But if he
should become a wind not always going but at some time
returning,[76] he will be made whole with the fresh growth
of grace as if his hair had grown again.

14. It is pleasant to give free rein to words, and to follow the strong man of the Lord to his death so that I may
weave an entire letter out of the subject of hair. We shall
marvel that in Samson's blindness and death the sacraments
of the divine mystery were prefigured.[77] When we read in
Scripture that he laid low more enemies when he died than
he had destroyed earlier throughout the whole period of
his life, I think we are chiefly to understand by this the
power of the Lord's passion, by which the house of the
devil caved in and the kingdom of death was destroyed.

Even before His physical coming, Christ had always
lived as He lives now, as God and the Word in the majesty
of His nature, in the presence of His Lord and Father; yet
in the line of generations from Adam to Moses lawlessness

was rife and the power of death had reigned. After Moses that power grew, for though the Law made men aware of sin, they did not avoid it. But the King of kings, the Steward of time, the Son of God, divided and destroyed this kingdom. Himself God, *He was made under the Law* to loose those who were slaves to the Law; *He was made of a woman*,[78] a woman by sex and a virgin in childbirth, so that the Creator of both sexes might make both holy; for He became man,[79] and of a woman He was born. By dying, He destroyed death itself. As Scripture says: *He broke down the enmities in His flesh, and hath made both one*.[80] He has made man and God one, for Christ Jesus, God and man, united them in Himself, and in Him the substance of both natures abandoned their disharmony and recognised the undying compact of the grace uniting them.

We had been plundered and robbed by the devil, and lay wounded on the road.[81] Our brothers the Levite and the priest passed by, for the Law did not redeem us by sacrifices or prophets. But the Samaritan did not pass us by, but for our sake shouldered even the obloquy of that name. He did not pass by, because He was not a hireling but the true and good Shepherd who had come prepared to lay down His life for His sheep. In pity He came to His own, who had been ignored and left untended by previous travellers. He took him up on His mule, which is the incarnation of the Word, bound him with the oil of grace and the wine of His passion, entrusted him to the innkeeper, the perfect master of the Gentiles, and healed him by the payment of two denarii, that is, with the two Testaments.[82] He promised that innkeeper fecund graces of blessed virginity from the incalculable harvest this good would reap, and countless crowns as well, because he, adding this counsel to what was commanded, *spent over and above* from his own pocket.[83]

15. So Christ was not a brother (the Lord differed from His slaves in status, and God from a mortal by nature), yet He was a man of whom it had been written: *He too is a man, and who will know him?*[84] So He is not our brother, though the love of God, in the humility of His heart, allowed even the title of brother to His servants when He said: *I will declare thy name to My brethren.*[85]

Yet we must not dare in our pride to call Him brother, even though He deigned to become a man. For even in His birth as a man He has nothing in common with us. He became flesh in a manner beyond the scope of our birth, being conceived and born of the Holy Spirit from the unviolated maidenhead of His holy mother. So He became man like us without any of our bodily disease. *He did not give to God his ransom*, for *He is the propitiation*, and is not *the price of the redemption of His soul*[86] but of ours, because as saviour He had no need of salvation.

We were *sold under sin*[87] and needed the price of redemption, and so for us He became man, taking the form of a servant and becoming the son of a maidservant. The blessed Sanctifier of the saints became for us a sin and a curse,[88] which He was not, so that we might be freed by Him both from the sin of transgression and from the curse of condemnation. He nailed to the cross in His own flesh both sin and curse.

I think that this is the meaning of the words *No brother can redeem but a man shall redeem*,[89] for those who had not been redeemed by a brother, that is, by a prophet or lawgiver who was only a man, were redeemed by this Man who is also God. *For God indeed was in Christ, reconcil-*

ing the world to Himself.[90] Only a man of this kind could prevail against the sentence of death and the sting of sin, to *blot out the handwriting*[91] of death and to humble the crafty one.

But He grappled with the devil not with the majesty of His own nature but with the clothing of ours. He extracted nothing from him by forceful mastery, but overcame him by the law of righteousness. Since the woman had been deceived and the man brought low by the woman,[92] the devil claimed the entire offspring of that first man, by the laws of death, as sinners. True, his motive was a wicked desire to harm, but his claim rested on the fairest right of victory. So his power prevailed until he should kill a just man in whom he could show no guilt worthy of death (for Christ was not merely killed when without sin but also born without concupiscence). The devil had made his captives subject to that concupiscence so that whatever was born of it he could keep as the fruit of his own tree; his desire for possession was base, but his right to retain it not unjust. So the devil is most justly compelled to relinquish those who believe in Christ, whom he most unjustly killed; they pay their debt by dying in this life, and their eternal life is in Him who paid the debt which He did not owe.

16. So I believe that for us He is the dead lion in whose mouth we find honey to eat. For what is sweeter than the word of God? And what is stronger than His right hand? In whose mouth other than Christ's are there bees and a honeycomb after death?[93] In His word is the blessing of our salvation and the gathering of the Gentiles.

Many have preferred to typify the Gentiles by this lion, for the people of the Gentiles who became believers was previously a fierce body but is now the body of

Christ.[94] In this body the apostles like bees stored the honey of wisdom garnered from the dew of heaven and the blossoms of divine graces; it was as if *out of the eater came forth meat*,[95] because races previously fierce towards God accepted with believing hearts the word of God they had received, and brought forth the fruit of salvation.

But those who see Christ prefigured in that lion make Samson represent the Jews, for he killed the lion as the Jews killed Christ.[96] They also ascribe to that mystical preparation the fact that Samson achieved the desired slaughter of the powerful beast at the very time when he was seeking marriage; the reason was that the agreed marriage between Christ and the Church could not be established unless the lion of the tribe of Juda had been killed.[97]

For the Lord is both the lion which prevailed and the lion's whelp which couched of its own accord and was roused by itself, of which Scripture wrote: *Who shall rouse Him?*[98] Of His own accord and on behalf of us He sacrificed to His Father the offering of His own body; and then this Priest most high, a Priest forever, took up His life again, as He testifies,[99] with the same power by which He laid it down. He is the lion's whelp, because He is the Son of God; He is also the lion, because He is equal to His Father. So I think the quotation is more appropriate to Christ as lion; *Out of the eater came forth meat, and out of the strong came forth sweetness.*[100] In other words, the meat and the sweetness came forth from our Saviour, for He whose word is life both chewed this food for us by teaching it and brought it forth by bestowing it on us.

Or, if another explanation is preferred, the meat came forth from the eater because this lion from the tribe of Juda, who is victorious on our behalf, rescues us from the mouth of the hostile lion. He hunts to preserve, seizes to loose, breaks to strengthen, bites to make whole, eating the element in us which corrupts us. So let us pray that we may become the prey of this lion so as to avoid being the prey of the hostile lion. Let us become the meat of God that we may not be the meat of the serpent. Let Christ eat us so that the devil may not devour us, for, as I have said, when Christ eats us there is devoured in us that which devours us.

Christ is our Life, and we shall not be able to lose our mortality unless we are swallowed up, for Christ devours our death. But we cannot become the food of Christ unless we do His will, so that He in turn becomes Our food. We live in Him always if we live by His commandments. Therefore, *out of the strong comes forth sweetness,* when the bitterness of our wickedness is transformed by Him into the sweetness of goodness, and we come forth as sweet food from the word of Him who has refashioned for life those whom He devoured by eating their sin.

He alone is powerful, and sweetly powerful, *who delivered the poor from the* greed of the *mighty,*[101] who annihilated the hostility of my body by the mystery of His dutiful love, even to the death of His own body. The food of life was eaten in the place where the hunger of wretched death withered, by Him who transformed my sin into grace, my transgression into justice, my weakness into strength, my death into life, my shame into glory, my exile into acceptance into the kingdom. Previously we heard: *Dust thou art and into dust thou shalt return,* but now we hear: *Your conversation is in heaven.*[102]

17. So I believe that the figure of Samson renewed in Christ, both with hair grown anew and in death, is apposite

also to every servant of Christ. *A man who has been over-taken in any fault,*[103] once his hair, so to speak, grows afresh, returns by salutary repentance to the renewal of grace, and *makes his arms like a brazen bow.*[104] Those arms are his faith in the true hope and hope unfeigned in the faith. He also keeps his hands in trim for battle by works of godliness, the performance of which *is profitable to all things.*[105] Then since he has attained muscular strength in his arms—a good conscience and strong faith—he will dare to attack and will be able to overturn the pillars of his enemies. These pillars are the supports of the enemy's house, in which he feasts as victor over us, mocking at his captives if he employs our limbs as weapons of his wickedness. So by the death of our subjugated flesh we dislodge this enemy from his own house. It is by the help of this flesh that the enemy enclosed within us disturbs our souls with inner war. He gains control over us by our voluntary sinning, and has our vices as his supporters against us. By the agency of our outer selves he attacks our inner selves.

18. But let us remember the contract by which we have sworn allegiance to the cross, buried with Christ through the grace of baptism, so that we may not deal with the world under the illusion that we live, and so that Christ within and not we ourselves may live. When He has been restored to us to adorn our heads, the house of the devil will fall, and with the death of our sins the whole retinue of our enemies will die. Therefore the death of Samson teaches me to die with my enemies; in other words, to mortify my flesh and to kill sin at the same time, so that my spirit can survive and I may triumphantly win salvation and say to my soul: *Turn into thy rest, for the Lord hath been bountiful to me.*[106]

And again, Samson's blindness, by which he lost his bodily but not his spiritual eyes, enlightens me to right understanding, so that by his example I may know which eyes I should prefer to have. For Samson would not have called upon the Lord to lend aid to his strength if his inward eyes had not been sound. Their light is Christ, *in whose light we shall see light.*[107] If this light always burns in the lamp of our bodies, the works of darkness will fall away, and *the prince of this world will be cast out*[108]—not, of course, cast out from this world, with which, as Scripture says,[109] he will be purged at the final condemnation, and his end mingled with those who are condemned, but cast out of our hearts, from which he is driven if we accept Christ.

19. Since, then, Satan's followers imitate their leader, we must imitate our Lord Jesus, for He has summoned us to share His inheritance, and has bidden us to take up His sweet yoke so that He might remove from us the oppressive yoke of the Law and of death. Our hair, too, like the yoke is light, for, as Divine Scripture teaches us, the hair of holy men is light but that of wicked men oppressive. The hair of holy men is a mark of strength, like Samson's, or of holiness, like Samuel's;[110] that of wicked men is a mark of oppression, like Absalom's,[111] or of foulness, like Nabuchodonosor's.[112] By this dissimilarity between men and between their hair, we are taught to adjudge men's works by their locks, for when the Assyrian king was condemned to the exile of a wild animal, his unshorn hair grew grievously stiff and bristled like a lion's mane. As a result, even in physical appearance he was changed into a wild beast, exiled not only from his kingdom but also from human feelings. His dilapidated hair was a lion's, his

hooked claws a vulture's, his sensations and his food made him an ox; for since he had resembled many beasts in character, he was compelled to resemble more than one in his punishment.

20. At length, however, Nabuchodonosor came to a knowledge of God, and his senses and his kingdom returned to him. He, too, stands as an exemplar of faith to us, so that we may fear to lose the kingdom within us by sinning, and remember to seek it again by repentance.

But Absalom, however handsome his bearing and haughty his head, could not say what Samson said: *If my head be shaven, my strength shall depart from me.*[113] Though Absalom had a very fine head of hair, he had not the strength deriving not from bodily hair but from the spiritual grace which a wicked man could not possess. For Christ is the strength and wisdom of God, who *did not enter into a murderous soul, because He did not dwell in a body subject to sins.*[114] And then the fact that he had to cut his hair, as Scripture reveals, attests that he cut it because of the burden of his sins. For you read as follows: *He sheared his hair because it was burdensome; and when he was shorn he weighed the hairs of his head, and they weighed a hundred sicles according to the royal weight.*[115]

Could there be a more explicit statement than this that one's hairs are numbered according to one's deeds, since Scripture has shown that this wicked man's head had no strength but merely a weight of hair? *He weighed,* says Scripture, *the hairs of his head.* For the wicked man his injustice is a source of glory. As someone has said, not merely his wicked deeds but also a reputation for wickedness pleases him. So you have the verse in Psalms: *Why dost thou glory in malice, thou that art mighty in in-*

iquity?[116] For the light of wicked men is darkness, their glory is a shadow, their high position is transitory, their head is the devil, and therefore their hair is a dead weight.

This is why Scripture says that the hair of that murderer was heavy *according to the royal weight*, in other words by the weight of the devil. For every wicked man is the kingdom of the devil. Likewise, says Scripture, *they that are clothed in soft garments are in the houses of kings*,[117] that is, the houses of *the princes of this air*[118] and the leaders of spiritual impiety. In their houses and kingdoms operate those who are obstinate in wickedness or effeminate in wantonness. Their riches are sin, their ways slippery, *their end destruction*, their glory in Hell, their home in the sepulchre.[119] The locks of such men are their sins, and therefore theirs cannot be the hair by which the consecrated warrior broke the bonds of the enemy, and their new ropes as though they were soft threads.[120] Rather, their hair is that of which it is written: *The cords of the wicked have encompassed me*.[121] For the soul is enmeshed and oppressed by its sins. This view the prophet fully approves when he says: *My iniquities are gone over my head, and as a heavy burden are become heavy on me.*[122]

21. You see how heavy are the locks of a sinner. But he whose hair is Christ is light and swift, and he rejoices, saying: *God, who girds me with strength and has made my way blameless, who has made my feet like the feet of harts, and who setteth me in high places.*[123] As I have said, the yoke and hair of Christ are light, because by serving Christ we perform the good works by which we wing up to the heights. So Paul says to Christians, even whilst they reside in the flesh: *But you are not in the flesh but in the spirit.*[124] The flesh, being subject to the soul which in turn is subject

to God, passes over into the spirit by a change not of our
substance but of our life. So I desire for myself both the
death and the blindness of Samson, so that I may live and
see for God, for it is possible that once Samson had recovered the strength of his hair to achieve the mystery to
come, he ceased to long for the recovery of his sight once
it was lost, because the strength of heavenly grace, so
healthy in inward vision, did not need bodily sight.

22. Accordingly we should follow this example and
train our senses on the Lord, blinding our bodily eyes by
turning away from the things of the world. It was the eyes
of the body which the prophet longed to lose when he
said: *Turn away my eyes that they may not behold
vanity.*[125] And the Lord Himself preferred blindness to the
seeing eyes of the Jews when He said: *If you were blind,
you should not have sin.*[126]

Let us recall the loss with which those in Paradise had
their eyes opened,[127] eyes which had a clear vision of God
as long as they were closed to sin. They experienced
shame in their puberty only when through the sin of their
transgression they lost the purity of a good conscience, the
light of which had clothed them. To use one's eyes for the
purposes of darkness, therefore, and to blind them to
heavenly things by keeping them bent on things of earth,
is to lose one's real sight. The soul is given clear sight to
behold God by the blindness with which it holds the world
in contempt. *For all that is in the world,* says Scripture, *is
the concupiscence of the eyes;*[128] and because of this the
Apostle teaches us to close our vision to this world and to
open it to Christ, who *enlighteneth every man that cometh
into this world*[129] (that is, the mind of every man who
comes).

The Apostle rouses us from our vision of immediate things to look up to eternal ones, saying: *Seek not the things which are in this world, for the fashion of this world passeth away.*[130] And again Paul says: *Seek the things that are above, where Christ is sitting at the right hand of God.*[131] In the words of Ecclesiastes: *All things under the sun are vanity.*[132] And by the same token, truth lies beyond the sun. So, too, those who reside in the truth, though their physical dwelling is within the world, lie outside the world in their heavenly intercourse. Their spirit flies forth, and they mount and go beyond the dancing stars or the poles of the heavens; they rise higher than the elements, not being subject to material things or to the wearing of the elements. Their life is riveted to Christ and they are above the world, abiding in Him who is the blessed God over all ages.[133]

23. You see how Paul who imitated Christ takes us from men to God both by his teaching and by the example of his virtue. He removed the veil from our hearts, so that *we might behold with open face the glory of God*[134] which is hidden from unbelievers by the covering of the Law and is uncovered for the faithful by the revelation of the Gospel. So now we have no need of that bodily hair. For *the old things*, says Paul, *are passed away, and behold all things are now new.*[135] For *a light is risen up in darkness to the righteous of heart; the Lord is merciful and compassionate and just.*[136] Now *God is a spirit*, and *where the spirit of the Lord is, there is liberty.*[137]

So hair was honoured whilst the spiritual veil of the Law had to be observed even in bodily appearance; but now it is a burden, since the Sun of eternal freedom has shone forth and Christ has become our Head to relieve us of our yoke and of the weight of our bent heads. Therefore as free men we now dare to proclaim with voices of joy and praise: *Let us break their bonds asunder and let us cast away their yoke from us.*[138] For *now is the acceptable time, now is the day of salvation,*[139] since now the Truth is with us not in the shadow of a cloud[140] but in the light of His body. The barber has appeared at the apposite time for this moment of grace in which our freedom has shown itself,[141] so that he can lighten me of the all too lengthy covering of my head. So even the body's appearance can attest the benefit of spiritual grace, and a clear uncovered forehead reveal the joy of inner freedom.

24. The Apostle's authority has allowed only women to have long hair, for though their faith like that of men removes the veil from their hearts, fitting modesty demands a covering for their heads and a veil for their brows. So the master who is perfect in faith and training teaches us that hair is unbecoming for men because Christ, *the head of every man*, cannot be concealed, for He is *that city built on a mountain* in the person of *the Church which is the body of Christ.*[142]

So hair is unbecoming to a man, but a glory to a woman. For she is no one's head, but the embellishment of her husband by the adornment of her virtue. We might say that she is placed at the base to support that body's chain which is linked to God by the head of Christ, to Christ by the head of man, and to man by the head of woman.[143] But Christ makes woman also belong to the head at the top by making her part of the body and of the structure of the limbs, for *in Christ we are neither male nor female.*[144]

By all means let women keep their tresses, so that like the sinning woman in the Gospel they can wipe Christ's feet and clasp the feet of Wisdom, so that they may be able to love nothing but Wisdom, embrace nothing but virtue, and kiss nothing but chastity;[145] so that sprinkled at least with the last drops of the heavenly word they can say: *Thy dew is for us a healing*.[146] Let our women have as their hair acts of spiritual virtues, fasting, acts of mercy, prayers. Such hair as this is also fitting for a man. Let Christ's grace, not the grace of their hair, and the precious jewel of chastity, not of costly stones, adorn them. Let their fragrance be of good works, not of perfumes. Let them remember that they are the daughters of *the king's daughter whose whole glory is within*.[147]

Let them realise why Paul ordered their heads to be clothed with a more abundant covering; it is *because of the angels*,[148] that is, the angels who are ready to seduce them and whom the saints will condemn. For quite wantonly these angels tempt the weaker vessels, just as the serpent assailed not Adam but Eve. So for this reason women are forbidden to teach in church, so that their spirits may not be puffed up and so that they may not dare to gaze on the decrees of wisdom, and then secede[149] through becoming haughty with pride. For it would certainly contribute to the confusion of the wicked angels if they saw a woman hiding her feelings in silence on the grounds of ignorance, and by her modest manner revealing the discipline of her understanding, so that the serpent does not dare to approach and tempt her again because he has no hope of beguiling her.

25. Paul's teaching is relevant here, that a woman ought to cover her head especially in prayer and prophecy.[150] Then she becomes pregnant with the spirit, and accordingly rouses the hatred of the tempter all the more when she leaves behind the boundaries of her womanly weakness,

and aspires to human perfection. It is not surprising that
Paul has the same view of prayer as of prophecy, for elsewhere he says that we pray by the spirit; for when we
pray, he states, we do not know how a petition ought to be
made, but the spirit teaches us.[151] So because a woman becomes spiritually pregnant also when she prays, Paul desires her appearance to reveal that she has *a power over her
head*,[152] so that the wiles and snares of the enemy may not
confront her if she steps beyond what Scripture calls her
vessel.[153] Her hair shows that by this power she is both
guided and defended. Strength is bestowed on her by that
very humility of heart by which through the guidance of
her self-control she restrains the arrogance of knowledge.
She prefers fear to depth of knowledge. It is safer for her
to be silent in the fear prescribed by faith than to have a
practised tongue, for it will be vain for her to weigh down
her brow with hair if she does not cover it also with
modesty.[154]

26. So let us all together be eager at heart to be adorned
by the hairs of which God keeps count. As He Himself
says: *The very hairs of your head are all numbered.*[155] But
on whose head would God deign to number the hairs rather
than Christ's, of which He Himself is head? Of Christ it is
said that His head is like *aurum cephas*, an expression which
I think means a gold of better quality, more pure, like that
from the land of Hevilath.[156]

This gold is the beauty of the saints, who shine like
glowing eyes in the head of the body, and are as *gold fire-
tried*[157] by God. For they have been burned in the furnace
of the world to be tried by sufferings, and, as Scripture
says: *God has found them worthy of Himself.*[158] He has
implanted on them the sacred stamp of His image, impress-

ing on their hearts and lips the word of His truth. He has made them also officials of His mint, so that they might fashion good coins for the Lord in His image and mint the living coinage of the celestial King, effacing from us the features of Caesar. Thus signed with the spirit of the Redemption, with our necks now free of the yoke, our foreheads protected by the inscription of salvation, we might sing: *The light of Thy countenance, O Lord, is signed upon us.*[159]

27. Let us strive, then, with all our resources to prepare ourselves that we may deserve to be the hair and the gold of the divine Head. Christ, by the grace of God, is that Head for us.[160] For from that very Head sprout forth the locks of which Scripture says: *His hair is as flocks of goats.*[161] The name of these animals is especially apposite to designate Christ's flocks, because their chief yield is milk; and everyone who believes that Christ is God embraces with dutiful faith the entire fulness of the Trinity in Him *whom God anointed with the Holy Ghost.*[162] And accordingly the very *mother of all the living,* the Church which is the body of Christ, overflows with the milk of love, and her goodly *breasts are better than wine.*[163]

I think that this verse means that the freedom of grace with its milk of mercy is sweeter than the austerity of the Law with its wine of justice. For *the letter killeth,* as Scripture says, and here you see the wine of stern judgment; *but the spirit quickeneth,*[164] and here you see the yield of the breasts and the effect of the milk. But as you prefer to understand the passage, the reference may be to the watery substance with which the first milk drunk by the newly born is mixed.[165] Goodly are the breasts, then, with which *the good Shepherd, who laid down His life for His sheep,* gave milk to the children *from whose mouths He perfected praise* for Himself *that He might destroy the enemy*[166] of the good and the defender of evil.

28. From amongst these herds of goats was the man of the flock who gave the children of Christ the delicate nourishment of milk when they were not yet ready for more solid food. To them he said: *I gave you milk to drink, not meat, for you were not able as yet. But neither indeed are you now able.*[167] But once we have grown through the sustenance of this milk, our footsteps will first be strengthened as we imbibe faith, and we shall grow to the flower of young manhood. Then, when our patience has been strengthened by faith and charity, we shall raise our hands to more vigorous action, and live on the stronger food of virtuous works.

So we may become the hairs of which Scripture says: *His locks are as black fir trees, like the raven.*[168] The raven is the crow, but this one is the good crow—not the one which did not remember to return to the ark,[169] but the one which remembered to feed the prophet.[170] The comparison is good which likens it to the hair rivalling the fir trees of which Scripture speaks: *Those goodly black firs, bringing ships to Tharsis. . . .*[171] So now this raven is the crow not of night but of light; his hair, so beautiful in colour, is holy, *a royal and priestly race,*[172] for with it he beautifies God's head as with the purple of His glory, because youthful grace clothes its prime of manhood especially with this colour of hair.

29. Yet we must not conceal the fact that in the Scriptures that bird is found symbolising now sin and now grace. It appears to bring death when it is summoned for the punishment of the wicked; for, as Scripture says, God sends

ills by evil angels.[173] Again, it is said to avenge a curse: *The eye that mocketh at his father and mother, let the ravens of the valleys pick it out.*[174] But the raven is of good augury when it nourishes the prophet with bread in the morning and with meat at night, or when the young of ravens call upon the name of the Lord.[175]

Its colour, too, is variously interpreted, for it is found sometimes amongst the holy and sometimes amongst the wicked. The spouse of Christ says that she is swarthy and beautiful,[176] and again, the Lord *made darkness His covert.*[177] On the other hand, we are warned by the Apostle *that the darkness overtake us not.*[178] However, the black and goodly firs which bring ships to Tharsis are like her who is swarthy yet beautiful; for her limbs[179] are the holy men who are black and goodly firs as well as flourishing palm trees and cedars that multiply,[180] because in the Church, which is the mountain of God, they are tallest in height of merit like the firs on their mountains.

And as firs make good timber for the construction of ships, so these leaders of the people were cut down from the mountain of the Law, as it were from Libanus; they fashioned the ark or ship of the Lord, which is the Church, to sail through the floods of this world once the Gentiles had been prepared for the word of God. Once they had assembled this structure of love, and faith had bound it tight, they taught it to cut through the waves of this world without rotting its timber.

30. But souls that are now schooled in the faith of the apostles are also black and goodly firs. They are now black not from sin, but rather I think from still dwelling in the body, or from the dust of battle or grimy sweat caused by

the inner struggle. They are goodly because of the spiritual life which exists even in the darkness of their bodies.

So, too, they are ships floating on the waves of the world, armed with the oars of faith in the truth and of works of justice both on the right hand, as Scripture says, and on the left.[181] The word of God is the rudder that steers them. They open the sails of their senses to the wind of the Holy Spirit, and they lash the sail of their hearts to the sailyard of the cross, using for ropes the bonds of charity.[182] Their mast is *the rod out of the root of Jesse*,[183] controlling the whole quadrireme of our bodies. If we are fastened to it through the truth of the prophets by voluntary bonds, as in the Homeric story, and if the ears of our hearts, not our bodies, are stopped up with faith, not wax, against the enticements of this world which beguile us variously but harm us equally, then we shall sail safely and harmlessly by the rocks of pleasures, the cliffs of the Sirens, so to speak.[184]

But let the rope which binds us to this mast be the strongest. Let us be fastened by hope, faith, and charity, believing in heart and proclaiming with our tongues the undivided Trinity, the threefold rope which cannot be sundered. With this rope our works should be interwoven; by it, too, the mast of our faith, the sailyard of our charity, should be raised, and the sails of our lives extended. So we may become the firs which were fastened to great rafts and brought from Tharsis to build the temple, or ships to rival the one which once brought chosen gold and Tyrian riches to Solomon.[185]

But as Jesus, our eternal King, overshadows Solomon, king only for a time, so ought our trade be carried on more eagerly and more profitably than that of old. *Behold, a greater than Solomon here*, says Scripture, *shall not pound us in pieces amongst the ships of Tharsis*,[186] if we transport to Him by good works the profit of our lives, which is the merchandise most precious to God. So He may receive from us His own prize, for He is the Pearl which all our negotiation in this spiritual traffic strives to win. If our resources are sufficient to purchase that Pearl,[187] we shall bear over this great and boundless sea the Burden which does not weigh us down but raises us. We shall dare to rouse the Lord who because of our sloth slumbers within us (provided that we deserve to convey Him even asleep), so that He may rebuke the winds of hostile spirits or even of our own feelings, save us from faintheartedness and the storm, and calm the seas for us as we strive to reach His tranquil waters. May He bring us to the harbour of salvation like merchant vessels bearing His riches. May He joyfully place green garlands on the prows that have conquered the waves.

31. Let us also be the right hand of Him who is wholly a right hand;[188] in our actions let us have no left hand so that we may deserve to stand on the right hand of the Judge,[189] or, rather, to be His right hand; thus, on the day of retribution, the Lord who repays may count our deeds as the hairs of His head, as He Himself stated in the Gospel.[190] These deeds must be proclaimed at the Judgment, when He will requite the deserving merits of spiritual virtues with divine blessings and with kingly payment.

Those merits are the most lovely locks of His own head, like the ones with which that woman who typified the Church wiped the feet of Christ after cleaning them with ointment and her tears. She pleased God not so much by

the value of her gifts as with her gesture of service. It was
not her ointment that the Lord held in regard in her case,
but the love which led her uninvited to enter the strange
house of the Pharisee. Modest in her lack of shame, dutiful in her impudence, she showed no fear of insult or refusal, but pertly entered, using the violence by which the
kingdom of heaven is attained. Hungering only for the
heavenly word, she hastened not to the Pharisee's table[191]
but to the feet of Christ. In them she washed and took her
food; I might say that she made those feet her shrine and
her altar. She watered them with the libation of tears,
brought an offering of ointment, and made sacrifice of her
love. For *an afflicted spirit is a sacrifice to God*,[192] and by
offering it to God she merited not merely the remission of
her sins but also the glory of having her name preached in
the Gospel.[193]

32. Because she prefigured the Church which was to be
called forth from the Gentiles,[194] she bore within her all
the signs of the mystery of salvation. She was anointed with
the chrism of her own gift; her tears of repentance served
as the washing, and the bowels of her charity as the sacrifice. She anticipated us in taking into her hands and mouth
the living, life-giving Bread Itself; she also anticipated us in
sipping the blood of the chalice before it became the
chalice of blood, for her kisses imbibed it.

Blessed is she who tasted Christ in the flesh, and felt
Christ's body on her own. She was rightly preferred to the
Pharisee, even though he gave food to Christ; for whilst
the Jew feasted, she fasted, and in her role as servant she
yearned not for food but for salvation, as I have described.

Blessed is she who deserved to symbolise the Church in
this additional sense,[195] for in the house and at the table of

the Pharisee it was not the host but the sinner who won justification and pardon. Her rude behaviour gained the greater blessing; for *the dispensation of the mystery established from eternity*[196] demanded that, in accordance with the prophetic blessing of their father Noe, Japheth should go to dwell in the tents of Sem;[197] in other words, that the Church, not the synagogue, should win justification in the house of the Law and the prophets, for though younger in years, she is greater than the Law in grace. So the very law of the Law itself[198] proclaims in the person of John: *After me there cometh One who has been preferred before me, because He was before me.*[199]

33. But the Church had done well to take the image of a sinner, so that even in her symbolism she might be consistent with her Head, for Christ, too, took the form of a sinner. But the Jew, who was to set neither his head nor his base in Christ, anointed neither the head nor the feet of Christ, whereas the woman of the Gospel steeped both in precious ointments.[200] So Christ confers neither the oil of grace nor the water of renewal on the synagogue, an image of which is represented by the Pharisee standing at the very fount of the oil and water of salvation; but for him the water and the oil of charity have run dry.

Christ was possibly[201] foretelling this when His prophet said: *The oil of the sinner shall not fatten My head*, just as He was able to say to His Church: *Thou hast anointed My head with oil.*[202] She had brought ointment not only of costly manufacture but also in a precious container. The ointment was fragrant with the grace and properties of many herbs or blossoms combined. Only the Church could perfect such a product. Scented with the varied blossoms and juices of heavenly graces, she breathes out to God her manifold sweetness from different races. Her breath is the prayers of holy men, like spices burnt on libation-bowls which are fragrant[203] with the spirit of truth. Permeated with the fragrances of such flowers or their dewy juices, she is acclaimed by the Bridegroom Himself with the flattering verses He uses also in the Song of Songs: *My dove, My undefiled, for My head is full of dew* (the head of Christ is God, and His hairs are His chosen saints, in whom the father takes joy in Christ) *and My locks are full of the drops of the night.*[204]

The dew, as we know, is water brought not by rain but by the cold, by which the grass is refreshed when parched by the day's heat. Only on a fine night is the earth sprinkled by the translucent drops of this dew. So we are to understand that those *drops of the night* in which Wisdom so gladly steeped His head and hair represent the saints whom Paul describes as shining amongst the stars,[205] which on fine nights shine as the dew falls. As for the night, what spiritual interpretation are we to give it other than the passion of the Lord, which also brought daylight? I think that Scripture is referring to it with the words: *Night shall be a light in My pleasures.*[206]

But one can also interpret the night as this world, which was made fine and cloudless by the conversion of the Gentiles, at whose earlier beliefs the night shuddered in her darkness. But now by the light of the Church, which shines with the entire reflection of the full moon,[207] and of the holy men who are like stars in a cloudless sky, the good works of the faithful drip down like dew in what I have called this night of the world. This dew gives life to the soul of each believer, and refreshment after the previous arid drought.

34. So Christ rejoices that His head is steeped in such dew; though He brings light to our dark nights, He is nonetheless glad that His hair is sprinkled with the drops of our darkness. For the good works of the faithful, which aid our brothers or cherish the needy, refresh and renew Him. This is why He finally rejected the comment of Judas, who, when the spirit of the devil had entered his soul, begrudged Christ's feet the ointment of the woman; for Christ is anointed, lent resources, and fed by works of love and mercy.

But the betrayer betrayed his own faithlessness before he betrayed the Lord. It was not concern for the poor but anxiety for his ill-gotten gains and the spite of his sceptical mind that had impelled his indignation. He assessed that ointment (and however costly it was, it was utterly cheap in comparison with the Lord's blood) as more valuable than the Body which brings salvation. So he was angry with the woman whose extravagance was motivated by love, and whose kindness the Lord Himself acknowledges. By this He teaches us that concern for the poor must be relegated, but only to Himself. He wished to show that Judas' heart was distorted in putting mercy before faith, for faith is the tinder of good works, and the Teacher comes before the teachings. But *the son of perdition*[208] showed how cheap he held Christ by his further saying that the ointment poured over Him was wasted. So Judas is not worthy of Christ's blood, for he cannot have as redeemer One whom he preferred to put up for sale. He signed a contract for death, so he is rightly debarred from the commerce of life. He was to be condemned by his own decision, by which he sold for thirty gold coins[209] the One whom the woman had anointed at a cost of three hundred, which was

his own estimate.[210] His judgment was awry, because he
counted the Lord Himself cheap, whereas he considered
dear the ointment anticipating His burial, which would
bring us salvation.

Like the devil, he was truly ignorant of God's grace, of
which he had no portion; with hatred rather than love he
regarded as dear the price of Christ's death, by which
Christ buys us, not sells us, at great cost, and saves us without demanding a return. He wishes to enhance our value
by making His gift cheap; He is all the more precious to
us because of the love which makes Him long to be accounted cheap so that all may buy Him.[211] For, as Scripture says: *The Lord hath made the poor and the rich, and
He hath equally care of all.*[212] So He says: *Freely have you
received* grace; *freely give.*[213] Peter was rich in the freely
given wealth of this grace. He had no money, but he enriched with health the poor lame man who desired only
beggarly alms.[214]

35. So let us forswear greed for gold that we may have
abundance of grace. Let us become cheap in the eyes of
this world by voluntary poverty, and become an ointment
precious to the Lord. We shall breathe forth Christ's
goodly fragrance to God if *we bear about in our body the
death of Christ, and manifest His life*[215] in our spirit, and
are scented with the fragrance of the Passion and Resurrection of the Lord. Now we apply ointment to the body of
Christ if we apply our persons and our lives to faith in His
truth and obedience to His teaching. Then we shall
through His body emit scents filling the whole of His
house, if we can ever say with perfect love: "*The world is
crucified to me,*[216] for I do not love riches, or worldly distinctions, or my own possessions, but Christ's; I love not

things visible but things invisible."²¹⁷ This will be the hair
to give us strength and aid our holy service, so that with it
we can wipe the feet of Christ and break the cord of sins,
thankfully saying in the spirit of freedom: *Thou hast
broken my bonds: I will sacrifice to Thee a victim of
praise.*²¹⁸

36. But while part of the course is yet to be run, whilst
there remains time to serve, let us nourish this kind of hair.
Let us imitate not only the love of that sinner of the
Gospel, that by great love we may discharge our great
debts, but also her untimely insistence, that we may snatch
salvation from the anger overhanging us. Let us seek the
Bread of life in season and out of season, beating on the
door of the Father of the house even at night. For Scripture says: *In the nights lift up your hands to the holy
places.*²¹⁹

Let us wear out the thresholds of all the wise who dwell
in Christ, as we are bidden,²²⁰ and everywhere lay hold of
the food of life wherever we can pursue the word of God.
Let us hang on the lips of all the faithful because the
Spirit of God breathes on every believer; and heavenly
wisdom must drop from the smallest servant of God, even
if it is only a drop to bedew my parched heart and to provide a draught more abundantly beneficial to me than the
rivers of this world's philosophers. For I prefer *to speak
five words in the Law than many thousands in a tongue,*²²¹
just as *it is better to live for one day in the courts of the
Lord above thousands in the tabernacles of sinners.*²²²

For *the Spirit breathes where He will, and I hear His
voice and know not whence He cometh.*²²³ I shall intercept
His breath wherever I can catch the slightest exhalation.
Let me only hear that a just man has entered the house of

an unworthy man or Pharisee, and I shall hasten to be first
to win the favour of the guest, in the hope that I can anticipate the kingdom of heaven. Wherever the name of
Christ rings in my ears, I shall hasten to it; whosesoever is
the house which I know Jesus is entering, I, too, shall hurry
there. Whenever I see wisdom and justice reclining in a
man's inner room, I shall run to the feet of Christ, so that
I may be stamped if only by the tip of Wisdom's foot. I
shall not disdain His feet; rather I shall pray that even with
them Christ may touch my head. The woman touched the
hem of His garment, and was healed;[224] others were healed
even by the shadow of Peter falling on them as he
passed.[225]

37. Let us stretch out our hair before Him. In other
words, let us strew before Him all the distinctions of our
decorations.[226] Let us cast ourselves down that we may be
raised by Him *who dwelleth on high and looketh down on
the low things.*[227] Let us tearfully confess our sins, so that
of us, too, the heavenly Justice may say: *With tears he
hath washed My feet and with his hairs hath wiped
them.*[228]

It was perhaps for this reason that He did not wash His
own feet when he washed his disciples', so that we can
wash them with our tears.[229] No inconsiderable merit is
won by that soul of which Wisdom can say: *Since she
came in, she hath not ceased to kiss My feet.*[230] What is this
kiss but the eternal pledge of that charity *which covereth a
multitude of sins?*[231] The Church was already preparing
these kisses for her Bridegroom when she sang: *Let Him
kiss me with the kisses of His mouth.*[232] This privilege is
rightly claimed only by that love of the Catholic Church
which is kept uniquely and perfectly for a single Man, and

which seeks the kisses of truth from the lips of the very Word, so that it may not be defiled by the poisonous deceit of heretics, which are the kisses, so to speak, of the lewd mouth of a stranger.

38. So let us plant chaste kisses on the feet of Christ, that we may deserve to rise from His feet to His head, and as we grow towards his upper limbs, may soon presume to ask for kisses on the face and mouth to which we have drawn near. When we have savoured the word of God in pure hearts, and tasted how sweet the Lord is,[233] our souls may then be fired with the love of Wisdom to the depths of our hearts. Refreshed by this sweet fervour, and pierced by the fiery arrows of the Lord's love, by which all foreign pleasure in the enemy's delights is destroyed, our souls may be pricked to the heart, and say: *I am wounded by love.*[234]

Blessed indeed is he who can anoint Christ's feet even with a kiss. Would that someone would burn my wretched mouth and cleanse my tongue with that heavenly coal,[235] so that I might deserve to touch even the heel of Christ with the tip of my tongue, to thrust my head beneath His holy soles, and cleanse them so that instead my head could be cleansed by His feet! And in licking God's feet I might purify my unclean lips on the feet of the chaste Christ.

39. So let us encourage each other and vie in saying: *Come, let us adore and weep before the Lord who made us.*[236] By weeping before Him we shall engender our joys, by anointing the soles of His feet we shall heal our wounds. For whatever we expend on Christ we bestow rather on ourselves.

That woman cleansed herself by washing Christ, washed away her sins by wiping His feet, and loved herself by loving Him. So she deserved to hear the words: *Daughter, thy*

faith hath made thee safe,[237] whereas Simon, who was a son
of the kingdom, did not. She won greater justification
from her service than he did from his feast. For the Pharisee
had not believed, but she did. In fact the Pharisee said:
*This Man, if He were a prophet, would know surely who
this woman is that toucheth Him.*[238] So Simon was not
justified by the feast to which he had invited Christ as if
He were a mere man. Perhaps he thought that Christ, to
the extent that Christ was for our sakes poor, was indebted
to him, because he considered it so great that he, a rich
man, invited a poor man to his table. But that woman
would not have hoped for the remission of her sins through
this great round of service, expense, and tears if she had not
believed in God in Christ; and so she found the head of
her salvation at the very tip of the Saviour's foot.

40. Poor Jew, where will you cast yourself? Our sinner
anticipated you by embarking on your tasks in your own
house. You feasted to show your arrogance; she fasted to
play the servant. The water that you had refused to pour
from your jugs she provided from her eyes. You did not
wipe Christ's feet even with a towel, but she did so with
her hair. You were unwilling to touch His feet even with
your hands, but she did not cease to caress them with her
kisses. Undoubtedly you ought to have provided this service to the guest you had received in your house, if you had
preserved the law of hospitality even according to the
example of your fathers; it is enough to cast up before
your pride the example of father Abraham.[239] So she was
preferred to you, for by her faithful love she proved that
she was more truly the child of your father.

The lack of kindness by which you disdained to wash
the feet of the Lord proves that you have fallen below the

standard of Abraham, for he washed the feet of the angels,[240] and the Lord Himself washed those of His poor servants. Yet on that occasion, too, the father of faith washed the feet of Christ as well; Christ alone of the three divine persons did Abraham see with his prophet's eyes and adore, and so He Himself rebukes you with the pertinent words: *If you were the children of Abraham, you would do the works of Abraham.*[241] Christ added: *Abraham saw My day, and was glad.*[242] Christ accounted blessed also *those who have not seen but have believed*[243] in company with those who did see. From this it is clear that in us survives the faith that we have gained, but in you the condition of bad faith.

41. So let the Jews who glory in the body rather than the spirit of their father Abraham keep their pride, their riches, their nobility, their justice. Only their flesh, and not their hearts, is circumcised. Christ, the crucified Christ, suffices us for salvation and glory; for from the stones He raised us up as sons to Abraham,[244] while the sons of Abraham were stiffening into the stones from which we came.

The blessing of Ephrem, who was set on the left, but at Jacob's right hand, is of profit to us; when Jacob with his arms fashioned the mystery of the cross and placed his left hand across to the head of Manasses, who with the confidence of the elder brother had taken his position on the right of his grandfather,[245] he designated the Jews; for the cross was to be for them a stumbling block, but for the Christians a glory. The cross was to remove the Jew from right to left, but me from left to right, for the Jews slipped into our wasteland, and we came into their crops. They have taken over our blindness, and we have succeeded to their grace.

Yet we shall not take pleasure at our salvation in such a way, O Jews, as to rejoice in your death. For your physical brother, who is our spiritual master, has taught us not *to boast against the broken branches*,[246] for it is not by our own deeds but by the kindnesses of God's mercies that we have grown on to the tree of which you are the root. But our common Lord, who is the Father of Christians and so God of the faithful, can graft you in turn on the native clefts of your own bark, and set you again in your own sod, which by beneficial adoption has implanted the marrow in us through the sap of your richness, so that a single root can sustain both of us together if we bear fruit for the Lord.

42. Meanwhile I prefer the wealth of our poor sinner's tears and love to the riches which you boast—filial disrespect and the letter of the Law. I prefer her fasting to your feast. I would rather be tied to the feet of Christ amongst her hair than recline with you at your table next to Christ, but without possessing Him. If I have no ointment for the feet of Christ now, I shall have no oil for my torch at His coming. It will go hard with me if my ointment is cheap, for it must be costly that I may deserve to share my burial with His; for unless I die in His death, I shall not live in His Resurrection. So let us love Him whom we have an obligation to love. Let us kiss Him whose embrace is chastity. Let us have intercourse with Him, with whom marriage is virginity. Let us be subject to Him, for if we are prostrate beneath Him we stand above the world. Let us be cast down for the sake of Him, for if we fall for Him it means resurrection. Let us die with Him in whom is life.

43. How shall we be able worthily to make recompense

to this Lord in whom we live when we are dead? For He in turn deigns to be to us whatever we His poor servants have been to Him. He mingles with us, and implants us in Him, so that what He has received from us is put to our own profit. He regards all that is given to us, *his least brethren*,[247] as having been given to Him.

Likewise He shares His glory with His people, giving us a participation in almost everything, even in His names. Just as He is called the Strength of God, so He deigns to be our strength, too: *God is our Refuge and our Strength*.[248] As we are His heirs, so He is ours, for you read in the book of Moses: *The people of Jacob are become the Lord's portion;* and again in the Psalms: *The Lord is my portion*.[249] Just as He called Himself *the Light of this world*, so He said to His own: *You are the light of this world*.[250]

Again, He says: *I am the living Bread;* and: *We are all one bread*.[251] Elsewhere He states: *I am the true Vine;* and to you He says: *I planted thee a fruitful vine, all true*.[252] Christ is the *mountain of God, in which God is well pleased to dwell,* and His saints are the *mountains of God, fruitful mountains,* from which *He enlighteneth us wonderfully from the everlasting mountains*.[253] Christ is the rock, for *they drank of the spiritual Rock that followed them, and the Rock was Christ*.[254] The favour of this name, too, He did not refuse to His disciple; He says to him: *Upon this rock I will build My church, and the gates of hell shall not prevail against it*.[255]

44. But why are we surprised that He granted His names to His servants, when He shares even His Father and His kingship with them? *For to those who received Him, He gave them power to be made the sons of God;* and for Himself He said to all men: *You are gods, and all*

of you the sons of the Most High.[256] But through the sinning of our own free will we *die like men and fall like one of the princes.*[257]

Lucifer was one of these angelic princes before he fell and became the devil by defection.[258] To him the words of Scripture are addressed: *How is Lucifer fallen from heaven, when he did rise in the morning?*[259] But we are not condemned to eternal death as he is, for he was the author of sin. He will be punished both on his own account and for the man who died by the sin with which the devil killed him.[260] But that man did not deserve to be finally excluded from Paradise and from the earth, for the justice of God more indulgently decreed that he sinned not through his own design but through another's. It is more sinful to deceive than to be deceived, to devise a sin than to execute it. So he who consented to the deceit was punished for a time for his improvement, but the deviser of death was doomed to eternal punishment. This punishment for his sin will never end, because the sin never ceases.[261]

So it was not an angel or ambassador but, as Scripture says,[262] the Lord Himself who came to raise the shipwrecked, to loose the fettered, *to save that which was lost.*[263] But in order to confound him who deceived us with reciprocated deceit, the only-begotten Son of God deigned through the mystery of His love to receive our frail nature, so that the devil might be vanquished by means of the nature which he had deceived; so that he who was, and is, always subject to the strength and laws of God might be subjugated to a Man.

45. *What,* then, *shall I render to the Lord for all the things that He hath rendered to me?*[264] For like a good Lord He has repaid me by giving blessings for evils, though

on Him we had heaped evils in return for blessings. He blessed us, and we cursed Him. He healed us, and we blasphemed Him. He pardoned the unholy, and *was reputed with the wicked.*[265] What, then, shall I repay Him for my sins which He has endured and for the blessings He has bestowed on me? What repayment can I make for His taking human flesh, for the blows He sustained, for the insults and the scourgings, for His cross and death and burial? Very well, let us repay cross with cross, death with death. But, of course, we can never make repayment, for we have *of Him and by Him and in Him all things,*[266] including ourselves who possess them. *He made us, and not we ourselves;*[267] our souls are always in His hands. Let us then repay with love our debts to Him; let our gift be charity and our currency grace. If we do not love, it will be the worse for us.

46. But when can I, poor needy wretch, hope to be able to repay a Lord like this, when even the apostles confess that they have not repaid Him? Hear, for example, one of them admitting that he has not repaid Him: *Who hath first given to Him, and recompense shall be made him?*[268] But thanks be to Him, for He discounts the interest on His great loan to us, and guarantees a profit on the huge sum that I owe Him; He seeks in return only our love, putting this in first place among His commandments and thereby showing that even we beggars can discharge to Him the debt we cannot pay.

So no one should cite as pretext the difficulty of payment, for none can say that he has no heart. No sacrifices or costly gifts or grinding toil is demanded of us; we have the wherewithal to pay, for our love is a commodity that we control. Let us bestow it on the Lord, and we pay our

debt. David, for example, summed this up when freed from
the power of all his enemies. In return for his complete
deliverance and safety he repaid the Lord with the wealth
not of his kingdom but of his heart. He uttered the Psalm:
I will love Thee, O Lord, my Strength.[269]

47. I go even further and say that the Creditor will be
our Debtor if we make free payment of heartfelt love to
Him as the reward for His goodness, which He proffers
gratuitously to us. But He is loved also in our persons, for
He said that the mark of His disciples would be that they
loved each other as He loved us.[270] This means that we
should have one heart and one soul in Christ, and that each
does for his neighbour what he wishes to be done to himself.[271] For this reason I boast of my love for you in the
Lord, for this alone allows me to pay in some degree to
God at least one of the great and countless debts I owe
Him. For I confess that to all other blessings I have not
been outstandingly or especially admitted, and that only in
my love for you am I perfect.

LETTER 24

To Severus[1]

The sinners Paulinus and Therasia greet Severus.

1. I have a further point to make to you—though no doubt you will welcome my criticism with your letter-files flung open. Doubtless, too, you are keen to shout my words from the housetops as loudly as you can—I am quoting your own words here. I intend to lay a complaint against you which you can judge yourself, and if you declare this complaint to be on a par with the rest of my idle chatter, you will simultaneously reveal your rashness.

It is to complain about this temerity that I write this letter. The close of my last one,[2] in which I discussed charity and perfection, has impelled me to begin this. The reason why I grumble at your excessive feelings of friendship is that your great affection leads you even to commit the sin of lying. Whether I call to mind your comments about yourself, as you seek with false censure to lessen your burdens, or those about me, as you increase my burdens with unjustified praise,[3] I shall convict you of sinning against charity from motives of charity. For *charity*, says Scripture, *is kind; love for our neighbour worketh no evil.*[4] You show me that it is kind, for I experience it and indeed glory in it.

But be careful not to contravene the rule of charity by seeming to do evil to your neighbours. If you pile a heap of sins on your neighbours by burdening them with un-

deserved praise, if you appear not to have the same intention for me as for yourself (for you think it right to give
me the flattery which you think useless for yourself), you
will justly be told: *If your love was just, but your ap-
portioning was not, you have sinned.*[5] Perhaps, however, in
doing this you have a deeper design of love, and by ascrib-
ing to me the good qualities I do not possess you may be
trying to apply the goad of shame, so that by reading what
I ought to be, I may learn to be good, and strive to align
myself to your description, and perhaps be able to become
what I am not through shame at not being as you describe
me.

Meanwhile, however, since my self-knowledge is aware
that your words are not trustworthy, my sense of shame
rejects them as flattery. As I have said, the palm of perfection would be apposite for·yourself; so why should you
presume to ascribe it to me as though the contest were
already fought and I were victorious, merely because I
appear to have unloaded all the baggage of my earthly
possessions?

And why should you lament that you on the contrary
are still unhappily clinging to the slimy dregs of hell below,
just because from your letter you appear not to have sold
one petty estate? Your forfeiture of your present right
even to that farm is equivalent to selling it, so that by the
greater fruits of your faith you showed to God a twofold
dedication. As both a seller and a donor of your farms, you
have applied your goods to different purposes, yet for the
single gain of life and within the limits of the same divine
command. So you are an owner without being mentally a
captive to your wealth, for the goods you have kept back
are possessed by the church which you serve.[6]

2. So weigh my accounts as carefully as your own in accord with the words of the Lord, so that you may neither lose trust in yourself as one loaded with the world's goods, nor felicitate me as one now free of them. Remember that there are *diversities of graces*[7] and different measures of gifts. God, who is the sole Steward, arranges these in the limbs of His body, distinguishing the different members by the offices He decides upon. But out of the different limbs he makes one body. He is enriched by the grace of His sacred body if manifold virtues are numbered in the single structure. *So the queen may stand on His right hand with gilded fringes, clothed around with variety.*[8]

Realise now the immensity of God's gift to you within the Church, for He has assigned to you a share of the destiny of those who have lived perfect in the Law, having possessions yet in such a way that they were not possessed by them. Lot, Abraham, and Job are examples of how such men put no love of property or relatives before the love and teaching of the Lord.[9] But you may share also the lot of those perfected by the fulness of the Gospel, for you have sold the estates which carried the greater wealth and allure.

3. So I am sure that there awaits you equal rest *amongst the midst of the lots*[10] of God, which is how Scripture describes the sleep of the clergy. For the clergy are the lots of the Lord which we read of in both Testaments,[11] and from which is fulfilled the inheritance of the Lord and the perfection of the saints.[12] So I am ready to adapt the words of the Lord against you, and to say to you: "You see the mote of grace in your brother's eye, and do not feel the beam of this same blessing in your own."[13]

As I have said, you have undertaken two saintly roles, by refusing to own the land you have retained, and by achieving perfection through that which you have sold. So in your apparent role of owner you are perfect, because your mind is free from the ties of possessions; mindful of how short the time is, you fulfil Paul's injunction by possessing without possessing,[14] for you keep possessions not for yourself but for those with nothing. You play host in your house so that your house may be a hospice. You are a traveller from your native land, and an exile in this world that you may dwell in Paradise and be a citizen of your former country. You do not crowd your houses with dining tables, or cram them with masses of furniture or wealth. You measure off a corner for yourself and fill the house with travellers and beggars. You live as a fellow servant with your own slaves. The temporary lodging which is your dwelling you do not possess like the father of a household, but you lodge there like a mercenary or a lodger, paying the Lord a regular rent for the favour of the lodging by serving your neighbours with body and mind.

4. But if a reward is to be offered us or a bargain struck in accordance with the nature of our work, if an assessment is to be made of what we have done and left undone, your inner perfection will be calculated as equalling the actions of those who have sold everything. For you have left nothing for yourself either by right of ownership or (what is more important) by intention. Your dealings with the world leave you free of it. Perhaps that constancy and inner faith, which saves you from burning though surrounded by fires, and from being caught though snares beset you, which allows you to touch pitch without being

defiled,[15] are to be adjudged the mark of a faith stronger than that of those who you think are strong. I think that these last are to be considered the weaker, because they could not trust their frailty and hastened to dispose of everything to which they feared to cling.

So you are *free among the dead*.[16] Though you have earthly possessions, you are no longer earth but rise above the earth. You are not defiled by the contagion of carrion; you do not dwell amongst the tombs of outcasts sleeping there,[17] for you have buried your life in heaven by hiding it in Christ. But let me not endure the odium incurred by perfection, but rather receive the pardon due to weakness, for you cannot deny that it is braver to forgo the property you possess than that which you have sold, and more courageous to reject what you have than to avoid having what you reject.

5. You should indeed consider the Lord's very words which lead you to claim perfection for me, and you will see that you have regarded the beginnings as the end. *If thou wilt be perfect*, He says, *go, sell all thou hast and give it to the poor*.[18] If He had ended His words at this point, I should be wrong to rebuke you; and I should take the initiative in demanding that you, whose soul is close to mine because of its similar vocation, should congratulate me on now, at the completion of the contest, holding in my hands the palm, which like the tenth groat[19] had been lost by our first human parent, but which was found when the lamp of the saving Word was lit within the house.

But notice how weighty are the words which remain, when the Lord of majesty Himself adds: *And come, follow Me*.[20] Then consider the difficulty of this. Open your heart and assess it, and you will realise that you have still

on my behalf greater causes for anxiety than for thanksgiving. For the goods, or rather the burdens, imposed on
me easily fell away when I gave up my cloak.[21] Since I had
not brought them with me into the world and could not
take them away with me,[22] I regarded them as a loan which
I was returning. I did not tear them off like skin from
flesh, but laid them aside like clothes from my body.

6. Now I must offer to God what is really mine, *pre-
senting my body*, heart, and soul *as a living sacrifice* to the
Lord, as Scripture says.[23] I must build myself into His holy
temple at the very cornerstone,[24] which gave us in Himself
the rule for our sanctification. *Be holy*, He says, *because I
am holy*.[25] What grace, then, will accrue to me if I am
faithful only in what does not belong to me, and do not
serve with what is my own, which entails loving God by a
free decision of the will with all my heart and all my inner
soul, as Scripture says?[26]

To this love the prophet provokes us when he says: *I
will freely sacrifice to Thee*.[27] For what God welcomes
and desires is that *our good deed be voluntary*,[28] so that we
may receive what is ours—a home in Paradise and the
eternal life for which we were created. If we are purged of
the possessions of this world to which we descended when
we were condemned, and if we recover that life, then we
shall in truth be restored to our fatherland as though from
exile. We shall return from distant travels to the home of
our birth, and we shall be able to say: *The Lord is our
portion in the land of the living*.[29]

7. So abandoning or parting from the temporal goods of
this world is not the completion but the beginning of the
course; it is not the winning-post but the start. An athlete
does not strip after victory; he undresses to commence the

contest, and he will gain the crown only after duly com-
peting.[30] A swimmer strips to cross a river barrier. He will
not swim across with all the encumbrances he has taken
off; he must cut through the force of the current, and endure the fatigue of swimming, by straining with his whole
body, moving adroitly all his limbs, striking out with his
feet, using his arms as oars, and gliding along on his side.

8. But I see that the manner of this journey was anticipated by the blessed patriarch Jacob. For I read that after
he had crossed the current, having sent ahead the burdens
of his anxieties (which were the hindrances of bodily
riches and relatives) he remained alone in his tent to
struggle with God. He succeeded in extracting a blessing
from Him and obtained the name Israel,[31] which is consecrated in heaven and on earth.

Now this account is regarded chiefly as prefiguring the
mystery of salvation, with Jacob representing the Jews, his
physical descendants. He prevailed over the Lord just as
the Jews prevailed over Pilate, as it is written, in extorting
from him the Passion of Christ when they said: *Crucify
Him, crucify Him. And,* it says, *their voices prevailed.*[32]
But it appears that in the context of the present discussion
we must regard the story as symbolising the precept of the
Gospel. In other words, by the exemplar of Jacob we may
understand that we can[33] be fitted for a struggle with God,
for we contend with Him precisely when we strive to fulfil His word, and we attempt to prevail against God's
strength by imitating Him.

So we cannot be suited to embark upon the path of life,
to lay hold of the word of God, to prevail against the
kingdom of heaven (which from the time of John suffers
violence from the plunderers),[34] unless before the evening

of our death we send ahead of us all the things which hinder and delay us through our love or anxiety for them, if they cling to us on the journey of this life. We must struggle to lay hold of and cling to Christ throughout the whole night of this world with anxious efforts of spiritual works and pursuits. We must refuse to be torn from Christ's love, as Jacob clung to His embrace, unless we exact a blessing from Him.

And I pray that, as a mark of the struggle for salvation, He may strike *the sinew of my thigh*[35] with the fear of His majesty; when numbed, the strength of my flesh will be weakened, and the grace of the spirit will grow strong. But the sinew of Jacob's smitten thigh shrank to symbolize the barrenness and degeneration of the Jews, showing that the section of his sons who seceded from their fathers' faith ceased to be fertile for God. So it is that she who was fertile with children was weakened,[36] and through abandoning the precepts of her Maker she has stumbled on paths of her own wandering.

9. But we ourselves must nonetheless be careful not to appear barren in the Lord's sight, or to limp on His path with halting foot. We must be barren rather in the fruits of the body, converting that numbness of our forefather's thigh, smitten by the hand of God, into the stiffness of temperance, so that drained of all desires which hamstring the strength of faith, we may strengthen our souls with the chastity in which Paul schools us,[37] and which even physical athletes sedulously observe. So since chastity is cultivated even by contenders for a frail and short-lived crown, we must preserve it with a more intense zeal, for we are wrestling for the crown that does not wither.

Therefore, since we are to fight in the Lord's presence

in the theatre of this world, in front of rows of men and angels, let us strip ourselves of detrimental works that we may clothe ourselves in healing ones. He who says: *Follow Me*,[38] wishes us to prepare ourselves so that *we may apprehend wherein we are also apprehended*[39] by Him. He summons us to where *He sitteth at the right hand of God*[40] in the glory of the Father, and He says to all men: *Come to Me, all you that are burdened and labour, and you shall find rest for your souls*.[41]

In so far as it lies with Him, He wishes all men to be saved,[42] for He has made us all. He came down to us that we might rise to Him. He took the shape of our flesh, which was a slave to sin, that He might fashion us to His flesh, which did no sin, so that we might truly be refashioned to our original glory, if only by emulation we attain the divine likeness to Christ.

For Genesis itself, the book which relates the handiwork of God, shows that in Adam there remained to us only the image of God. At first, whilst the labour of creating man is still progressing,[43] both the likeness and the image of God are mentioned; but in the following verse man is said to have been made only in God's image. Scripture certainly showed foreknowledge of the future here, revealing that the word "likeness" was withdrawn from Adam because he was about to sin. It was to be kept for the men who live in Christ, who by His loving obedience reconciled to His Father the world which had been estranged by the disobedience of our first parent.

Accordingly that likeness to God, which had been lost by a slave whose puffed-up pride made him desire equality with the Lord, was recovered by the Lord Himself, who emptied Himself to take the form of a slave. Man, who through the devil's trickery had fallen by his own pride, rose again by his faith in a lowly Lord, when the devil was brought low by the humiliation of the highest Lord. So Christ, who suffered for us and for us *became obedient even to the death of the cross*,[44] recommended to us the way of life and perfection of virtue involving not only the sale of estates and donation of the moneys from them, but also the act of following Him. And because He had said: *When I be lifted up, I will draw all things to Myself*, He therefore says: *Come, follow Me*.[45]

Blessed is he who follows so close as to say: *My soul hath stuck close to Thee*.[46] Only the love which is *the end of the commandment and the fulfilling of the law* can make that claim, for love *from a pure heart, and a good conscience, and an unfeigned faith* so penetrates and clings to God that it loves nothing outside Him, and it says: *I am always with Thee*.[47] So our entire toil and consuming task lie in watching and examining[48] our hearts. We cannot see their darkness, or the lair of the enemy concealed there, unless we clear our minds of the cares of externals and turn them inwards upon themselves. For Scripture's words are not without point: *With all watchfulness keep thy heart*.[49]

10. I think that you have now realised how fatiguingly and unremittingly the struggle with this enemy proceeds every single day, how large is the ambush in my heart, how strong the vices and how weak the virtues there, how headlong its relapse to wickedness, and how sluggish its struggle towards God. Now the disharmony caused by the conflicting law earlier enclosed within me comes to light.

Now I feel the power of that hostile law which lays its hand on me and strives to drag me captive to the law of sin.

I recognise that it is through my unhappiness that Paul burns, that it is through my disposition that he cries out in grief for me: *Unhappy man that I am, who shall deliver me from the body of this death?*[50] But Paul is also the master who reforms and refashions me. He shows me the path out to salvation, if only *to will is present with me,*[51] so that through the grace of God I may deserve to find perfection through Jesus Christ our Lord.

We must win from Him our prayer that He may prevail over our enemies, submerge the darkness, destroy in us the foreign elements which are our own, and build up those that are His. I realise that even God's friends have had to merit this favour through prayer. They were enduring their hearts with patience at the moment when they said: *Create a clean heart in me, O God, and renew a right spirit within my bowels.*[52] When the Psalmist has gained his request, he is untroubled, and says: *Prove me, O Lord, and know my heart; see if there be in me the way of iniquity.*[53]

But to avoid the impression that he has won this self-confidence by his own strength rather than by God's grace, he also says: *For Thou, O Lord, hast possessed my reins.*[54] For, as the Lord Himself has said, we can do nothing without Him because He is the true Vine and we are His branches.[55] If we abide in His love, we do not wither, but live by the sap of His eternal root; we shall not be cut out in anger for the fire, but rather be pruned by instruction to bear fruit. The sharp edge of the Gospels' knife will cut away the foliage, so that when the luxuriance of our vine is restrained, we may sprout forth more fruit.

11. So when the Lord begins His husbandry in us He says: *I am come to cast fire on the earth.*[56] He means that by His fire He is clearing our sin-choked hearts as if they were a field bristling with thorns, by bringing fire to our sins and light to our senses. The loving Farmer wields the knife of salvation to attack the stems of our former actions, so that His words of fire may burn the superfluous stubble of the former harvest and prepare our souls as a field for a fresh sowing. So these seeds may sprout forth as an abundant and fertile crop of virtues, once the ploughshare of God's word has been pushed into the earth and the thorns rooted out. After the roots of harmful weeds have been destroyed, the harvest can be multiplied and made worthy of the barns of heaven. But because we are not merely God's husbandry but also His building (for we are both cultivated and erected by His grace and spirit and word), He intends to build us up on the journey on which He summons us after Him; and He prepares us by the act of persuading us to sell and get rid of our possessions.

And because anxiety and affection for them blunt the edge of one's mind, and trouble the soul by diverting it from its inner concerns to externals, He further says to us, through His prophet: *Be still, and see that I am the Lord.*[57] Clearly He seems also to say: *You cannot serve two masters.*[58] It is not idleness that He urges upon us, for He warns us to watch and pray earnestly that we may not be put to the test.[59] He is urging us to relax by being at leisure from the world and busy for Him; to desist from worldly occupations, our concern for which causes us to take a holiday from God.

12. So we must destroy our old life that we may build

up the new. Because darkness has no intercourse with light, nor mammon with Christ, we must exchange the old for the new. We must transform our pattern of business and leisure, and involve ourselves in the things we have eschewed so that we may eschew our previous involvements. We must end our former life, and in turn start to live for the works and preoccupations to which we have been dead; for we have been dead to what brings life, and have lived amongst the dead by performing lethal works. So our holy teacher makes the gentle and fair demand that as we formerly yielded our members to serve wickedness, so now we should yield them as instruments of justice;[60] once we have changed masters, we must also change our pursuits.

It is not by a change of masters that we lay aside freedom or slavery. Once we have redirected our freedom and our slavery for the better, we can seek happiness only when we break the bonds of wickedness, when by submitting to the yoke of righteousness we accept the reins of fear of God. By amending our path to the direct way, we must start to free ourselves from the sin to which we were slaves in our wretched freedom, when we warred on righteousness.

13. So now in turn we are slaves to God and insurgents against this world. We are commencing the contest, and with our trust in the Lord we challenge that very enemy whose slaves we were. You are surely aware, my brother (for I speak to you as a fellow soldier, and your experience is the same as mine), how great is the conflict within me, and how great is the enemy—not flesh and blood, but powers unseen and the spiritual wickedness of which Paul speaks,[61] with which the vices of our flesh conspire as

instruments. So they are called *the rulers of darkness*,[62] be-cause, according to Paul, sinners are called darkness, and the evil spirits rule them because they are like themselves.

But the entire *fashion of this world*, which *passes away*[63] and entices hearts through the eyes, is stretched out before us by the devil's nets; fashioned in his likeness, it is a noose and a sword for the mind. Let us believe the prophet, that we walk in the midst of snares,[64] and that our life is spent amidst swords hidden with death-dealing cunning. This world, blossoming with varied pleasures and venomous with treacherous charms, intercepts us. The snake, "whose names and baneful skills are legion,"[65] intercepts us with countless ambushes, and often fiercely attacks us in open contest, assailing us with white-hot darts if he does not catch us in his hidden snares. For *his mighty arrows are sharp and his coals lay waste*,[66] that is, they burn our souls with the harmful fires of desires and rob us of the dwelling of the Holy Spirit.

When this happens, very different are the guests who steal into us; *a man's enemies become they of his own household*.[67] Now they puff us up with the wind of ambi-tion, now they ignite us with the torches of lusts, now they bind us with the chains of greed. Should greed even by herself, equipped as she is with every sin, capture us, enough wickedness is provided for the devil, and death for man.[68]

14. Unhappy mankind, what can you do then, set amongst such formidable enemies? How in your weakness will you stand up against the strong, defenceless against armed enemies? The blessed Job, though wounded by many of the devil's darts, remained heart-whole and cried: *Naked came I out of my mother's womb;* who then will

arm me against the numerous columns of the aerial enemy, and prevent me from *returning naked* as I came to the earth?[69]

See now how I revive, gain strength, and arise. *The Lord is my Light, the Lord is the Protector of my life; if armies in camp should stand together against me, my heart shall not fear.*[70] I shall not lose heart even if I lack arms of my own resource, for I have the armoury of Christ. From it I can make use of the arms of light with which to storm the princes of darkness and the columns of night as they oppose me in the heavenly regions, the regions, that is, of the spirit, which they strive to vanquish by the entice-ments of earth.

Against them, however, I shall have as arms-bearer and standard-bearer the man who was God's chosen vessel.[71] He will bind my loins with the girdle of chastity, he will cap my head with the helmet of salvation, he will shield my breast with the breastplate of justice. He will protect my whole body with the sword of faith, he will arm my right hand—or rather my whole person, transformed into Christ's right hand—with the sword of the spirit and the word of truth,[72] so that *a thousand shall fall at my side, and ten thousand at my right hand.*[73] He will shoe my feet for the preparation of the Gospel,[74] so that I may both walk over the thorns and thistles of this earth, treading on them without hurt, and safely enter upon the rough and narrow way with feet protected; and I may crush the hostile serpent's head beneath my feet without fear of being bitten, by means of the very heel for which the cunning one keeps watch.

I do not arrogantly claim this promise for myself, out of the boldness of my weakness, but for every believer, by reason of the strength of Christ.[75] For just as *He calleth those things that are not as those that are*,[76] so He is able to destroy the strong and lofty things of this world by means of His weak and lowly subjects, as He has always done and does. For this reason He has given us a master[77] who imitated Him, so that through him we may attain imitation of the Lord Himself.

15. The master himself teaches me to stand in the line of battle, run in the stadium, and wrestle in the contest, by bruising his own body.[78] *He forgets the things that are behind, and stretches forth himself to those that are before.*[79] He is so firmly embedded in the rock that he boasts even in infirmities. He is strong when he is weak, and, as he proclaims,[80] he is able to do all things in Christ who strengthens His own, fights for us, and conquers in us. This was why Paul said: *So run that you may all obtain.*[81]

It is just the opposite in an earthly contest. A wrestling match cannot end without differing outcomes for the contestants; the glory of the one is the shame of the other. But since we, being many, are one in Christ, we all run as one and all share a joint journey to the one good. So we are told: *So run that you may all obtain.* As Paul also says,[82] there cannot be a cleavage in the body whose head is Christ. He is the summit common to all His members, the single structure of which goes with Him. Since the members cannot be at odds with each other, let us run together that we may all obtain, without hostile rivalry and with equal success. Just as in the struggle of the race we are the toil of Christ, so when we reach the goal we can be His triumph, and He can bless us *in the crown of the year of His goodness.*[83]

16. I realise, however, that in this struggle it is in our

interests to be conquered as much as to conquer, for both
enemy and friend dwell in us. What is more friendly to
me than the spirit which wars on the flesh and prevents it
from dragging me to the law of sin? What is more hostile
than the flesh which *lusteth against the spirit*[84] in support
of death?

So *better to me are the wounds of a friend*, which Christ
endured to heal me, *than the voluntary kisses of an
enemy*,[85] by which the evil-counselling flesh beguiles me
through the enticements of its delights, so that it may
betray me, as if by the murderous kiss of Judas, to my
enemies who are ready to lead me captive. The Lord acknowledged that kiss not to welcome the peace of the betrayer but to take back His own from one estranged, yet
this is a salutary exemplar of perfect goodness to keep
before our eyes—how, with the same kindness with which
He bids us also to love our enemies, He bestowed a friendly
kiss on the enemy of peace, and returned love for hatred
though experiencing hatred in return for love.

17. So it is easy to identify the victors when Christ and
the spirit are allies against the devil and the flesh;[86] for it is
better to be conquered by good than to prevail by evil. So
the man who loses his tunic to another[87] is apparently defeated in this world, but he who gives his cloak as well to
the man who takes his tunic, triumphs in Christ. Human
vengeance consists in returning injury for injury; but the
revenge of heaven is to love your enemy.

Selling your inheritance and giving the money to the
poor is foolishness in the eyes of the world, but wisdom in
God's; on the other hand, to sit on your riches, increase
your money by usury, extend your possessions at public
sales and your boundaries by force is in the eyes of this

world diligence and pure gain, but in God's eyes sin and punishment. So if you conquer by evil, though victorious you are conquered, because your victory is won through sin, and so you have been defeated by greed. But if you are conquered, you will conquer, if only you yield to what is right and the will of God prevails over your will.

So let us empty ourselves of our strength to be filled with God's. Let us be overcome physically so that we may win salvation. Let us remember that we are the limbs of Him who conquered when condemned, who prevailed by yielding, who rose again to glory by falling into death; He ensured that we would rise to our resurrection by the headlong fall of His passion.

18. Let us follow this Lord when He calls us, so that, by killing in us the cause of our death and quickening in us the source of life, He may teach us to conquer by yielding and to come to life by dying. *This is our God, and there shall no other be accounted of in comparison of Him; He was seen upon earth and dwelt amongst men.*[88] He says, because flesh and blood cannot reveal it to us: *Be still, and see that I am God.*[89]

At this point I am emboldened to ask the question: Who art Thou, O God, who *made heaven and earth,* who *appeared in the burning bush,* who *had done great things in Egypt and wondrous works in the land of Cham,* and *terrible things in the Red Sea?*[90] Up to this very day, O Lord, there is none who refuses to believe in You. Not only the Jews, a people fashioned in the Law (however distant they are at heart, though sedulous with their tongues),[91] but even nations who live without the Law proclaim by natural instinct that You are the one Lord of supreme power.[92]

What problem is there, then, in seeing that You are God? *The skies proclaim Your glory;*[93] and again: *Your invisible possessions are seen, being understood by the things that are made.*[94] What prevents men from possessing this truth? What hinders them from being solicitous for such matters,[95] when even in the heat of business men can readily behold the bright truth of God and see the clear light of His highest providence? *Day to day uttereth speech, and night to night sheweth knowledge;*[96] and I am bidden to 'be still' that I may see that You are the Lord, when even the nights (as we may call the princes or hirelings of darkness) know this light.

19. However, though Truth Itself has often appeared with many tokens of Its divine nature, Its testimony that It cannot be perceived unless we embrace retirement is no idle word. It is easy to see that so great a God is God; as I have said, every soul observes it, no mind is blind to it, and even the faith of unbelievers accepts it. But the mind which is busied and surrounded by a cloud of earthly cares does not observe that God is in Christ, or Christ in God. For the Word made flesh is stupidity to the wisdom of this world;[97] so it pleased God to confound the wisdom whose arrogance prevented the world from knowing the wisdom of God, and *by the foolishness of our preaching to save them that believe.*[98]

20. This is the treasure in the field, to obtain which we must even buy that field.[99] The price of our salvation is our admission that God, Son of God, took flesh to save flesh. This is the pearl which must be bought[100] by throwing up our inherited possessions; but the purchase is not made as soon as the money is put down, because many obstacles impede the transaction. For the sea lies between buyer and

seller, or there is theft by a brigand, or a keener buyer gets there first, or a richer one is preferred.

So do not think that I have already bought the jewel because you see that I have the price ready. Do not think that I have already built the house because I have cleared the site for it. I dug out my visible riches—furniture, money, inherited property—as if they were crumbling walls or useless paving, so that I might more firmly lay the foundations of a steadier edifice, in the living earth, so to say, of a purified heart.

But just as when paving is dug we see uncovered from the earth numerous knotted lengths of tree trunks or relics of fallen masonry beneath some grimy mass of stones, or many dangerous creatures, especially vipers' young in their nest, so when our hearts are freed from the possession and anxiety of worldly goods and we are delivered from the preoccupations which drew us outside ourselves, on examining our inmost selves we find deep in our consciousness the knots of ancient sins, the lurking places of our spiritual enemies. Now that inner part of the house, together with *the creeping things there without number*,[101] begins to show itself to me. Now the entire darkness of my unhappy state comes to view. Now at last I see how far I am from God, and how dead by comparison with the living.

21. I would have you be aware of these facts. Breathe forth your solicitude for me from a troubled heart, in awareness that the Lord sings our praises only at the end;[102] pray that I may be made perfect by the grace of the spirit in which I have made a beginning, and that I may obey the final letter of the command as I seem to have obeyed the initial counsel. For it is counsel He gives, not a command;

He does not say: "Be perfect," but: *If thou wilt be perfect. . . .*[103] The freedom of the will, which is above the law when it is good, is not coerced but persuaded, and is a law unto itself. But you can assess the difficulty of following Christ from the statement of John, when he says: *He who says that he is following Christ ought himself also to walk even as Christ walked.*[104] And another master tells us how Christ walked: *He did no sin, neither was guile found in His mouth. Who, when He was reviled, did not revile in return; but delivered Himself to death to him that judged Him unjustly.*[105] But from His own acts and commandments we can discover how He walked, since He came to project His life as an exemplar and mirror for ours. *I am not come,* He said, *to destroy the law but to fulfil it,*[106] and He teaches us in His own words what that fulfilment is: *Unless your justice abound more than that of the Pharisees, you shall not enter into the kingdom of heaven.*[107]

Fulfilment means to add what is missing. The Law says: *Thou shalt not kill;* but He says: *Nor shalt thou be angry with thy brother without cause.*[108] The Law forbids adultery, but Truth Itself condemns inquisitive eyeing of women.[109] This shows you how superior is the faith to the Law. The praise of the faith is not of men but of God; for the circumcision of the Law is outwardly, but that of faith is hidden.[110] The Law breaks off the branches of sin, but faith digs out its roots, making us spotless not in deeds but in our consciousness. So we are truly refashioned to man's original dignity, which is likeness to God, by being cleansed not only in body but also at heart. So Paul attests that we have laid aside the appearance of the earthly man, and are putting on that of the heavenly;[111] and elsewhere he says that man, when now clothed with Christ, is the glory of God.[112]

22. See, then, how much effort is needed for me to complete my extensive journey. For, as I have proved, I have just begun, not reached the goal, as you say. I am ordered to go beyond the justice of the Law *to be made the justice of God*.[113] I must not proceed according to the Law; but the law lies within my will, to follow Christ and imitate God. And He who wishes us to be juster than the very law of His justice, and be perfect like His Father, asks us not only to avoid the sins of men, but also to fulfil the virtues of God.

You realise that for those struggling in the contest the difficulty of doing this is as great as the glory of those who have endured the conflict and won through. So in the meantime, whilst I am still wrestling, whilst there are *combats without and fears within*,[114] do not think or speak too highly of me, but have fear.[115] Share my labours in spirit, share my work in prayer that He who *chose the weak things of the world to confound the strong* may use me, too, to *destroy the enemy and the defender*.[116]

23. Pray humbly that He may give me understanding on this path on which He summons me, that I may see that He is indeed God who *was crucified through our weakness yet liveth by the power of God*.[117] Pray that He may weaken in me the strength of sin so as to strengthen the spirit of His virtue; that He may interchange my poverty and wealth, so that I may abound in the righteousness that I lack, and may lack the wickedness in which I abound; that I may be stripped of sins and clothed in virtues; that He may bring me help against my own wishes, and not *give*

me up to the desires of my heart;[118] that He may grant me victory against flesh and blood, the devil and death, as He granted it to Abraham against the four kings.[119] The father of faith prevailed over them through the same mystery by which our faith, if strengthened with perfect spirit, will subdue the same number of elements in our bodies through the word of God. As Abraham prevailed over the kings on behalf of his kinsman, so faith will triumph over the outer man on behalf of the soul, which thrives when victorious over the same number of senses. The four kings symbolise the four elements composing the outer man.[120]

But just as Abraham conquered the opposing chiefs not by numbers or strength of legions, but even at that date by the mystery of the cross, whose shape is expressed by the number three hundred as represented by the Greek letter T[121] (and by the strength of the same mystery the ark, constructed three hundred cubits long, overcame the flood, as now the Church sails over this world),[122] so may we, too, raise our eyes to Him, relying not on our own resources and strength but on the single awareness of Christ crucified, so that He who *saves them that hope in Him* may *show forth His wonderful mercies over us.*[123] For He is the Lord who abolishes wars and is mighty in battle,[124] who gave us both confidence to fight and the path to victory when He bore human nature triumphant within Him, and said: *Endure, for I have overcome the world.*[125]

LETTER 25

To Crispinianus[1]

1. Though I am unknown to you personally, I already know you in spirit. Victor, my dearest son in the Lord, ensured that I knew you, though distance separates us, by telling me of your scrupulous life. So I have begun to love you as a future comrade in Christ, for Victor recounted to me how he was an associate and attendant of your mess in that worldly military service in which you are still occupied. This has induced me to take the liberty of writing to you through him. For I hope that you will come to the true path by the same road as he, since in him you have sent one of your comrades ahead to us, and the Church holds him as your pledge that she may gain you after him.

There is nothing, my blessed son, which can or ought to be preferred to Him who is the true Lord, the true Father, the eternal Commander. To whom is it right to devote our lives more than to Him from whom we received them, and for whom we must preserve them to the end, because we live by His kindness? If we have been a soldier for Him in this world, we shall then deserve to pass over to Him. But if we love this world more, and prefer to be a soldier for Caesar rather than for Christ, we shall later be transported not to Christ but to hell, where the cause of the princes of this world rests.

2. So we ought not to put loyalties or fatherland or distinctions or riches before God, for Scripture says: *The*

73

fashion of this world passeth away.[2] And those who love this world will also perish with it. This is why the Lord Himself speaks these words of the Gospel in witness: *He that loveth father or mother more than Me is not worthy of Me. And whoever doth not take his cross and come after Me, cannot be My disciple.*[3]

Of the riches of this world, which some embrace and love as the highest and necessary good, He says: *Treasuries shall not profit wicked men, but justice delivers from death.*[4] Again He says through a prophet: *All were destroyed who were exalted with gold and silver.*[5] In the Gospel, too, He cries out in condemnation of the rich men of this world: *Woe to you that are rich; for you have your consolation. Woe to you that are filled; for you shall hunger. Woe to you that now laugh; for you shall mourn and weep.*[6]

3. Therefore do not any longer love this world or its military service, for Scripture's authority attests that *whoever is a friend of this world is an enemy of God.*[7] He who is a soldier with the sword is the servant of death, and when he sheds his own blood or that of another, this is the reward for his service. He will be regarded as guilty of death either because of his own death or because of his sin, because a soldier in war, fighting not so much for himself as for another, is either conquered and killed, or conquers and wins a pretext for death—for he cannot be a victor unless he first sheds blood. So the Lord says: *You cannot serve two masters,*[8] the one God and mammon, that is, Christ and Caesar, even though Caesar himself is now keen to be Christ's servant so that he may deserve kingship over a few peoples.[9] For it is not some earthly king who reigns over the whole world, but Christ God, for *all things*

*were made by Him and without Him was made nothing.
He is King of kings and Lord of lords. Whatever He
pleases He does in earth, in the sea, in the deeps.*[10]

4. Let us follow Him, then. Let us be soldiers for Him.
The soldier who wears armour for Him is never unarmed.
On them that fight for Him He bestows the glory of
eternal life, the distinction of the heavenly kingdom, the
riches of His inheritance, and an everlasting share in the
knowledge of God. But Scripture says: *He that loveth
money shall not be justified,* and *he that seeketh after
earthly possessions shall become entangled in them.*[11] So
divine Wisdom speaks through the mouth of Solomon in
Ecclesiasticus: *Many have been brought to fall for gold,
and the beauty thereof hath been their ruin. Gold is a
stumbling block and casts down those that follow after it.
But only fools shall perish by it.*[12] So flee from it, my son,
as from the appearance of a serpent. Trust in Christ, who
in the Gospel solemnly states to all men: *A man's life doth
not consist in the abundance of things which he possess-
eth.*[13]

5. Perhaps, however, the confidence of youth, your
family tradition of distinctions, and your increased riches
prompt you to say: "I am still young and have time to
complete my army service, marry, have children, and
afterwards serve God." You are answered not by me but
by the Lord speaking through His prophets and apostles.
The prophet says: *Delay not to be converted to the Lord,
and defer it not from day to day, lest His wrath come on
a sudden.*[14] The Gospel indicates with what eager haste we
should seek conversion when it says: *From the days of
John the Baptist until today, the kingdom of heaven
suffereth violence, and the violent bear it away.*[15]

Such violence is welcome to God, for it disturbs no one and is achieved without harm to any. Direct your hands to the plunder which is sinless and brings salvation. Why should you trouble about the provision of soldiers' pay which involves the violence you loathe, when doubtless your integrity makes you mild in levying even the regular taxes?[16] Whereas without rousing anyone's hatred and with God's grace you can be violent in seizing the kingdom of heaven. When it *suffereth violence,*[17] Christ rejoices at being attacked, because with His abundance of love and power He is capable both of donating what He holds and of retaining what He gives. For when He allows His saints to reign in His kingdom, He will reign amongst those whom He has adopted as comrades in His heavenly kingdom. Scripture says that God's kingdom will be shared with His saints and that those saints are themselves God's kingdom.[18] If God is good and you are converted, you will discover this by reading, and understand it by believing.

6. But who would presume to boast of the bloom of his youth and early manhood? Divine Scripture warns us with these words: *All flesh is grass, and all the glory thereof as the bloom of hay. The grass is withered and the flower fallen, but the word of the Lord endureth forever.*[19] So the prophet, too, longs rather for the surroundings in which the glory of the renewed body can remain eternal after the resurrection, and he cries: *How lovely are Thy tabernacles, O Lord of hosts. My soul longeth and fainteth for the courts of the Lord!*[20]

7. So far as the bonds of marriage and the other thorny and empty anxieties of the temporal state are concerned, Christ warns us through His spokesman Paul not to postpone our vows uselessly for long in this world, and bids us

realise that *the time is short.* He adds: *It remaineth that they who have wives be as if they had none; and they that weep as though they wept not; and they that rejoice as if they rejoiced not; and they that buy as though they possessed not; and they that use the world as if they used it not.*[21] When he says this, he indicates that those who are free ought not to become entangled, whereas he is persuading those who are entangled to dissociate themselves. If then you are already *bound to a wife, seek not to be loosed.*[22] But if you are still free, do not seek entanglement.

It is not to condemn marriage that Paul compares the bond of such a compact to the great mystery of Christ and the Church.[23] But he asserts that *it is good for the present necessity for a man so to be as he was.*[24] He says: *I would have you to be without solicitude;*[25] in other words, to think of nothing but God and our salvation. A wife and children, though they too are dear ones sent by God, are nonetheless most grievous burdens and anxieties. So Paul also says: *Such shall have tribulation of the flesh.*[26]

For our physical relations torture and weary us the dearer they are to us. Once you take a wife, you pray for children. If you don't get them, you bewail your barrenness; if you do get them, you fear to lose them.[27] Likewise when you have blood relations to care for, your mind gets no respite from torture. If your relatives are good, you love them but fear you may lose them; if they are bad, you hate them and pray you will lose them. But in either case you must be perpetually exposed to enduring wretchedness. For you are miserable if you lose a good wife, and more miserable if you fail to lose a bad one. Poised[28] between these two fates, the man who has experience of neither is better off. In the same way parents are very often most unhappy about their children. They lose the good ones, or else have such sons that they are forced to envy childless couples.[29]

8. Listen, then, my son, and give me your ear. Break off all ties which bind and entangle you in this world. Change your secular military service into something better—start being a soldier for the eternal King. I hear that you now help and protect civilians; I pray that you may become the count of Christ.[30] Again, you in secular military service are wont to pray for advancement to the rank of protector,[31] but if you prove yourself before God, you will begin to have Him as your Protector. See to what kind of military service I invite you as comrade, for God will be to you what you hope to be to a man.[32] Once you begin to follow Him, you begin your service as a count, and the end of your service will be kingship not on earth or in time, but in eternity and in heaven.

LETTER 25*

To Crispinianus[1]

Paulinus sends greetings to Crispinianus, his son in Christ the Lord.

1. I had hoped that when your former comrade-in-arms, Victor, returned here from his native land, I would get a letter from your honoured self to make me happy because of your action, that is, because of the progress of your faith. It was this motive which made me venture long ago to send you a letter by the hand of this same brother Victor; and now I write again, presuming to heap on you afresh my advice, at the insistent command of God recorded in Scripture: *Thou shalt love thy neighbour as thyself*.[2]

How else can I prove that I love you as myself, except by desiring for you what I adjudged best for myself? My decision was to renounce this world with all the pomps and allurements of its emptiness, to flee from the anger to come, and take refuge with the sole Salvation of the human race, Jesus Christ the Son of God, our Lord and God, who was crucified and rose from the dead to free us from eternal death and to guide us to eternal life, and beyond this to make us His heirs fashioned to His image and sharing in His glory.

So, my dearest son and brother, we must abandon all that entangles us in this world, all that kills us as we pursue the desires of our flesh. We must dismiss from our minds

79

the vices of our pleasures, thrusting them behind us like dung. Then we may account useful the loss of our worldly possessions, in which lurk the means of sin and the cause of death, and count Christ a gain. In Him are our honour and our treasure, in Him are the eternal kingdom and the true light which enlightens the eyes of our souls, so that we understand that *better is the just man's little than the abundant riches of sinners,*[3] and that *it profits a man nothing if he gain the whole world and suffer the loss of his own soul.*[4]

So I considered it necessary to obey my blessed brother and good fellow citizen Victor, and to send another letter to you, dear friend, daring in this labour of love to write to you even in rebuke. For when I showed anxiety about your progress, Victor told me that by God's kindness you were still aspiring to the Christian life, but not practising it, that you were continually contemplating eternity and embarking on the path of life which is the way of Christ. But if you do not wish to retire from military service, realise that you must change your service, not drop it; change it to that military service which is better accordingly as God is a greater King than is man.

2. *So repay to Caesar the things that are Caesar's,* so that you may begin to *render to God the things that are God's.*[5] Do tell me, dear brother, what you are waiting for. For what better hope do you delay your decision? Until what date do you postpone what is good for you? How long a life do you promise yourself? Even if you were sure of living as many years again as you have lived, you ought nonetheless to realise that time flies, that the remaining years of your life will slip away with equal speed, and that after the most short and grievous course of this life there

will follow ages in which we must live or die without cease. But those who love this world must inevitably become exiles in the next; for since Scripture says that *no one can serve two masters*,[6] that there is no fellowship between Christ and mammon, it is certain that he who has loved the temporary, transient things of this world cannot obtain the blessings of the age to come.

If you do not believe me, believe the Gospel, for there the Lord shows us in the person of our father Abraham that men are allotted changes of condition. Those who have been afflicted in this life have refreshment prepared for them hereafter, whereas those who have had barren riches here are repaid in hell with poverty rich in punishment.

For example, the unkind man of wealth who had been stingy to the poor man and generous to himself while he lived on earth, later died and was transported to hell, and as he lay submerged there he saw the beggar Lazarus afar off.[7] No longer did he spurn him, but marvelled that Lazarus was rich in joy whilst he himself had no part in life. For here on earth he had cast Lazarus out in scorn and refused to feed him when he was hungry; he had not tended his sores, nor had he pitied his fellow man when the dogs licked his wounds. So the rich man was revealed as inferior to the dogs, for the animal madness[8] of greed had obliterated his human feelings. On this earth the man who feasted richly and clothed himself proudly in royal garments showed disgust at the poor wretched beggar, but later the rich man was wretched and saw the poor man happy, resting in the light whilst he himself roasted in the darkness. Lazarus was happy in the bosom of Abraham, whilst the rich man roared in the bosom of hell. Forgetful

of his pride and empty life, that wretch who deserved no
pity acknowledged the poor man in vain and too late. He
bewailed his own joy on earth, but could not now find the
cure of repentance. For Scripture says: *There is no one in
death that is mindful of Thee, O Lord; and who shall confess to Thee in hell?*[9] So, too, the prophet says elsewhere:
*Because they have not called upon the Lord, there they
have trembled with fear where there was no fear.*[10]

3. So whilst we linger in the body on earth, we must
attend to our salvation, and seek out the remedies that will
benefit us; and accordingly as we have sinned extensively
and so provoked the Lord, let us make the satisfaction we
give Him still greater by due repentance. But once sinners
are in hell there is no longer opportunity for repentance,
but only for punishment.

So, as I have said, the rich and the poor change roles.
The rich man in death burns and supplicates the poor man
whom he had despised, mocked, and passed by whilst he
lived a life of luxury and the poor man was begging and
often faint with the pain of the rich man's blows. How
right it is that he who did not feed his needy neighbour
upon earth now feeds the fires and worms of hell! So now
the begging is transferred to him. Now he is grievously
rich in the number of his torments, and he begs the gift of
a little water from his beggar who has now plenty of the
riches of life. But he gets a just response, and is not refreshed by the mercy of the poor man whom he had never
refreshed from his wealth.

Why is it that though he burns throughout his body he
asks that only his tongue be sprinkled with drops from
even the little finger of the poor man? Surely it is because
he had sinned against Lazarus especially with his tongue,

for as Lazarus lay before his gate he ordered him to be thrown out, or laughed at his foulness and afflictions; both these sins he committed with his tongue, not thinking that he and the poor man were made by the one God, and that the Father, who resists the proud and gives grace to the humble, is kinder to the poor. He did not consider that the words of Scripture were for himself: *He that giveth to the poor lendeth to the Lord.*[11] And again: *He that oppresseth the poor provoketh God who made him.*[12] So he was pushed into the depths, and now as the son of hell heard Abraham, the father of refreshment, say: *Son, remember that thou didst receive good things in thy lifetime, and likewise Lazarus evil things; but now he is comforted but thou art tormented.*[13]

So Christ again says in the Gospel: *Blessed are they that mourn, for they shall be comforted.*[14] And He says on the other hand: *Woe to them that laugh, because they shall mourn.*[15] So, too, David says: *They that sow in tears shall reap in joy.*[16] And Ecclesiastes equally justly proclaims that *it is better to go to the house of mourning* (that is, where past sins are dissolved by healing grief in the humility of an afflicted heart) *than to the house of feasting,*[17] where profligacy and luxury further increase the sins which are to be punished with eternal fires.

4. Therefore, blessed son, I long for you to recover your senses from your love of darkness and to be freed from association with human error, for you know the words of Scripture: *Blessed is the man who hath not walked in the counsel of the ungodly.*[18] For if you wish to join with those who sow only in tears, you will be their comrade also on the day of repayment. *Coming, they shall come holy and with joyfulness, carrying their sheaves.*[19]

But what a man sows in this life he will reap in the next. So Paul says: *He that soweth in his flesh, of the flesh also shall reap corruption. But he that soweth in the spirit, of the spirit shall reap life everlasting.*[20]

Believe me, you will not be able to rejoice with Christ unless you cease to rejoice with this world. Unless you weep now, you will not laugh forever. Unless you humble yourself, you will not be exalted. Unless you despise the empty glory of the world, you will not win the undying glory of Christ. If you prefer transient riches here, you will endure poverty forever in the next world. If Christ comes upon you in the broad and spacious way, He will be compelled to judge you there. I pray it may not be so.

LETTER 26

To Sebastianus[1]

Paulinus and Therasia send greetings in the Lord to their holy brother Sebastianus, most deservedly the object of great affection.

1. Blessed is the Lord God of Israel, who chose and adopted you as *the vessel of his choice*,[2] separated you from the womb of your former mother, and gave you the wings of a dove, so that you could fly far away from the din of this world and say: *Lo, I have gone far off, flying away, and I abode in the wilderness.*[3] Yet your wilderness is not lonely, for it is not desert but a place set apart, so that it may be untouched by the darkness of this world and attended by God's light, avoided by wailing devils, and thronged by glad angels.

The Lord Himself, our God, has allowed us, though we are far distant, to approach you with affection; for the goodly odour of your fame has reached us through Victor, our dearest brother in the Lord, who has told us of the work of your vocation and of your sequestered abode. Straining to emulate the saints of old, you have established your peaceful residence and spiritual camp beyond a rushing stream, just as long ago those sons of the prophets under the leadership of Eliseus set theirs beyond the Jordan.[4] And your blessed brother the deacon serves you with the obedience of a woman of Sarephta or of a Sunamitess.[5] Blessed is he whom the Lord commanded, as one of the

winged messengers of heaven, to feed you as you sit apart,
like Elias at the river, with the bread of devotion, and to
fly repeatedly to your cell with diligent footsteps on this
duty, as the dove flew back to the ark of Noe, bringing
the fertile branch with its goodly foliage.[6]

2. You two are blessed by the Lord, who *maketh men
of one manner to dwell in a house,*[7] and has redoubled in
you the bond of true brotherhood. He has made you
brothers in the womb of the Church, distinguishing you
by separate duties within the one faith, so that with your
differing functions you might sustain each other. By fasting and prayer you are to help your deacon with the arms
of the spirit; and he is to sow for himself the seeds of
heavenly blessings, by providing you with the sustenance
of the body, though you feel no need for outlay on your
corruptible flesh because your hunger is for justice and for
the kingdom of God. Yet the Lord who made our inner
selves has also made the outer man, making *the spirit willing
but the flesh weak;*[8] and so though the soul lives by the
Word of God, which is Christ God, the living and true
Bread, God rewards it for such obedience by serving your
body, your earthly frailty, with small amounts of food so
that He is fattened by the great extent of your fasting. For
He said: *Not by bread alone doth man live, but in every
word of God,*[9] because whilst taking account of the greater
weakness of our flesh, the Creator was equally pointing out
that bread is necessary for that flesh.

3. On the one hand, He showed that human life does
not rest solely on bread, so that we should not put care of
the body before that of the soul, which feeds on the word
of God; on the other, when He said: *Not in bread alone,*
He was also teaching that man's sustenance rests on bread,

and that even if the preoccupation of the soul does not seek
it, the nature of the body still demands it. So blessed is he
whose wealth of soul is advanced by the needs of your
human condition, for you are still a man and must be fed
on that visible bread, even if your inner self is filled with
the Bread that is eternal.

Indeed, your virtue of the spirit would fail to grow if
your weakness of the flesh did not lurk beneath it. Likewise our ministrations to the faithful would be ineffective
if our brothers' poverty did not often provide the opportunity of giving such service. This is why Paul says that
holy men will attain an equality, when he encourages God's
Church to attain the consolation of this blessing. He says:
*Let your abundance supply their want, that their abun-
dance also may supply* an addition to *your want.*[10]

4. Further, I dare to say that you and your deacon are
separate images of John and the Lord, John crying in the
desert and the Lord teaching in the temple. One of you has
been called to the slavery of attendance, the other to the
freedom of the monk. But both of you are called to the one
kingdom and glory of God. Both are free because both are
under grace, and both are slaves because both are under the
law of faith. Both are free from sin and slaves to righteousness. Both *regard the day unto the Lord* by fasting, and
both give thanks by the feasting of uprightness to the Lord
who *giveth food to all flesh,*[11] and gives living food to those
who hunger for true life. One of you listened, and so he
says: *I will go to the altar of God, to God who giveth joy
to my youth.*[12] The other was taught by the same prophet
to say: *I am alone until I pass.*[13]

5. So because you have been chosen and loved by the
Lord to *bear each other's burdens,*[14] you must also pray for

me with that perfect charity with which you fulfil the law of Christ and feed, sustain, instruct, and enrich each other. Join your hands, so strong in prayer, that you may prevail over the crowd of my sins. The merciful, pitying Lord ministers and gives the acquaintance and love of holy men to His sinners so that their powerful advocacy may deliver from deserved damnation even the guilty who are without excuse. May you abide in the Lord's kingdom which He has made to dwell in you by the pledge of the Holy Spirit lodging there. In Him you cry: *Abba, Father*,[15] for you are the Lord's blessed sons, sons of devotion, peace, and light.

LETTER 27

To Severus[1]

Paulinus greets his loving brother Severus, respected and always greatly longed for.

1. *I will bless the Lord at all times, and will not forget how He repays me, because He has not repaid me according to my sins,*[2] for He satisfies my longing with the numerous continuing consolations derived from your affection. Only a few days after our holy brothers Posthumianus and Theridius,[3] whom we both hold dear, had returned here, two other brothers, Virinius and Sorianus,[4] arrived. So almost simultaneously I reaped a huge harvest of joys, for all these, who, as I have said, arrived together, brought the pleasure of their presence which was sweeter to me even than the letters of your affectionate self. So *my spirit hath rejoiced in the Lord, and my mouth is enlarged over my enemy,*[5] who has not been allowed to say: *I have prevailed against him.*[6] Instead it is my prayers of heartfelt longing that prevailed, for I received from you, for whom my soul cares most, the discerning judgments and communications for which I had longed.

2. So in order that we may owe each other only mutual love as Scripture commands,[7] I shall answer all your letters, dealing first with the one which arrived first. You rebuke me by asking why I have left you orphaned of the couriers[8] who brought your letter, or why I have weaned them from you. But you will realise that I am blameworthy on neither

count, for on my love for you I have never imposed limits, nor have I ever competed with you by claiming these couriers as mine. Besides, I would freely have granted you what was yours, if your possession had been prior to mine. For they would not have left me by remaining with you, since you are wholly mine in Christ the Lord, through whom I in turn am yours.

Nor would I have obtained such great pleasure in welcoming them as I would have lost if I had snatched them from you prematurely, even though it was right to seek them as comrades on the path to salvation. Indeed, it is my opinion as well as yours that I should be most justly stripped of your love if I preferred any blessing to accrue to me rather than to you. But when they had slipped into my ranks through the Lord's unexpected kindness, and I discovered in them those qualities which soon became known to you as well, I went so far as to loathe myself for having been luckier than you to this extent, namely, that whilst these men were worthier of your presence and fellowship than mine, yet I was keeping them, or I had laid claim to them first.

To put the matter briefly, I wanted you to share with all speed the joy of this grace by which I accounted myself happy; so whilst they were here I rebuked them for admitting that they were strangers to your friendship and acquaintance, and when they set out, the most earnest instruction I gave them was that they should hasten to your sight and embrace, and that they should prefer acquaintance with you to all their property and preoccupations on their native soil, so that, however tardily, they might repair their long-standing loss. And now, thank the Lord, I welcome them again as *they come with joyfulness;*[9] and the

blessed sheaf, which they carry in from their bounteous
fields, taller than all the other crops of their life, is their
great joy in knowing that they had trusted me in seeking
you out before all else. What thanks they rendered first to
God for not merely satisfying but overwhelming their
desires, for they found in you more blessings than they had
anticipated! What thanks they gave to me for having been
the sponsor of their great gain! What thanks they accorded
themselves for having obeyed me to their own advantage!

3. I cannot express the pleasure with which they filled
me as they recounted your activities and words, and told
me of your heart made perfect by knowledge of the divine
love. This has made you humble and exalted, poor and rich,
slave and free—a fellow slave to your servants, a slave to
your brothers; rich towards the poor through the bowels
of your mercy, poor towards the rich by your spirit of
meekness; humble in the strength of your devotion, exalted
in the lofty height of your virtue; a slave to God, but free
of mammon. They proclaimed that in you Martin wholly
breathes, Clarus blooms,[10] and the Gospel is brought to
ripeness. How completely *they anointed my head with the
oil of gladness!*[11] So *all that is within me blessed the Lord.*[12]

I had a double cause for thanksgiving. I realised that I
had done you the greatest service by acquainting you with
brothers who you have proved are most dear to you, and
I saw that they were pleased with themselves because they
regard your acquaintance and love as a God-sent gift.
Amongst the other works and gifts of God in you, they
greatly admired your boys, who flourish *as olive-plants
around you.*[13] Our God has made you to them what He
Himself is to all men, so that they both reverence you as
lord and love you as a father. But I confess that as they

told me this, I grieved for my own unhappiness, for my sins were too heavy and made me barren of such sons. But *I became as one comforted*,[14] for I consider it a blessing to be close to your happiness.

4. But you must now prevent my wickedness from widening the gulf between us, so prepare the whole of your group of holy young recruits, with whom you delight God night and day, to direct keen prayers on my behalf against my sins, and to pray that God may *confirm what He has wrought in us*;[15] in other words, that through your love, in which I now find rest and in which I boast, I may be refreshed and rejoice on the Day of Judgment.

LETTER 28

To Severus[1]

Paulinus greets his holy brother and affectionate fellow soldier Severus.

1. Victor[2] is returning from me to you that he may return from you to me. He is our joint pledge of affection, our faithful attendant, our regular consolation. Victor is mine in you and yours in me. For our letters he acts as foot-courier or two-legged post-horse, a Victor over the longest journeys! He can well be called both Victor and Vanquished, for he is conquered by the love with which he overcomes hard journeys and great toils. *In the sweat of his face doth he eat his bread*[3] that he may refresh us with his yearly journeys from one to the other, untiringly bearing to and fro the interchange of our letters, with which we each bestow on the other's mind and heart that mutual visitation which is the tribute of the obligation we owe each other.

May our servant Victor be blessed in the Lord; may his soil not bear him thorns and thistles, for he is untiring, whereas *the ways of the slothful are strewn with thorns*.[4] Our Victor does not say: *There is a lion in the ways*,[5] for he is so ingenuous that in his faith and chastity his journey is untroubled, so that *he is not afraid of the terror of the night and the dart that flieth in the day*.[6] So the Lord protects him in all his ways and entrusts him to the guardianship of angels, so that he may never *dash his foot against a stone*, and so that no watchful *serpent in the path may bite his heel*.[7] Instead he shall tread on that snake with impunity, and crush him underfoot with *feet shod with preparation for the Gospel's journey*.[8] So I shall praise and bless in the Lord our Victor's feet, and of these feet, too, I shall make bold to say: *How beautiful are the feet which bring good tidings*[9] to me of peace in your regard, for they announce your health and the peace within you, when they report your faith through which Christ our Peace remains within you.

It is Christ who *makes both one*,[10] either of us or in us—whether we are two in one heart, or whether we unify the twofold substance of soul and body by the fusion which Christ achieves in us through the fire of His Spirit, of which He says: *I am come to cast fire on the earth*, and *what does the good Lord will but that it be kindled*[11] in us, enlighten our darkness, and destroy our sins, *because the Lord our God is a consuming fire?*[12] May this Lord bestow the privilege of becoming a consuming fire in me and for me. May my heart blaze with this fire to afford me eternal light, so that my soul may not blaze with it for my eternal punishment. For the day of the Lord shall be revealed by this fire, and *the fire shall try the work of every one of us of what sort it is*.[13]

2. Let us beg this Lord to teach us to do His desires, so that *His good spirit may lead us into the right way*,[14] that our work be found not as wood or hay or straw, but rather as silver and gold and precious stones, and so that we may be found living within the walls of the heavenly and free Jerusalem, *which is built as a city which is compact together*.[15] For He who dwells in this city is revealed as the One in Three, so it is called *the city of the great King, the*

city of the Lord of hosts, which the Lord Himself has in Scripture's words *founded for ever.*[16] Christ is become not only the Foundation but also the Tower and the Gate of this city. As Scripture says: *For other foundation no man can lay* but Him *who is our Tower of strength against the face of the enemy.*[17] Christ says: *I am the Door of the sheep; no man can come to the Father but through Me.*[18]

If then our house and our mind is founded on Him, and a structure worthy of this great foundation is built upon Him, the Gate by which we shall enter His city will be *He who shall rule as forevermore.*[19] *He will set us in a place of pasture,* for He has begotten us for Himself *by the water of refreshment;*[20] and He nourishes us with feasts of salvation that we may reach that table which He has prepared for us against those who oppress us. Of this table He says: *Blessed is he that shall eat bread in the kingdom of God.*[21]

For Christ is both the Kingdom and the Bread by which we are nourished and by which the serpent withers away. The serpent's hunger and punishment is the Food of our life, Christ Jesus, who was made our Food that we may live on this Bread and walk in accordance with It, and be able to say with Paul: *But our conversation is in heaven.*[22] For when we know and seek the things which are above, we cease to be earthly, so that we are no longer the meat of the serpent. The serpent in turn was given *to be meat for the people of the Ethiopians,*[23] so that he may be devoured by those whom he devours.

But for us the opposite is the case and brings salvation, for we both consume and are consumed by Christ. Because He is the Life, He consumes our mortal form in order to clothe us with immortality and to shape us to His image. He has given us power over all the strength of the enemy;

we can grind the foe underfoot without harm through the same grace by which *He gave power to be made the sons of God to them that believe in His name, which is above all names.*[24]

Let us dwell in Him, for He is also *the city which cannot be hid*, for it is *seated on a mountain*, and *the foundations thereof are in the holy mountains.*[25] This city *the Highest Himself hath founded*, as Scripture says, because *Wisdom hath built a house for Himself.*[26] This is *a house not made by hands.*[27] If we dwell in it through those acts which we must perform to deserve citizenship with the saints, our work will not be burnt. That fire of Wisdom, as we pass through it to be tried, will not engulf us to punish us with fierce heat. It will receive us as men approved, and will lick us with caressing touch, so that we can say: *We have passed through fire and water, and Thou hast brought us out into a refreshment.*[28]

3. But to end this letter with the name with which I began it, let me return to Victor, on whose behalf I owe you an apology. Do not blame his feet because he returns to you later than was agreed. Those feet have remained here longer not through the vice of idleness but through eagerness to obey.

But recall not the time when you claimed he left you, but that at which you actually sent him, and you will realise that I have kept my accounts square with that alternating hospitality for Victor on which we agreed. For he did not, as you wrote, appear here in time to ask me for a roof for the winter. As he himself stated, he was sent back to you from Narbonese Gaul where he had met brother Posthumianus.[29] Then he said farewell to you afresh when he could have proceeded here direct from Narbonese Gaul.

So it was the end of winter when I welcomed him here, and I thought it necessary to keep him during the spring months. Then it seemed only a short time till the Easter solemnities were over; and I had been very ill at that time, so I was not equal to the task of replying to you. I accordingly prolonged his delay over some days of the summer, so that you and I could strike a balance; I could steal that amount of Victor's time with you which you had appropriated from the days of winter.

So if it is autumn before he greets your dear self, I shall allow him to spend his winter with you again; for, as you see, God's will enjoined that those periods of hospitality for the friend we both love, which we had allotted to each other, should be changed. The sanctity of our agreement[30] remains unbroken, whilst Victor gains a greater advantage. Now the situation is appositely reversed, so that your words which were unjustly kind to me and disparaging to yourself may have truer application. For you who are truly warm in spirit will bring him better health by cherishing him with the fiery heat of your faith during the cold season, whereas I in my coldness will be more suited to him during a summer stay.

4. But I pray that I may be even cold rather than luke-warm, that the Lord may not vomit me forth,[31] and that I may relieve my neighbour's heat. But as things are, because of my glut of words I arouse disgust in those who are neither hot nor cold, and who seek to avail themselves of the time of my sojourning on earth. Because my faith is so slight and lukewarm, I must inevitably be regurgitated by those who seek to savour my companionship in the hope of spiritual sweetness.

So I marvel the more at what is either your longing to

shoulder, or your patience in enduring, the burden of my stupidity. But I pray that the increase in the great reward won by your most unwearying charity may not mean for me an increase in sin arising from my multitude of words;[32] for you give the impression not of being wearied but of being refreshed by those volumes, so great in number and size, previously conveyed to you by our Victor, and you have again demanded that I should trouble you further with the pen, if I can, and send more words through the same book-bearer.

5. But you flatter yourself overmuch about your poor servant when you further bid me, as if I were more learned than you on the subject, to instruct you on those points not of national but of universal history on which you are ignorant. But he who knocks on the door of a poor friend and observes his empty cupboard should feel responsibility for his own hunger. My studies were never directed towards the investigation and collation of historical information. Even in the old days, when I doubtless read what I ought not to have read, I always steered clear of the historians.[33]

But I have given some thought to your project, which as you told me has engaged you in analysing and comparing the accounts of past ages in the interest of our Faith;[34] and what I could not provide myself I have sought from the richer store of a loving brother. That note, appended as a memorandum to your letter to me, I have forwarded to Rufinus,[35] a priest who is the companion of holy Melania[36] on her spiritual journey. He is a truly holy, pious, yet learned man, and so we are on terms of intimate friendship. He is equally fluent in both Greek and Latin literature, both the secular and the sacred. So if he cannot account

for the vagaries in the reckoning of years and reigns which
rightly trouble you as gaps in history, I fear that consulta-
tion of any other authority in the West may be in vain. If
he meets my demand on him, I shall forward it to your
dear self at the first opportunity, if the Lord is kind, whatever his reply to me is on this matter.

6. Meanwhile I have sought to carry out one of your
instructions, and have sent you some of the writings which
I fear attest my indolence and foolishness more than they
signify my heavenly service, or at any rate my human
wisdom. Yes, I send my trifles to you (which is the same
as entrusting them to my own heart), not that my darkness
may corrupt your sensibilities, but that it may be dispersed
by them.

I use the word "trifles" to describe both the expression
and the content of my work. Yet the subject matter is
sacred, and worthier of your talent and eloquence than of
mine; but though clothed in the grimy garb of my language, it still maintains the glory of God's light and its
inner beauty, though encased in a cheap and impoverished
frame. So you are getting two books from me. One of
them comprises verses of birthday poems drawn from the
yearly invocations to the patron of our house.[37] To him I
pay the most sweet tribute of voluntary service every day
in body and spirit, and once a year with my tongue, on the
feast of his admission into heaven, when I offer to Christ
*the sacrifice of praise, and pay my vows to the Most
High.*[38]

The other book is one of those which I am exposed as
having written for my friend the blessed (in other words,
Christian) Endelechius,[39] but I cannot be taxed with having published it. He was the one who sponsored this little

work in the Lord, as his letter, published as preface to my book to outline the subject, explains to the reader. Yet I confess that I gladly undertook this task imposed by a friend, so that I might proclaim in the person of Theodosius not so much an emperor as a servant of Christ, a man whose power lay not in the pride of despotism but in humility of service, a man who was first citizen not in kingship but in faith.[40]

45405

LETTER 29

To Severus[1]

Paulinus greets his loving brother Severus.

1. In your letter which spoke of the burden I bear, your uncontrolled love called forth my rebuke. But that love is tempered by your kind gifts, which are suited and well-directed to my profit. The cloaks woven from camel's hair[2] were a gift necessary for this sinner, who needs to utter the prayers and wear the dress of lamentation, so that when I am prostrate in the sight of the Most High their profitable itch may remind me, as I am pricked with their sharp bristles, to be pricked also with dismay by my sins; and as the garments chafe me outwardly, to be likewise chafed in spirit.

There are many other profitable ways in which they help to fashion faith as recorded by saints of old. I think of Elias when sent on an errand, and of John who was sent before Christ. The first was girdled with a prickly belt of hair; the second, as Scripture says, was clothed in a shaggy covering of camel's hair.[3] I remember also *David and all his meekness,* in which *he sacrificed a contrite and humbled heart to God, made haircloth his garment,* and *covered his soul in fasting,*[4] so that he could invest it with the repletion of the spirit.

So we learn that such fasting, by which we abstain from all that is forbidden by God's law, is the clothing of the soul. We know this from the stripping of our first parents,

101

Lincoln Christian College

who were made naked once they ceased to fast from the forbidden food.[5] Now the prophet himself instructs us with what kind of fasting he has protected his soul from the nakedness which brings confusion,[6] when he says to the Lord: *I have restrained my feet from every evil way, that I may keep Thy word.*[7]

2. The hair of this gift of yours also impresses on my mind the camel of the Gospel, which *passes more easily through the eye of a needle than a rich man enters the kingdom of heaven.*[8] This makes me think of the riches now remaining with me only in my sins. And because I cannot aim at the virtues like those of the men of God,[9] I desire that there should at least accrue to me the grace of the publican[10] who with afflicted heart accused himself before God and repeatedly beating his bruised breast did not dare to raise to heaven eyes bent down through shame at his guilt. The foulness of his sins was like the camel's hump. But so effectively did he contract himself into the necessary humility, level out his reformed soul, and direct his way, that he obtained a hearing from God and squeezed through the eye of the needle, that is, along the path of the Word or of the cross, which leads to life by the narrow strait.[11]

For, as Scripture says, *the prayer of him that humbleth himself pierces the clouds.*[12] On the other hand, the Pharisee, so rich in his boastful spirit, presented an account of the good works which he owed—for by the law of good works he did owe them—on the grounds that he had performed voluntary works beyond what was necessary. And because he proclaimed his own merits and accused another's, so that he did not so much entreat God as accost Him, he could not gain admittance there because the entrance is too narrow for those who are fat. Portly boasting could not be given entry where pinched humility betook itself and entered, because it was more pinched than the pinched emaciation of a sorrowful heart.

3. May your prayers intercede for me, so that the needle of the Lord's cross may be threaded with the word of salvation, and repair my soul which is extensively worn and haphazardly pinned with the thorns[13] of feeling. For I think that the faith and word of Christ's cross are the needle by which the clothing of our life is repaired, by which our mind is pricked, and by which we are sewn on God Himself through the intercession of the Mediator Himself. The eye of the needle, too, lies in Christ, for through Him and in Him lies the path to life desired by many but attainable by few; on that path the humility of wickedness enters more easily than the pride of righteousness.

So I owe you greater gratitude for being my spiritual physician, since even your bodily gifts to me are spiritually useful; for you have sent these cloaks to me to incite me to prayer and to the practice of humility, as if you were sending a bag of dung to the barren fig tree.[14] I think that this parable reveals the perennial profit of loving humility, which fertilises the barren soul so that it should not become complacent like the Pharisee with an empty show of pride, or be like a tree which yields no fruit yet blossoms with unproductive foliage.

The blessed Job teaches us how good and useful such dung is for cultivating salvation, for after he sat on a dung-hill he ceased to be tempted.[15] He had exhausted the hatred of the tempter by his perfect humility, which can rise more easily than be thrust down. For by sitting in the dirt it cannot fall further, but can rise up from there through Him who *raises up the needy from the earth, and lifts up the poor out of the dunghill,*[16] and relegates the proud to the dung because, as Scripture says, every proud man is unclean in the sight of God.[17] So he who accuses his own wickedness is more righteous in God's sight than he who proclaims his own justice. The Pharisee accused himself with his self-praise, whereas the publican defended himself with his self-accusation.

4. So let us not flatter ourselves because of our works, but rather always *commend our spirit into His hands,* for *with Him is the fountain of light.*[18] Let us seek from him an understanding of our journey, for *by the Lord are the steps of a man directed.*[19] But even if we shall be able through His help to perform His commands, we must even so confess our uselessness, for we cannot enter an account of the service we owe if we are only carrying out His commands.

He whose love makes no voluntary addition to the necessary task he must perform is an unprofitable and wicked servant. He will have no reason to hope for reward if he has discharged only the duties of his state. Therefore, as I often write to you, even if we fulfil His commands, we must always fear and say to the Lord: *Enter not into judgment with Thy servant, for in Thy sight no man living shall be justified.*[20] Whilst even humble confession will be able to gain us admission before God as men without self-esteem, useful and industrious service will fail to commend us, for we shall be branded as idlers.

The people of Ninive are a further proof of the great cure which the sinner finds in the mercy of God, provided he does not spare himself. For they were reconciled to

God by their decision to repent, and so deserved to escape the threatened destruction, because they anticipated God's sentence with their own, and punished themselves with voluntary lamentation.[21]

5. I cannot worthily repay you in words or deeds, but with the sole quality in which I equal you, that love which is my sole endowment, I have sent you a tunic. Kindly accept it (for I have worn it) as a shirt obtained from the foulness of a dunghill; for it suits your blameless life, being woven from soft lambswool which soothes the skin with its touch.

But let me mention an additional value and grace which it possesses, so that it may be approved as more worthy of your use. It is a pledge to me of the blessing of the holy Melania,[22] famous amongst the holy women of God. So the tunic seemed more worthily yours, for your faith has greater affinity with her than has my blood.[23] Yet I confess that though I earmarked it for you at the very moment I received it, I disregarded this intention to the extent of wearing it first. I knew that by thus wronging you I would visit you more effectively than if I honoured you with the tunic all new and unworn. I also wished to snatch a prior blessing from the garment which was now yours, so that I might boast that I shared your clothing; for I was putting on the shirt which with God's kindness you will wear, as if you had already worn it.

6. But the Lord conferred a further grace as a result of your gifts and letter. Our brother Victor arrived here about the very time when I welcomed that holy lady who was returning from Jerusalem after twenty-five years.[24] What a woman she is, if one can call so virile a Christian a woman! What am I to do now? Fear of being unbearably

tedious forbids me to add more to the volumes written
about her; yet the worth of her person, or rather God's
grace in her seems to demand that I should not exclude
with hasty omission a mention of this great soul. Just as
voyagers, seeing some notable spot on the shore, do not
pass by, but briefly draw in their sails, or lift their oars, and
linger to feast their eyes in gazing, so I must alter the
course of my words to tell you about her for a moment. In
this way I may be seen to make some return for that book
of yours,[25] so splendid in its matter and style, if I describe
the woman who is a soldier for Christ with the virtues of
Martin, though she is of the weaker sex. She is a noblewoman who has made herself nobler than her consular
grandfathers by her contempt for mere bodily nobility.

7. I think that I should begin to proclaim her praiseworthy holiness by praising her ancestry, for this, too, has
a bearing on the grace which God has heaped on her. The
most learned Luke attests that this order of topics is
adopted not from the practice of rhetoricians but from the
example of the Gospels.[26] Luke began his description of the
merits of blessed John the Baptist with his illustrious ancestry. He would not have you think that he mentioned
the noble father of the Lord's forerunner as a mere historical detail. He links up the revered distinction of John's
ancient nobility and gives the genealogy of both parents.
When he says that *the priest Zachary was of the course of
Abia*,[27] in my opinion he does it to demonstrate his high
merit from that very fact. He appends the name Abia because of Zachary's office, which was undoubtedly a distinction amongst the Jews, for it was because he was descended
from Abia that he obtained and held that honoured priest-

hood. Finally, he adds: *And his wife was of the daughters of Aaron.*[28]

You notice that the evangelist, by mentioning the birth of these holy persons, has pronounced on their merit, so that before proclaiming their own deserving acts he set down their ancestral names. *And his wife,* he says, *was of the daughters of Aaron.* The merit of the priest is increased by mention of the nobility of his marriage. Before praising Zachary's life, he first praised his lineage, so that he might emerge more worthy of respect because his inbred holiness accorded with that of his holy parents as if it were some inherited righteousness. Zachary recalled the name of Aaron, outstanding amongst priests' names, because by his office he succeeded to Aaron's distinction and through his wife he continued his race.

Again, Elizabeth, who with her husband drew the harmonious yoke of truth along life's path, was to be chosen to bear her child by means of an angel, of whom it was written: *Behold, I shall send an angel before thy face.*[29] And she was to show herself all the worthier to have a priest as husband and John, ranked before the prophets,[30] as her son, because not only her righteous life but also her privileged family made her suitable to receive God's gifts.

But apart from John's origin, which flowed forth from a divine source,[31] two of the evangelists start their account of the birth of the Lord Himself, by which He deigned to be the Son of man, by recounting His ancestors from the beginning.[32] Each writer, with equal faith and grandeur, records differing courses of His body's blood;[33] for it was right that the only-begotten Son of God, Firstborn of the whole creation, Head of the whole body, should hold the primacy also in distinction of bodily race, and that the one Son of God in heaven, born before all ages by a beginning which cannot be fathomed, should likewise claim for Himself on earth the crown of splendid titles, being on the witness of the two authors the famed Offspring of kings and priests.

So it is our own procedure, not that of outsiders, that I shall clearly follow if I proclaim the worldly as well as the spiritual nobility of this maidservant of God; for it is clear that the Lord conferred this distinction also on the glory of His work, so that the world which glories in such honours might be confounded. So to despise the world she employed the attributes which vain men employ to despise God. Moreover, as the exemplar of salvation she wielded greater authority before the eyes of the proud. Here was a woman of higher rank who for love of Christ had sublimely lowered herself to practise humility, so that as a strong member of the weak sex she might arraign idle men, and as a rich woman embracing poverty and a noblewoman embracing humility she might confound the haughty of both sexes.

8. Her grandfather was the consul Marcellinus,[34] and the pomp of her family and opulence of wealth ensured that she married whilst still a young girl. Soon she became a mother, but that transitory happiness she enjoyed only briefly so that she might not love earthly things too long. For quite apart from the bereavements which she mourned in company with her surviving husband[35] after labour vainly ended in premature births, her griefs so accumulated that she lost two sons and her husband in a year; only a baby boy[36] was left to provide remembrance of, rather than solace for, her loved ones.

But since the Lord brings forth from the seeds of our ills the sources of heavenly blessings, through the loss of her human love she conceived a love of God. She was made wretched to become blessed; she was afflicted to be healed. For the Lord says: *I will strike and I will heal.*[37] So great is the love of our highest Father that even His anger springs from mercy, and He punishes to spare. For example, the blessed Paul was blinded to be enlightened; the persecutor fell that the apostle might rise; on a journey he found the true journey, and on the path of impiety he recognized the path to peace.[38]

In the same way the good Lord, who ever up to this moment, as He has witnessed, *performed the work of His Father*[39] with the same outpouring of His love even on us His least ones, laid hold of this holy woman, too, with fatherly love, not because He considered her unfaithful, but to make her perfect. In His mercy He assailed her with trials to crown her with patience, for *He scourgeth every son whom He receiveth.*[40] So after accompanying her three dead in tearful procession, robbed of both husband and sons, she arrived in Rome with her one child who stimulated rather than allayed her tears. For he either experienced grief before his proper time, and could already bewail the death of others before being able to know his own life, or he was inappropriately happy in the ignorance of childhood, and smiled in pathetic joking while his mother wept.

9. She was taught by these proofs not to bound herself with this frail world and to put her hope only in God, the sole Person whom we cannot lose involuntarily. So she clad her son and herself in the knowledge of salvation, so that she loved her child by neglecting him and kept him by re-

linquishing him.[41] By commending him to the Lord she
was to possess him in absence more firmly than she would
have embraced him in person if she had entrusted him to
herself.

In her situation she imitated so far as she could the faithful vow of the barren Anna.[42] For disastrous fertility had
made her very like a barren woman; and because she was
afraid, now that her fertility was nullified, to become as
Anna had been before she attained the fruitfulness she deserved, she dedicated to God a different gift but with similar love. Whereas Anna wished to conceive a child, Melania
was troubled about the dear one she had borne. Anna
wished to begin being a mother; Melania, not to cease being
one.

You may regard the two cases as dissimilar, because
Melania's son, unlike Samuel, is not set in the temple to
serve the Lord, but rather enjoys the riches and distinctions of the world; but you should nonetheless realise that
love and faith are equally balanced on both sides. For
Melania has paid to God through her own person what the
glorious Anna paid through her son. The dedication of
Samuel to God was subsequently compensated by several
children;[43] but Melania's only son was the sum of her
childbearing, the end of her labour. When Anna consigned
her firstborn to a position in the temple, she had other dear
ones at home to console her, as well as the fact that she was
not far separated from her son though he was consecrated,
and that she paid a return visit annually to the temple. But
once Melania had torn her one son from her breast and set
him in Christ's bosom so that the Lord Himself might
nourish him, she bestowed no subsequent personal care on

him, for she thought it a sin of distrust to give her own attention to one whom she had entrusted to Christ.

The extent of her faith in this gesture can be gauged from this: though she had crowds of very influential and affectionate relatives at Rome, she thought it right to entrust her child to none of them for the proverbial rearing, tutoring, and protecting. So convinced was she that he had been taken up by Christ, she deserved to keep him because she did not wish to enjoy him, and she also has deserved to see him again now, because of that loving faith with which, once she left him with God, she had not longed for him in this world.

So He who can grant to believers more than they hope for *has done great things for her.*[44] He has allowed her to see her son even here, as He granted Solomon, for electing to follow Wisdom, all the other wealth which he had not sought, and precisely because he had not sought it. God rewarded his right understanding, by which he had preferred the highest things to the lowest, by adding the lesser to the greater. So Solomon deserved to become the owner of all his wealth because he had elected to seek out the highest things. This is the example which warns us to be wise when we are taught to choose. For if we prefer the lesser to the greater and the lowest to the highest (that is, earthly to heavenly things), as punishment for our foolish desires we shall be deprived of both highest and lowest blessings. Quite justly we shall not get the things we did not desire, and we must rightly be robbed of the things our disastrous love of which causes us to neglect the better choice.

Like Melania, father Abraham got back his one son

whom he had offered to God, because when the demand
was made he readily offered the child.[45] The Lord is content with the perfect sacrifice of heartfelt love, so the
angel's hand intervened to stay the father's right arm as it
was poised for the blow. The angel snatched up the victim
and in its place set a hastily furnished sheep, so that God
should not lose His offering, nor the father his son. There
was this further reason, that the mystery to be fulfilled in
Christ and rehearsed in Isaac (so far as that image of God
could rehearse it) could be given shape through a ram. For
the lamb which was to be later sacrificed in Egypt to
typify the Saviour[46] was thus already anticipated by a beast
of its own species—the ram which replaced Isaac as victim
to prefigure Christ. So the ram was found for Abraham,
since the highest sacrament was not his due, but it was
killed for Him for whom the fulfilment of the sacrament
was being preserved.

10. Melania had many struggles, too, with the hate-
filled dragon during her training for this service, because
the envy of the spiteful enemy did not allow her to depart
without difficulty and in peace. The devil attempted,
through the utmost pressure of her noble relatives, whom
he equipped to detain her, to block her design and prevent
her from going. But she was lent strength superior to the
power of the tempters. She gladly threw off the bonds of
human love with the ropes of the ship, as all wept. She
joined unwearied battle with the waves of the sea, so that
she could conquer these as well as the billows of the world,
and sailed away. Abandoning worldly life and her own
country, she chose to bestow her spiritual gift at Jerusalem,
and to dwell there in pilgrimage from her body. She became an exile from her fellow citizens, but a citizen

amongst the saints. With wisdom and sanctity she chose to be a servant in this world of thrall so as to be able to reign in the world of freedom.

11. Of her many divine virtues I shall recount just one, so that from this you can assess all her achievements. During the notorious reign of Valens,[47] when the rage of the Arians assailed the church of the living God using that king of impiety as their lackey, Melania was the leader or companion of all who stood fast for the faith. She gave refuge to fugitives or accompanied those arrested. But after she had hidden those who were the objects of greater hatred from the heretics because of their notable faith, and those who helped to conceal them had incurred loathing, the torches of the devil fired the serious discord.

She was ordered to be haled forth for holding the state law in contempt and to suffer the fate awaiting her hidden protégés unless she agreed to produce them. She advanced fearlessly, desirous of suffering, and rejoicing at the unjust proclamation. Though she had not anticipated arrest, she flew along before her would-be escort to the judge's tribunal. His respect for the woman before him troubled him, and his surprise at her bold faith caused him to drop his heretical rage.

About the same time she fed five thousand monks,[48] who lay in hiding, for three days with her own bread, so that by her hand the Lord Jesus again fed in the desert the same number as of old.[49] But now His kindness was all the greater as the hidden monks were being accorded less freedom and affection than that former five thousand who had voluntarily assembled before the Lord in freedom and in peace.

But Melania did not fear arrest. Untroubled she provided the assistance which was forbidden. She wished to obtain no recognition or glory from her work, but the scale of her assistance brought fame, and she was renowned by as many attestations before men as the number whom she fed in league with God. Let us assess the extent of her merit. Abdias is famed in the history of the Kings[50] for hiding a hundred men of God from the anger of an equally impious king, and feeding them; are we to doubt, then, that Melania, who bettered that total countless times over, has brought forth fruit a hundredfold?

12. I shall now hasten over her other achievements and days, and in imitation of her journey I shall embark on the crossing on which she made her return, so that I may conclude my words more speedily by recounting her arrival here.

In this event I witnessed the great grace of God. She put in at Naples, which lies a short distance away from the town of Nola where I live.[51] There she was met in welcome by her children[52] and grandchildren,[53] and then she hastened to Nola to enjoy my humble hospitality. She came to me here surrounded by a solicitous retinue of her very wealthy dear ones. In that journey of mother and children I beheld the glory of the Lord. She sat on a tiny thin horse, worth less than any ass; and they attended her on the journey, their trappings emphasizing the extraordinary contrast. For they had all the pomp of this world with which honoured and wealthy senators could be invested. The Appian Way[54] groaned and gleamed with swaying coaches, decorated horses, ladies' carriages all gilded, and numerous smaller vehicles.

Yet the grace of Christian humility outshone such vain brilliance. The rich marvelled at this poor saint whilst our

poverty mocked them. I beheld the world in a turmoil fit
for God's eyes, crimson silk and gilded trappings playing
servant to old black rags. I blessed the Lord who exalts the
humble, lends them wisdom, and fills them with good
things, whilst the rich He sends empty away.[55]

Yet on that day I was astounded at the spirit of poverty
shown by those rich people towards their mother's welfare,
for they took pride more in her holy poverty than in their
own conspicuous wealth. God's glory seemed to ensure
that I beheld the riches of my sister in poverty now possessed by her children, so that she was already obtaining a
reward for her faith by beholding her victory over the
utter emptiness of this world, when at close quarters she
saw all that she had left for Christ, all that she had continued unremittingly to despise.

Those silk-clad children of hers, though accustomed to
the splendour of a toga or a dress according to their sex,
took joy in touching that thick tunic of hers, with its hard
threads like broom, and her cheap cloak. They longed to
have their woollen garments, so valuable with their golden
embroidery, trodden down beneath her feet or worn away
with the rubbing of her rags. For they thought that they
were cleansed from the pollution of their riches if they
succeeded in gathering some of the dirt from her tawdry
clothing or her feet.

13. We have a cottage here raised off the ground, which
runs quite a distance along to the dining hall, and has a
colonnade separating it from the guest rooms. God in His
kindness seemed to make this bigger, and it afforded modest
but not too constricted accommodation not only for the
numerous holy ladies who accompanied Melania, but also
for the bands of rich people as well. The ringing choirs of

boys and maidens in the cottage made the near-by roof of our patron Saint Felix resound.

Nor did the other type of guests, however different their manner of life, protest, though they were dwelling in the same lodging. Even in them there was a pious sobriety emulating our disciplined silence, so that if they declined to watch and sing with us because they were overcome with sleep and mental indolence, they did not dare to register dissent from the voices at worship. They were calmed by that fear of the faithful which restrained the hubbub of their secular anxieties, and made them join, if only under their breath, with the peaceful voices as they sang the Psalms.[56]

But I hasten to return to the perfect dove of the Lord. Be sure that there is such divine strength in that weak woman's body that she finds refreshment in fasting, repose in prayer, bread in the Word, clothing in rags. Her hard couch (for she lies on the ground on a cloak and quilt) becomes soft as she studies, for her pleasure in reading reduces the hardship of that stiff bed. That holy soul is at rest when she is awake for the Lord.

Up to now the daughter of Sion has possessed her, and longs for her; but now the daughter of Babylon possesses and admires her.[57] For now even Rome herself in the greater number of her population is the daughter of Sion rather than of Babylon. So Rome admires Melania, as she dwells in the shadow of humility and the light of truth, as she offers incentives to faith among the rich and the consolations of poverty among the poor. Yet now that she is amongst the crowds of Rome, she yearns for her silence and obscurity at Jerusalem, and cries: *Woe is me that my sojourning is prolonged!* Has my journey been postponed

that I might now *dwell with the inhabitants of Cedar?*[58]
(For I have discovered that Cedar in Hebrew means darkness.)

So I think she is to be felicitated on the virtues I have
mentioned provided that she is fearful about her present
abode, and as long as so outstanding a soul bestows more
on Rome than she draws from it. She must *sit on the rivers
of Babylon yet remember Sion.*[59] She must keep the instru-
ment of her body above all the ambushes and attractions of
hostile Babylon, secure in the steady course of her committed life, which we may call the willows always thriving
on true moisture. So she may flourish unceasingly, and
with the enduring constancy of faith and the grace of
virtue, *her leaf will not fall off.*[60] Just as on the journey of
this life she is a model, so at its end her praise will be sung.

14. My brother, I could not allow Melania to go in
ignorance of you. So that she might savour more fully the
grace of God in you, I made you plain to her through your
own words rather than mine, for with my own lips I de-
claimed to her your life of our Martin. She is most inter-
ested in such historical works.

In the same manner I portrayed you both to the revered
and most learned bishop Nicetas,[61] who arrived from
Dacia, a figure rightly admired by the Romans, and also
to very many holy men abiding in God's truth. I did this
not so much to tell of you as to boast of myself, for it is
my boast that I have your love and affection, and your life
accords with your tongue in attesting that you are the
servant of truth. *May the Lord grant me to find mercy of
the Lord on that day*[62] through the grace which He Himself creates, so that as I am now refreshed in the bowels of
your charity, I may likewise be saved from the fires I de-

serve by the cooling finger of your inheritance. For I hope that in His kindness the Lord will judge me favourably because you are righteous and because I have great love for you, even though I am unworthy, and cannot presume to hope for a share in your crown.

LETTER 30

To Severus[1]

Paulinus greets his holy and loving brother Severus.

1. The blessed Apostle was told: *Much learning doth make thee mad.*[2] In this passage the real madness is clearly in them who regarded God's wisdom (which Paul was recounting) as foolishness, because they were void of faith in the truth, and did not deserve to understand the Wisdom of God, which is Christ. But though by Christ's kindness I differ in character from them whose lack of faith led them to regard the master of sanity as mad, I shall nonetheless exploit our free intimacy, which the harmony of our faith makes all the closer, to adopt similar words if not a similar attitude, and say: "Severus, dear Severus, your great affection for me is driving you mad. You make a fool of yourself in your attitude to me, your child in awareness but not in age. You are like a grandfather who treats a long-awaited grandson with too much affection. I say this with all respect to your wisdom."

2. For what reply can I make to your request that I have my portrait painted and sent to you? By the bowels of charity I ask you, what consolations of real affection are you trying to get from appearances without life? What image of myself would you like me to send—the earthly or the heavenly Paulinus? I know that you long for that incorruptible appearance which the King of heaven loved in you. The only representation of me which can be neces-

sary for you is that in which you yourself are fashioned, by which you love your neighbour as yourself, and desire to outshine me in no respect, lest some inequality appear between us.

But[3] I am poor and wretched, and since I am still caked with the filth of my earthly image, because in bodily feelings and worldly actions I resemble the first more than the second Adam, how shall I dare to paint myself for you when I am found guilty of denying the image of the heavenly man through earthly corruption? Shame encloses me on both sides. I blush to paint myself as I am, and dare not paint myself as I am not; I hate myself as I am, and am not what I long to be. But what good will it do me in my wretchedness to hate wickedness and love virtue, when I prefer to do what I hate, and idly neglect the attempt at doing what I love? I am in conflict with myself, distracted with inner war, while *the spirit wars against the flesh and the flesh against the spirit*,[4] and the law of the body attacks the law of the mind with the law of sin.

How wretched I am, for even the wood of the cross has not helped me to dissolve the poisonous taste of that hostile tree! That ancestral venom descended from Adam, with which the erring father infected the whole of his human race, remains in me. In the state of natural goodness I kept my inner eyes open to innocence and closed to wickedness; but by choosing evil from that unpropitious food of the forbidden tree, I was both blinded and unhappily enlightened to wickedness, and I drank in the knowledge of good and evil which brings death.

3. I only wish that my sin of forbidden lust had been at least dissolved by this remedy of attaining knowledge of good and evil by the tasting that brought harm, and of

then preferring the good; especially as I had heard the saving plan of God urging me, in my choice of fire or water, life or death, to put my hand to the water and prefer the gift of life. But from my sin of stupidity sprouted forth the guilt of recklessness; for though I had agreed to choose the good I preferred to seek what was harmful. What pardon for my sin remains to me in my wretchedness, then, when I have no longer the excuse of ignorance? I recognised the good yet did the wicked thing, though it was equally open to me to do what was good if I had not through perversity of will despised my soul's profit. This perversity, through lack of necessary control, led me to do what was unfitting. So it was right that I should lose the eyes of innocence, through which I saw no evil, and receive instead these eyes of iniquity by which I recognise sin as the punishment for my guilt.

4. For Scripture states that the original parents of the human race saw yet did not see. *The woman saw that the tree was good to eat and fair for the eyes to behold.*[5] *She saw*, says Scripture, so she had eyes. Yet what is appended later on? *When they had eaten, their eyes were opened.*[6] So they had been blind. So we realise, since blindness and sight cannot exist simultaneously in the one body, that we who possess sight have certainly some blindness, and on the other hand the blind have a kind of vision. This is why, as I see it, the Lord said: *For judgment I am come into this world, that they who see not may see, and they who see may become blind.*[7] For He *is come* into this world *to seek what had been lost*,[8] and to give fresh light to what had been blind.

In short, this was the Physician needed by the man who cries out in the prophet's words: *Enlighten my darkness,*

O Lord. For *the Lord is merciful and compassionate. He is a Light risen up in the darkness*[9] of human blindness, to raise up the broken, to loose the enchained, to enlighten the blind. How had He come to make blind those who see? The Gospel indeed tells us that He restored the sight of many blind persons, and took it from none. Yet it is written in the Law: *I will kill, and I will make to live.*[10] And this is also in the Gospel, for He *is set for the fall and resurrection of many;*[11] and there is also that passage I quoted before: *For judgment am I come into this world, that they who see not may see, and they who see may become blind.*[12]

So the Lord came that the old things might pass away, and the new arise. And what He had said was fulfilled: *I will kill, and I will make to live.*[13] For by taking the form of our old man, He killed him. He fastened him to the cross, and by plundering Himself of His flesh He *exposed the principalities and powers to open show.*[14] He triumphed over the old man in Himself, and brought to life the new man by the resurrection of the dead, rising to the heights and setting him in the heavenly places.[15]

5. This, then, is why He came, to enlighten the blind and to make blind those who see, so that our eyes which had been opened to sin should be blinded, and on the other hand so that the eyes which had been blinded should be opened. For it is good for me to be blind if I see no sin; it is good to have eyes if I see righteousness. So pray, dear brother, that the Lord may achieve in me both the blinding of my sight that I may not see what is empty, and the enlightenment of my blindness that I may see justice. May He kill in me *the old man with his deeds,* so that my flesh may take new vigour in Christ and *my youth be renewed*

like the eagle's.[16] For *this is the change of the right hand of the Most High,*[17] when we shall be transformed from ourselves *into the new man who is created according to God* and whose image is the heavenly one, and shall *put off the old man who is corrupted according to the desire for error.*[18]

I ask that God should crush in me the likeness to this old man, and reduce to nothing my earthly image[19] in this walled city.[20] May He renew in me and perfect His image, in which I am not ashamed to be painted. If I put this image first I can indeed say: *My heart and my flesh hath fainted away; Thou art the God of my heart and the God that is my portion forever.*[21]

For when my heart and my flesh—in other words, the action of my will and the harvest of my flesh—have fainted away by the blessed change achieved in man by the hand of the Most High, then shall I be free of bodily attachments, and cleansed in heart I shall dare to say: *Thou art the God of my heart and the God that is my portion forever.*[22] May the words of Simeon in the Gospel be fulfilled in me, that Christ *may be set for my fall and resurrection,*[23] the fall, that is, of my outer man, and the resurrection of the inner, so that the sin flourishing in my ailing soul may fade away, and the immortal man, now fallen through the ascent of sin, may arise. For when the outer man stands the inner man falls; and therefore *when our outer man is weakened the inward man is renewed day by day.*[24] The master who was perfect in this respect says: *When I am weak, then I am powerful.*[25]

6. But thanks be to the Lord, because He has painted my portrait in a picture that lasts and lives, not on tablets that crumble or on wax that melts, but *in the fleshly tablets*

of your heart.[26] There, in the unity of faith and grace, I am impressed and fashioned after your soul; and you will keep me and behold me there with inseparable and ever-present regard, not only in this life but also in eternity.

Even in this life, if you are fired with such a great desire to possess also the consolations of sight, you will be able to describe my appearance to painters, however inexperienced or ignorant, by sketching my outline which dominates your mind. You can lay before them your memory in which you keep my portrait, like a face to be copied from the clear features of seated models. But if the hand of the artist[27] strays through being too ignorant to understand your description, in the eyes of others he will paint a poor likeness; but for you, who always think of me and embrace me in mind, it does not matter what likeness he paints with unskilled hand and calls Paulinus, for in your knowing heart it will still be I.

LETTER 31

To Severus[1]

Paulinus greets his holy and loving brother Severus.

1. In telling me of your other activities and desires, our brother Victor has reported to me that you desire for our basilica, which you have built in the village of Primulia-cum[2] on bigger lines than your previous one, some blessed object from the sacred relics of the saints, with which to adorn your family church in a manner worthy of your faith and service. The Lord is my witness that if I had even the smallest measure of sacred ashes over and above what we shall find necessary for the dedication of the basilica soon to be completed here[3] in the Lord's name, I should have sent it to you, my loving brother. But because I did not possess abundance of such a gift, and because Victor said that he had great hope of a similar favour from the holy Silvia who had promised him some of the relics of many Eastern martyrs, I have found instead a fragment of a sliver of the wood of the holy Cross to send you as a worthy gift. This will enhance both the consecration of your basilica and your holy collection of sacred ashes.

This goodly gift was brought to me from Jerusalem by the blessed Melania,[4] a gift of the holy bishop John[5] there; my fellow servant Therasia has sent it specially to our venerable sister Bassula.[6] Though presented to one of you, it belongs to you both, for you are both animated by a single vocation, and the faith which brings you together

into a perfect man[7] empties you of your sex. So from your
loving brethren, who long to associate with you in every
good, receive this gift which is great in small compass. In
this almost indivisible particle of a small sliver take up the
protection of your immediate safety, and the guarantee of
your eternal salvation. Let not your faith shrink because
the eyes of the body behold evidence so small; let it look
with the inner eye on the whole power of the cross in this
tiny segment. Once you think that you behold the wood
on which our Salvation, the Lord of majesty, was hanged
with nails whilst the world trembled, you, too, must trem-
ble, but you must also rejoice.

Let us remember that *the rocks were rent*[8] when this
cross was seen; so let us imitate the rocks at least, and rend
our hearts with fear of God. Let us recall that *the veil of
the temple was* also *rent*[9] by this same mystery of the cross.
We must realise that the rending of this veil was revealed
to us that, hearing the voice of the Lord and the mystery
of His boundless love, we may refrain from hardening our
hearts, and may sunder ourselves from things of the flesh
and rend in two the veil of unbelief. So, when we have
uncovered the surface of our hearts, we may behold the
mysteries of the saving gifts of God.

2. But I do not also bid you imitate the arrangement by
which I have enclosed this relic, which imparts a great
blessing, in a golden casing. Rather in this adornment I
have imitated your faith. I sent you your own exemplar
clothed with gold, for I know that you have within you,
like gold tried in the fire, the kingdom of God—in other
words, faith in the cross, by which we enter the kingdom
of heaven. As Scripture says,[10] if we suffer with Him we
shall also reign with Him. So this is given not to strengthen

your faith, because you believed before you saw, but because of the merit of your faith, which you received by hearing the word and now prove in action. This is why I have sent you this gift of wood bearing salvation in the Lord, so that you might both physically possess the cross which you hold in spirit and carry with the strength of your vocation.

3. I think it relevant here, because our faith seems to demand it and it is worth knowing, to recount the special history of the uncovering and finding of the cross after the time of the Passion.[11] If this history is not known, one can easily gauge how difficult it is to prove that this is the wood of the Lord's cross. It is certain that if it had fallen into the hands of the Jews (who were taking every precaution to crush belief in Christ), it would inevitably have been broken into pieces and burnt. Nor would the men who sealed the tomb have been careless enough to ignore the cross. They would not have allowed His passion to be venerated through the survival of the cross, when they cannot bear His resurrection to be venerated, though it is proved by the tomb found empty and the shattered seals they had affixed to it.

This is why[12] the search for its hiding place is made in our day, because if it had not lain hidden it must clearly have been destroyed, especially during the years of persecutions which succeeded upon the hatred of the Jews and almost exceeded their savagery. For we can easily hazard the violence with which those who assaulted even the site of the cross would have destroyed the cross itself, if they had found it surviving.

The emperor Hadrian thought that he would destroy the Christian faith by insult to the place of Crucifixion,

and so he consecrated on the site of the Passion a statue of
Jupiter.[13] Bethlehem was also polluted with a shrine to
Adonis.[14] The intention was that what is in a sense the
root and foundation of the Church might be destroyed if
idols were worshipped in the places where Christ was born
to suffer, suffered to rise again, and rose again to reign as
Judge or judge as King.

How wretched I feel, when I recall that the almighty
Lord did not refuse even these sufferings for our sake!
Where He had hung crucified to win the salvation of the
human race, men showed their contempt by sacrilege. The
statue of an evil spirit stood over the cross, before which
the world had been shaken and the sun banished, the
tombstones made to dance through the awakening of the
dead, and nature herself made to totter. The altar erected to
the statue smoked with the ashes of cattle; the title of God
was conferred on statues of the dead, whilst the God of the
living, who is also the Resurrection of the dead,[15] was
blasphemed with abuse as a man who had not merely died
but even been crucified.

In Bethlehem, too, where *the ox had recognised his
owner and the ass his Master's crib*,[16] the princes of men
denied the God who is their Saviour, and worshipped the
ill-famed loves and deaths of men.[17] Where the Chaldaeans
had knelt with their riches, adoring the cradle of the
eternal King revealed to them by a new star, the Romans
ritually perpetrated barbaric lusts. Where the shepherds
on that glorious night had greeted the infant Saviour, singing in harmony with the host of angels in heavenly joy, a
mixed crowd of harlots and eunuchs lamented for Venus'
lover. How sad this is! What human devotion will be able
to atone for such impiety? Where the sacred Child, the

baby Saviour, had uttered His cries, that ill-famed rite
shrieked with the wanton grief of those counterfeiting the
laments of Venus. Where the Virgin had borne her child,
adulterers were worshipped.

4. This wickedness of an earlier age continued to the
time of Constantine, shortly before our day. He deserved
to be prince of the princes of Christ as much through the
faith of his mother Helena as through his own. The outcome proved that she was inspired by God's plan when she
set eyes on Jerusalem. As co-regent with the title Augusta,
she asked her son to give her a free hand in clearing all the
sites there on which our Lord's feet had trod, and which
were stamped with remembrances of God's works for us.[18]
She sought to cleanse them of all the infection of profane
wickednesses by pulling down temples and statues, and to
restore them to their rightful allegiance so that the Church
might at last be famed in the land of its beginnings.

So when the agreement of her son, the emperor, was
promptly forthcoming, the Augusta, his mother, applied
the money of the treasury to her holy tasks, completely
draining the imperial purse. With all the expense and all
the veneration which the queen could summon, and which
piety urged, she covered and adorned by the construction
of basilicas all the places where our Lord and Redeemer
had fulfilled for us the saving secrets of His love by the
mysteries of the Incarnation, Passion, Resurrection, and
Ascension.

A striking phenomenon is afforded by this building. In
the basilica commemorating the Ascension is the place
from which He was taken into a cloud, and *ascending on
high, led our captivity captive*[19] in His own flesh. That
single place and no other is said to have been so hallowed

with God's footsteps that it has always rejected a covering of marble or paving. The soil throws off in contempt whatever the human hand tries to set there in eagerness to adorn the place. So in the whole area of the basilica this is the sole spot retaining its natural green appearance of turf. The sand is both visible and accessible to worshippers, and preserves the adored imprint of the divine feet in that dust trodden by God, so that one can truly say: *We have adored in the place where His feet stood.*[20]

5. But hear of the great, truly God-sent miracle in the history of the Cross. When that revered queen reached Jerusalem, with care and devotion she avidly visited all the places in the city and vicinity which bore the marks of God's presence. She was eager to absorb through her eyes the faith which she had gained by devoted listening and reading; but most eagerly of all she began to seek after the cross of the Lord. But what method or plan of discovering it was at hand, when no suitable informant could be found, since both the long interval of years and the persistence of wicked superstition had removed all recollection and interest in religious awareness and observance?

But the Lord Himself is aware of and awake to all that is hidden in earth and in men's minds; so this faithful woman through her devoted love deserved to experience the breath of the Holy Spirit. After carefully but vainly searching for this object which God had removed from men's knowledge, she became eager to obtain information solely on the site of the Passion. So she sought out not only Christians full of learning and holiness, but also the most learned of the Jews to inform her of their native wickedness in which, poor men, they even boast.

Having summoned them she assembled them in Jerusalem. Her resolve was strengthened by the unanimous
witness of all about the site. There and then (undoubtedly
under the impulse of a revelation she had experienced) she
ordered digging operations to be prepared on that very
site. A force of civilians and soldiers was quickly mustered,
and the work of digging soon completed. To the general
astonishment, but precisely as the queen alone had believed, deep digging opened up cavities in the earth and
revealed the secret of the hidden cross.

But three crosses were found together, as they had once
stood together with the Lord and the thieves fastened to
them. So the thanksgiving for their discovery began to be
compounded with troubled doubts. The devoted faithful
were rightly afraid that they might perhaps choose the
gibbet of a thief in mistake for the Lord's cross, or outrage
the cross of salvation by discarding it as the stake of a
thief.

The Lord looked with mercy on the pious anxieties of
those whose faith put them in a ferment, and especially on
her who was outstandingly agitated in the devotion of her
heart. So He poured light on her counsels. So inspired, she
ordered a man newly dead to be sought out and brought to
her. Her command was instantly obeyed; a corpse was
carried in and set down. As the body lay there, the first
and then the second cross was placed on it, but death
spurned the wood which had supported the guilty. Finally
the Lord's cross was revealed by a resurrection, for at the
touch of the wood of salvation mortality fled, death was
shaken off, and the corpse brought upright. Whilst living
men trembled, the dead man stood up; like Lazarus of old

he was freed from the bonds of death, and there and then joined the group of spectators watching him, a man brought to life.[21]

6. So it is surely clear that, since the Lord's cross had lain hidden for so many generations, concealed from the Jews at the time of the Passion and screened from the sight of the Gentiles who undoubtedly dug up the ground when building a shrine there, it must have lain unnoticed through the agency of God so that it could now be found by a devoted search. As was fitting for Christ's cross, it was discovered and authenticated as His by the proof of resurrection.

Then it was consecrated in worthy surroundings by the foundation of a basilica on the site of the Passion. The basilica, gleaming with gilded ceilings and rich wth golden altars, preserves the cross which is placed in a hidden sanctuary. Every year during the Lord's Pasch the bishop of that city brings it out to be venerated by the people; he leads them in this show of respect. Only on the day when we celebrate the mystery of the cross itself is that source of mysteries brought out to mark the holy and solemn occasion; but occasionally devout pilgrims who have come there merely for that purpose beg that it be shown them as reward for their long journeying. It is said that this request is granted only by the kindness of the bishop; and it is likewise by his gift alone that these tiny fragments of sacred wood from the same cross are made available to win great graces of faith and blessings.

Indeed this cross of inanimate wood has living power, and ever since its discovery it has lent its wood to the countless, almost daily, prayers of men. Yet it suffers no diminution; though daily divided, it seems to remain whole to those who lift it, and always entire to those who venerate it. Assuredly it draws this power of incorruptibility, this undiminishing integrity, from the Blood of that Flesh which endured death yet did not see corruption.[22]

I hope that the cross will not only be a reminder of its blessing, but also generate for you incorruptibility, so that in looking on it you may be fired to faith by recalling also the blessed thief. He turned his robbery to good account. Through the faith of a moment and the rapid declaration of it, he preceded the saints whose journeys were prolonged with many labours. Quite fittingly he was the first, before the very martyrs and apostles, to *enter the kingdom prepared for them from the beginning*.[23] He became a pious plunderer in his sack of heaven. This was because, when he saw Christ crucified and suffering the same punishment as himself, he proclaimed Christ as the Lord of majesty that He was, in that condition which had confounded and weakened the faith even of the disciples. When the thief asked to be remembered in the kingdom of God, he believed in the glory of the Resurrection before it took place, whereas the apostles believed after it took place, when they both saw and had proof of it.

Their doubt, however, was concerned not with the fact of the Resurrection of the flesh, but with its nature.[24] For they who were to be sent out to the world to instruct all nations[25] had to embrace the faith they were to proclaim not only by hearing but also by seeing, so that they might more firmly teach what they had more certainly learnt.

LETTER 32

To Severus[1]

1. When I had enclosed those poor verses,[2] the open page made advances to my tongue and hand to fill out the empty spaces, and it struck me that I had something to write. I am highly delighted that we have together exhibited the one appearance of heart and body, and of works and dedications as well, by simultaneously bestowing basilicas on the Lord's folds. But you have also constructed a baptistry between your two basilicas, so that you surpassed me in the erection of visible buildings as well as in invisible works.

I thank the Lord, however, that he has granted me even defeat as victory. For when I am surpassed in grace by him whom I set before myself in esteem but on a par with myself in love, I prevail in my prayer. You are the one of whom I speak; you, I say, are the greater and better part of me. You are my rest and joy. You are a pillow for my head, and a dwelling for my mind which I hope and trust in the Lord will remain accessible to me not merely in this life but also forever, through His gift and in His body and spirit. So should you achieve anything considerable through the grace of the Lord, you do it assuredly in company with me, and certainly on my behalf.

2. But here I am afraid that through your love for me, of which I regularly complain, you may set a rough stumbling block amongst your works, by which you level

the steep paths and make straight the crooked ways of the world. For you seek to tarnish the gleaming inscriptions of your dedication in Christ with my name, and to set my wickedness amongst your toils of righteousness, so that you desecrate even your holy place with the countenance of the wicked.[3] It is right that Martin should be portrayed in that place of renewal[4] for men, for he bore the image of the heavenly man by his perfect imitation of Christ; so when men lay aside the old age of their earthly image in the baptismal font, the portrait of a heavenly soul worthy of imitation should strike their eyes. But by what right am I there, since I cannot match the innocence of children or the wisdom of men, and since I am distinguished from spotless souls by my wickedness and from perfect ones by my weakness? *For what fellowship hath light with darkness?*[5] Or wolves with lambs? Or serpents with doves—a true comparison of myself with Martin? Have you not mingled milk with gall?

However, there is a good side to this. When men are set in the same place they are not mixed with each other like liquids in a cup. If they differ in their deserts, the sweetness of the good man is not poisoned by the bitter taste of the wicked one. On the contrary, the sinner when associated with the just man appears fouler, while the just man in comparison with the other shines more brightly. For this reason I am less troubled by your fault of affection, because you have done no wrong to the blessed Martin, but rather added to his glory; for you have set his revered portrait facing my contemptible countenance, so that by comparison with my darkness, his brilliance, gleaming with outstanding radiance even *in the brightness of the saints*,[6] might shine forth all the more brightly.

Indeed, if I did not know that you had had this portrait done through the great zeal of your excessive love for me, I would charge you with devious malice. I would have said that by depicting me close on the opposite wall, you had contrasted my lowly figure shrouded in mental darkness with Martin's holy person; and that by so doing, you had painted only him and done a caricature of me, exposing me to merited contempt once Martin's countenance is sighted, and demonstrating the heinousness of this absurd comparison.

3. But I do not wish to cause this idea of yours, which springs from your love, to incur the laughter it can and should provoke, merely because your great love for me deceives you and will lead you to express falsehood. So for this reason only I have obeyed your demand, and have sent some modest verses describing such a picture as yours is. These verses can reveal your design. For you were eager to give a healthy formation to the persons renewed by baptism, so you placed before them two completely different portraits, in order that on leaving the sacred font they might simultaneously see the exemplar to avoid and the model to follow. So here are my lines to use if you like them:

"All you who wash your souls and bodies in this font should behold the paths set before you for good deeds. Martin is here so that you may see a model of perfect life, whereas Paulinus schools you in how to merit forgiveness. Martin should catch the eye of the blessed, Paulinus of sinners. So Martin must be the example for the saintly, Paulinus for the guilty."

Or again, on the same subject:

"Severus, so rich in wealth lavished on Christ and so

poor in that devoted to himself, here sets this fine roof over
the consecrated waters. He built this shrine for the works
of heaven, so that here men may be refashioned by water
and by God. So he has adorned it, making it worthy of the
sacrament, by painting twin portraits above, so that when
men attain new birth they may learn of the gifts of life.
One man's revered portrait bears witness to Martin; the
other represents the lowly Paulinus. Martin arms our faith
by good example and courageous words, so that our faith
may be unsullied and win the palm of glory. Paulinus re-
deems his sins by casting away his pence, and so teaches us
how our possessions are of less account than our salvation."

4. It will be a certain proof that you are to be the object
not of laughter but rather of approval, if only you are
shown to have painted cheek by jowl these wholly different persons from one motive only. This would be to
make manifest in Martin the shape of right living and the
aggregate of virtues, and in me contrition for and admission of my conscious guilt; in other words, to exhibit a
model both for the blessed and for the wretched, so that in
Martin courage can be mirrored and in me cowardice may
find consolation. So those who are able to fulfil virtuously
God's command may look on Martin, while those who
aspire to remedy their sins may be consoled through me.
For only redemption can assist those of us who like captives are tied with the bonds of wickedness and stripped of
the confidence of innocence.

I beg you, however, not to turn my obedience into sin
by removing those verses of yours, so filled with light and
redolent of the honeycomb, as you threatened to do. I pray
that your threat may betray modesty rather than true intention. If you think that my verses should be added, let

yours remain to sparkle like gems amongst mine, giving value to what is cheap and adorning blackness with brightness. I indeed accepted the free hand you offered me. I told my tongue not, as the prophet bids, to preserve its rest and *take heed to its ways*,[7] but rather to burst its protective bridle, provided that it was ministering to you. I love you so deeply that I feared more to sin through disobeying you than through excess of words.[8]

5. So I have also written some little verses for your basilicas like votive inscriptions for sacred fountains. If any of my lines shall seem apposite, the credit for this, too, is brother Victor's, for it is through his eyes and words that I have witnessed all that you have done and continue to do in Christ the Lord. So you will assess these additional verses which I have inserted about the basilicas as written by him, for he dictated the contents by telling me of your works. The following lines will describe the baptistry, for the previous ones described only the murals there.

"Here the spring which fathers newborn souls brings forth water living with divine light. The Holy Spirit descends on it from heaven, and mates its sacred liquid with a heavenly stream. The water becomes pregnant with God, and begets from seed eternal a holy offspring in its fostering fount. Wondrous is God's fatherly love, for the sinner is plunged into the water and then comes forth from it justified. So man achieves a happy death and birth, dying to things earthly and being born to things eternal. His sin dies, but his life returns. The old Adam perishes and the new Adam is born for eternal sway."

"Severus, most chaste of Christ's dwellers in body, mind, and faith, has in joy built this house for God. He is himself wholly a temple of God, and thrives with Christ as

his guest, bearing in humble heart the glad Lord. And just
as he worships one Mind under three names, so here he has
dedicated a threefold work of sacred building.[9] On the
twin structures he has set for his people splendid roofs so
that their number might harmonise with the sacred Laws.
For just as the one Proposer stipulated two Testaments,
joining Christ with God in the one faith, so Severus has
set his baptistry with tower-shaped dome between two
churches, so that Mother Church may joyfully receive in
twin bosoms the newborn offspring brought forth by
water. The twin-roofed basilicas represent the Church
with her two Testaments; the single baptistry lending grace
adjoins both. The Old Law strengthens the New, the New
fulfils the Old. Hope lies in the old, Faith in that which is
new. But Christ's grace combines Old and New, so the
baptistry is placed between the two. From it the priest our
father raises from the consecrated water children snow-
white in body, heart, and dress.[10] These novice-lambs he
leads round to the festive altars, and introduces their un-
initiated mouths to the Bread of salvation. Here the crowd
of elders, a gathering of friends, shares the rejoicing. The
fold bleats in fresh chorus: Alleluia!"

6. After I had written these verses to celebrate the
handiwork of your dear self, I could not leave unmentioned that which is made by no hand, the grace of God in
your church. By that grace He bestowed Clarus[11] on you
as permanent guest in your church. So I presumed to write
some verses to his holy memory, not because I could say
anything worthy of his godlike merits, but to express my
eager and abundant love for his soul. These verses I now
boldly send to your affectionate person. When you read
them out, in the Lord's presence, to this holy soul who

lodges forever with you in the Lord, you must excuse my recklessness and praise my obedience.

"Clarus the priest is clothed in that inner light which reflects his name.[12] His mortal body lies in the tomb. But his mind, freed from the prison of the body, finds joy amongst the stars, for its purity has gained the haven of the holy men who are approved. His sacred bones are at rest beneath the eternal altar; and so when the chaste gift of Christ is devoutly offered there, the fragrance of his soul may be joined to the divine sacrifice."

Here are more verses on the same subject, so that you may select those you prefer. But I know that in this matter your hesitation ought to be prompted not by choice of particular verses for the inscription, but by the necessity to do no injustice to any of God's saints.

"A priest lies here, Clarus by name and famed[13] by his merits, Martin's companion in meditation and now his partner in praise. The altar is a worthy home for this devoted man now dead, whose limbs lie beneath it. But his spirit rejoices in the upper air. Above the stars, he shares with the Master he resembles his disciple here below."

"Clarus, renowned in faith, highly renowned in deeds, most renowned in your harvest, your name is reflected by your merits. It is right that a pure altar covers your body, so that God's altar may conceal the temple of Christ. But you are not restricted to the abode where your body lies, for your spirit flies to the reward you have merited above. Whether you lie in the bosom of our fathers, or are buried beneath the Lord's altar, or feast in a sacred grove— wherever, Clarus, you are set in heaven or Paradise, you live happily in eternal peace. In your kindness receive these prayers of sinners who ask you to be mindful of Paulinus

and Therasia. Love these persons entrusted to you by the
mediation of Severus, though when you were here in the
flesh you were unaware of their merits. Let the love of a
friend held in common kindle in both of us an eternal cove-
nant in the highest Lord. You cannot separate men who
are united; should you seek to drag away one, he will draw
to his forced destination those who cling to him. So embrace Severus and Paulinus together as brothers indivisible.
Love us and join with us in this union. God summoned us
together, Martin loved us together. So, Clarus, you must
likewise protect us together. Our equality lies not in merit,
but in love; but you, holy Clarus, will be able to ensure
our equality also in merit, if you become Martin's partner
in the toil of paternal love, so that your prayers may prevail over my sins. So I may attain the destiny of Severus,
and your wing may ever protect me in its folds."

7. Doubtless the Lord has through your faith granted
your heart's desire by enhancing the beauty and holiness
of your buildings through your acquisition of sacred ashes
from the holy remains of glorious apostles or martyrs. I
know that it was in expectation of this favour that you
have built our second basilica, bigger than the first, at the
village of Primuliacum. Yet I think it worthy of the work
of your faith, and of the dedication of that building now
faithfully completed (which I am sure huge crowds attend), and also appropriate to the relics of the saints, that
you should also venerate that fragment of the cross which
I sent, and which lies consecrated in your church in company with the relics of the saints. If you decide to do this,
these little verses will announce your decision:

"The revered altar conceals a sacred union, for martyrs
lie there with the holy cross. The entire martyrdom of the

saving Christ is here assembled—cross, body, and blood of
the Martyr, God Himself. For God preserves His gifts for
you forever, and where Christ is, there also are the Spirit
and the Father. Likewise where the cross is, there, too, is
the Martyr; for the Martyr's cross is the holy reason for
the martyrdom of saints. That cross has won for men the
Food of life, has won also the crowns which gain a portion
with the Lord for His servants. The flesh which I eat was
nailed to the cross; from the cross flows that blood by
which I drink life and cleanse my heart. Christ, may these
gifts of Yours unite with Your Severus. May he bear your
cross and witness to it. May he live on Your flesh; may
Your blood provide his drink; may he live and work by
Your word. Through Your kindness may he be borne on
that upward journey on which he beheld Your Martin and
his companion Clarus rise."

8. But you may desire to have this blessing from the
cross available for your daily protection and healing, and
once it is buried within the altar it may not be always accessible according to the need. In that case it would be a
sufficient grace for the consecration of the basilica if we
entrusted it to the apostles and martyrs. If their revered
ashes are stowed beneath the altar unaccompanied by the
cross, this superscription will reveal that they are hidden
there:

"The splendour of God's table conceals those dear relics
of the saints which have been taken from the bodies of the
apostles. The Spirit of the Lord hovers near with healing
powers, and demonstrates by living proofs that these are
sacred ashes. So twin graces favour our devoted prayers,
the one springing from the martyrs below, the other from
the sacrament above. The precious death of the saints as-

sists, through this fragment of their ashes, the prayers of the priest and the welfare of the living."

9. Here, then, are your verses. They are unworthy of your holy and splendid buildings, yet they accord with that conviction about me which you prefer to trust rather than me. If you have no shame in inscribing them on the public walls of your church, I shall have my revenge. For I believe that you will be ashamed of my trifling lines, and that you will repent of your wish which you extorted from me, once you behold, pink with embarrassment, your immaculate buildings, as yet gleaming with the spotless beauty of your labours, darkened and—to use an expression worthy of my verses—befouled by my lines of childish ignorance which will provoke many to laughter or disgust.

You must not strain to deceive people so that the reader may think that you have written the verses; and since their ineptness, which no one associates with you, can inform the reader, he must not put the blame for my poems on to you, though you should incur censure as publisher or scribe.

But I should not like anyone to judge me a transgressor of that law which enjoins *never to do to another what thou dost not wish for thyself*.[14] So you will have proof, by the evidence which lies before Victor's eyes, that my own basilica endured the same treatment from me before yours. So you can show our inner unity additionally by the fact that by compliment or insult I compared myself with you and sinned against your basilicas only as rashly as I did against my own.

But you must regard our Victor as the author or as the guilty one—the author of what your most indulgent attitude to me regards as a favour, or the one guilty of injustice if one contemplates my most unworthy gift. For Victor, that most holy spokesman of our love, assumed that your pleasure on seeing him back from me would be greater the more bent he was on his return under the unjust burden of the trifling verses I send you. For he desired to add to his load by carrying inscriptions and sketches of my basilica to show to you. And he will be justified if on his arrival, weary and bent, he utters this complaint: *"Behold, for the sake of the commands of thy lips I have kept hard ways. The wicked have wrought upon my back; they have lengthened their iniquity*[15] to the extent of all these letters."

10. So I have thus accumulated my sins by bestowing the injustice he sought upon our brother, who was most eager for this burden so that his soul might be lightened by the affliction of his body. For this demand of his, by which he maintained that my buildings in the Lord ought to be made known to you as you had desired to reveal yours to me by inscriptions and paintings, seemed to be truly in keeping with our unity of purpose. So this motive has induced me to interconnect my basilicas with yours not only by their simultaneous construction and the fashion of their dedication, but also by describing them by letter. So in this additional way the fusion of our minds, however remotely we are separated, may be symbolised; and though these buildings, which in the same spirit we have toiled at and erected in the Lord's name, are separated and far distant from each other, they may be visited and, as it were, joined to each other by a chain of letters.

Well then, the basilica, now dedicated in the name of Christ our Lord and God to our common protector and lord of our house,[16] is thronged as an addition to his four basilicas,[17] and is venerable not merely through the respect paid to the blessed Felix but also because of the consecrated relics of apostles and martyrs kept under the altar in the tripartite apse. A vault adorned with mosaics provides light for the apse, the floor and walls of which are faced with marble. These are the verses which describe the scene depicted on the vault:

"The Trinity shines out in all its mystery. Christ is represented by a lamb, the Father's voice thunders forth from the sky, and the Holy Spirit flows down in the form of a dove. A wreath's gleaming circle surrounds the cross, and around this circle the apostles form a ring, represented by a chorus of doves. The holy unity of the Trinity merges in Christ, but the Trinity has its threefold symbolism. The Father's voice and the Spirit show forth God, the cross and the lamb proclaim the holy victim. The purple and the palm point to kingship and to triumph. Christ Himself, the Rock, stands on the rock of the Church, and from this rock four plashing fountains flow, the evangelists, the living streams of Christ."[18]

11. On the girdle below, where an inserted ridge of plaster joins or separates the borders of wall and vault, the following superscription reveals the holy of holies which has been set beneath the altar:

"Here is reverence, and fostering faith, and Christ's glory; here is the cross, joined with those who witnessed to it. For the tiny splinter from the wood of the cross is a mighty promise. The whole power of the cross lies in this small segment. It was brought to Nola by the gift of holy Melania, this greatest of blessings that has come from Jerusalem. The holy altar conceals a twofold honour to God, for it combines the cross and the ashes of the martyrs.

How right it is that the bones of holy men lie with the wood of the cross, so that there is rest on the cross for those who died for it!"

12. The whole area outside the apse of the basilica extends with high-panelled ceiling and with twin colonnades running straight through an arch on each side. Four chapels within each colonnade, set into the longitudinal sides of the basilica, provide places suitable for those who privately pray or meditate on the Lord's law,[19] and for the funeral monuments of the clergy and their friends so that they may rest in eternal peace. Each chapel is designated on the front of the lintels by a couplet which I have not wanted to quote in this letter. But I have jotted down the lines inscribed on the entrances to the basilica, because if you wished to adopt them they might be suited to the doors of your basilicas. For example:

"Peace be upon you who enter the sanctuary of Christ God with pure minds and peaceful hearts."

Or this, taken from the representation of the Lord over the entrance, the appearance of which the lines describe:

"Behold the wreathed cross of Christ the Lord, set above the entrance hall. It promises high rewards for grinding toil. If you wish to obtain the crown, take up the cross."

The following verses are found at a more private door to the second basilica, where there is what I might call our private entrance from the garden or orchard:

"Christ's worshippers, take the path to heaven by way of this lovely sward. An approach from bright gardens is fitting, for from here is granted to those who desire it their departure to holy Paradise."

This same door is adorned with further lines inside:

"Each of you that departs from the house of the Lord, after completing your prayers in due order, remove your bodies but remain here in heart."

13. The outlook of the basilica is not, after the usual fashion, towards the east,[20] but faces the basilica of the blessed Lord Felix, looking out upon his tomb. But the apse winds round, extending with two side apses on right and left in the spacious area around. One of these is available to the bishop when making his sacrifices of joy, whilst the other takes the praying congregation in its large recess behind the priest. The whole of this basilica opens on to the basilica of our renowned confessor, giving great pleasure to the eye; there are three external arches, and the light floods through the lattice by which the buildings and courtyards of the two churches are connected. For because the new church was separated from the older one by the intervening wall of the apse belonging to some tomb,[21] the wall was penetrated on the side of Saint Felix's church by as many doors as the new church has at its front entrance. So the wall is pierced to provide a view from one church into the other, as is indicated by the inscriptions posted between the doors on each side. So these lines are set at the very entrance to the new church:

"This beautiful house lies open for you to enter through the triple arch; this threefold door bears witness to devoted faith."[22]

14. Again, there are the following inscriptions on either side of that one, beneath crosses painted in red lead:

"The cross on high is circled by a flowery wreath, and is red with the blood which the Lord shed. The doves resting on this divine symbol show that God's kingdom lies open to the simple of heart."

"With this cross slay us to the world and the world to us, bringing life to our souls by destroying our guilt. If your peace thrives in our hearts made pure, O Christ, you will make us also your pleasing doves."

15. Within the lattice, which now bridges the short distance previously dividing the adjoining basilicas, over the central arch on the side of the new basilica are inscribed these lines:

"As Jesus our peace has destroyed the dividing barrier, and made us one with Him, sweeping away our divorce by means of the cross, so we see this new building no longer sundered from the old, but joined to it and united by the doors. A fountain gleaming with its attendant waters plays between the holy churches, and washes the hands of those who enter with its ministering stream. The people worship Christ in both these churches of Felix, governed by Paul their bishop[23] with his apostolic words."

The following couplets are inscribed over the other arches which stand on each side. On the one:

"On eyes bemused a new light dawns. He who stands on the single threshold sees twin churches simultaneously."

On the other:

"Twin churches now lie open by means of three sets of twin arches. Each admires the decoration of the other over the threshold which they share."

On these arches at the front, facing the basilica of the Lord Felix, these verses are set over the centre:

"You whose devoted faith constrains you in great crowds to hymn blessed Felix with diverse tongues, stream through the threefold entrance in loose-knit throng. For though you come in thousands, the huge churches will have space for you. Paul the bishop consecrates them for immortal purposes, as they stand close joined to each other by means of the open arches."

On the other arches are these two couplets:

"You who have left the old church of holy Felix, now pass to his new abode."

"That single faith which worships One under three names receives with its triple entrance those of single mind."

16. The following lines are inscribed in the two sacristies which, as I mentioned,[24] enclose the apse on each side. They describe the purposes of each of them. To the right of the apse we read:

"This is the place where the sacred food is stored; from here is brought forth the nourishing repast of the holy service."[25]

And on the left of the apse:

"If a person decides piously to meditate upon the Law, he will be able to sit here and concentrate upon the holy books."

17. Let us now leave this basilica at Nola and pass to that at Fundi, a town equally dear to me whilst I had property there,[26] which was then more frequently visited by me. So I had longed to found a basilica there as a pledge of my affection as a resident or to commemorate my former estate there; for the town was in need of a new one, since the existing church was tumbledown and small. So I thought I should append here these modest verses which I have composed for the dedication of that basilica at Fundi; for building is still in progress, but it is almost ready to be consecrated if God be kind.

The reason chiefly impelling me to send these verses is that my Victor liked the painting which is to be visible in

the apse of the church, and he desired to convey the poems
to you in case you wished to depict one or other of them
in your newer basilica, which Victor says also incorporates
an apse. (You must decide whether I should say *absida*
here or *abside;* I confess my ignorance, for I don't remember ever reading this latter form of the word.)

This little basilica of Fundi also will be consecrated by
sacred ashes from the blessed remains of apostles and
martyrs, in the name of Christ the Saint of saints, the
Martyr of martyrs, the Lord of lords. For He Himself
has guaranteed that He will in turn acknowledge those
who acknowledge Him; so there is a second inscription
describing this grace of His, quite separate from the painting. This is the description of the painting:

"Here the saints' toil and reward are rightly merged, the
steep cross and the crown which is the cross's high prize.
God Himself, who was the first to bear the cross and win
the crown, Christ, stands as a snowy lamb beneath the
bloody cross in the heavenly grove of flower-dotted Paradise. This Lamb, offered as an innocent victim in unmerited
death, with rapt expression is haloed by the bird of peace
which symbolises the Holy Spirit, and crowned by the
Father from a ruddy cloud. The Lamb stands as judge on a
lofty rock, and surrounding this throne are two groups of
animals, the goats at odds with the lambs. The Shepherd is
diverting the goats to the left and is welcoming the deserving lambs on His right hand."[27]

These are the verses on the relics:

"Under the lighted altar, a royal slab of purple marble
covers the bones of holy men. Here God's grace sets before
you the power of the apostles by the great pledges contained in this meagre dust. Here lie father Andrew, the

gloriously famed Luke, and Nazarius, a martyr glorious for
the blood he shed; here are Protasius and his peer Gervasius,
whom God made known after long ages to His servant
Ambrose.[28] One simple casket embraces here his holy band,
and in its tiny bosom embraces names so great."[29]

18. These and other works of the same kind, distinguish-
able on earth from things of earth, are the temporary
buildings at which I have toiled, dear brother. But *blessed
be the Lord day by day, who alone doth wonderful
things.*[30] *As He turned the rock into pools of water,*[31] so
He transforms earthly things into heavenly, deigning to
make this change in company with us though all things on
earth and in heaven are His. So all our physical labours on
earth are through Him being built up secretly in heaven,
and will be revealed to us when we see with the naked eye
what we now anticipate through faith.[32] We sow on earth,
therefore, and reap in heaven. Here we strew and there we
gather. Here we dwell but our conversation is there. We
gird ourselves here and are soldiers there. We fight here
and conquer there; or if we conquer here, we are crowned
there. So what we build by our hands here we store up for
ourselves there by faith.

And if we build our structures, however earthly, with
spiritual prayer and study, this becomes a blessed preparation for the heavenly mansions.[33] For even as we erect these
buildings in the Lord because we have received the faith,
we are ourselves erected by the Lord through the growth
of this same faith. The centurion of the Gospel exemplifies
for us the certain expectation that we may win eternal
reward especially because of such building. He was able to
merit the healing of his son,[34] and the praise of his faith by
the Lord Jesus Himself, precisely because the Lord's people

(at that time comprising only the Jews) commended him by witnessing to his building of a synagogue.

19. Why, then, do we poor souls remain idle and yawning? Why do we stand inactive in the noisy forum of this world as though we were not hired labourers? Or, if we reflect that we owe the master of the house his denarius and so perform some work in his vineyard, why do we flaunt that work not as a debt but as a favour, and even contemplate adding it to the Lord's credit account, as though we were doing something of benefit to Him rather than to ourselves? Wretched creatures that we are, we think that we bestow gifts; in performing our business we gain a reputation for generosity, but we are convicted of the utmost greed. Indeed, we are greedier than the keenest usurers of this world, for it is a more handsome transaction to purchase heavenly possessions for earthly, and to purchase blessedness for misery and need, than it is to swap earthly objects for other earthly ones, to trade for things now decaying others which will decay; it is better to lend money to the Lord than to man. *He who puts out money to usury and takes bribes against the innocent*[35] is condemned in the Law. But see how the grace of the Gospel shows us how these crimes are transformed into innocence and holiness, and that repayment not of punishment but of reward follows, if only those sins are converted towards God's precepts for salvation by the keenness of faith. Put out your money for usury, but for Christ; then usury brings salvation.

20. Again, in the world judges who are bribed by gifts from defendants are condemned. But if one is detected in some sin, and if having no confidence in your innocence

you offer the price of your salvation to our Judge, you
need not fear to commit the injustice of bribery against
God's justice. Christ gladly accepts from you the reward
of your salvation, because He prefers *mercy and not sacrifice.*[36]

But perhaps you ask where you are to find Him, and
how you are to bribe Him when you cannot see Him.
Scripture says: *Rise, thou that sleepest, and arise from the
dead, and thou shalt come upon Christ.*[37] In other words,
shake off the sleep of physical idleness. Lift your mind,
now downcast with earthly thoughts, from the cares of the
dead, which are the life of the flesh. Raise and direct your
soul to the Lord and *thou shalt come upon Christ.* By act-
ing according to His precepts, you will see Him in every
poor man, touch Him in every needy person, entertain
Him in every guest, since He Himself bears witness that
what is done to His least brethren in His name is done to
Him.[38] So now you know how you are to see Him though
He is invisible, and to lay hold of Him though He cannot
be grasped.

So now let us be paupers here, that we may be enriched
later in heaven. Let us weep now, so that we may later rejoice. Let us be hungry now, to gain our fill then. *The
poor you have always with you,*[39] says Christ. You observe
that you have no excuse for ever delaying a kindness, for
the poor man is at hand if only our will is not lacking.

21. So let us now throw off anxiety and make gifts to
Christ who is in need even in the persons of His poor, so
that we can share in His glory which will abound in them.
This is why the Lord Himself gives us warning with the
words: *Make unto you friends of the mammon of in-*

iquity.[40] You see how the Almighty makes light from darkness and justice from wickedness, so that *when you shall fail they may receive you into everlasting dwellings*.[41]

For the human race is governed by a kind of alternation of riches and poverty. This the Gospel story makes clear in the case of the rich man in hell and the poor man in the kingdom of heaven, so that we may understand the design of Him who created both. By this design He created the rich for the poor and the poor for the rich, so that he who has plenty may provide sustenance for the needy, and the poor man may be the means for just action to the wealthy. So, as Paul puts it, *there may be an equality*,[42] and the eternal wealth which must in the next life compensate the poor for their indigence here may flow back to meet our need, if only our wealth in this world has given aid to their poverty.

Let us, then, sow seeds of the flesh in them, that we may reap spiritual harvests from them.[43] Let our hands now occupy themselves with earthly gifts, that our souls may be refreshed with heavenly ones. Let present hope build possessions for the future. Let us construct dwellings here to cover our heads in the next world. Let the poor man be fed in this world, where he is needy and I am rich, that he may feed me in the next, where he will be filled and I shall want. Note this spiritual transaction and deny, if you can, that we are greedy who sell our land and tithes to purchase exemption from payment and obtain eternal life in the kingdom.

22. We put down crumbling sand to build on it an eternal house, to reach the stars by means of cheap quarried stone. By this stone we do not vainly build that tower of confusion and pride[44] which is doomed to destruction.

Rather we base ourselves on the Cornerstone Himself,[45] so
that through Him who is *a tower of strength in the face of
the enemy*[46] we may rise to His fulness. He Himself bids us
build this tower only after prior reckoning of the cost, in
case we fail and stop building and have to endure the
stigma of rash thoughtlessness, and the deserved mockery
for our cowardice with its vain show of daring. The cost
we must pay is unflinching faith.

So he who believes according to God's truth, who makes
the Lord Jesus his Hope and Wealth and Strength, builds
a structure which all coheres and grows and rises and
mounts to the fulness of God. *Unless the Lord build the
house*, therefore, *we shall* sweat and *labour in vain that
build it.*[47] And even when the building is completed (and
this is achieved only with the Lord's aid), there is a danger
that we may sit back and complacently abandon our efforts; so divine Scripture adds that unless God also guards
the house when it is built, the watchful care of those who
preserve it will be vain.

23. So let us entreat the Lord that, while we build a
visible lodging for Him outside ourselves, He may build
within us a lodging which is invisible—in Paul's words, *that
house not made with hands*,[48] the entry to which will at the
end give us understanding, when *we see face to face what
we now see in a dark manner and know in part.*[49]

But now, whilst we are still established in the tabernacle
of our earthly bodies, we dwell, so to say, amongst the
tents in the desert, under the canvas of that ancient tabernacle;[50] and the word of God goes before us through the
parched region of this world, *in a pillar of a cloud, to over-
shadow our heads in the day of battle, or in a pillar of fire,
that we may know his heavenly way on earth.*[51] Let us pray

that through these present tabernacles of the Church we may *go into the house of God*,[52] where dwells our highest Lord Himself, the Cornerstone *made for us by the Lord*, the stone hewn from the mountain and grown into a mountain, which *is wonderful in our eyes*.[53]

May He offer Himself to our building both as its foundation and its top, for He is *the beginning and the end*.[54] I pray that on this rock (for Christ, too, is the Rock, without which no man can build a steady house) our hands may not heap stubble or hay or straw, like *the hands that served in baskets*[55] in Egypt, lest we waste our efforts, to use the proverbial phrase,[56] on worthless building of foul construction and, bent beneath the burdens of servile toil, we turn our backs on the Lord.[57] For on the one hand He refreshes with light those who turn to Him, but on the other He blinds those who turn away.

24. But as we build we must consider what we can erect from our frail and earthly material to be worthy of the divine foundation, so that being given life by the Cornerstone Himself we may be smoothed out to become stones for the construction of the heavenly temple.[58] Let us fuse together the gold of our thoughts and the silver of our speech in Christ, so that once we are cleansed in the furnace of this world, He who approves the souls that please Him may transform us into gold tried by the fire,[59] worthy of the stamp of His image, and we by reason of our enlightened works may offer ourselves as precious stones to Him. Let us not be foolishly hard as teak in heart, or withered in works with the dryness of hay, or fickle and weak in faith or charity with the frailty of unsubstantial straw.

But to ensure that the work which we willed is not laid

out for burning, but rises unshaken and with toil un-troubled, let us beg from the Most High that peace for our building in which the famed wall was of old built into the temple, *so that neither hammer nor axe nor any iron implement is heard upon it*,[60] nor, as afterward happened during the rebuilding of the temple through the hostile hatred of the Persians, may an enemy attack hinder and postpone the fresh construction of the building.[61] For we shall become a house of prayer and peace only if no distracting anxieties of the flesh enfeeble us, only if no din of this world disturbs our tranquillity.

Our hammer is the thought we take for food and clothing; our axe and iron implement are our longing for things of earth, our fear of death by night, our spiteful malice, and the possessions of this world, through the gnawing anxiety or contented love of which the soul is devoured and the mind enchained. The tranquillity of a well-ordered will, which is strengthened when our thoughts are disciplined in the silence of religious life, and the concentration of prayer, which proceeds unhindered from a free and chaste heart, are uprooted by the din of bodily cares which are like the distracting noise of the hammer or the blow of the axe. But *because He that is in us is greater than he that is in the world*, the Lord can *crush Satan under our feet*,[62] so that on our behalf that prophecy may be fulfilled: *The hammer of the whole earth is destroyed*.[63]

25. But it is profitable for us that the Lord Jesus should often revisit with the whip of His fear that temple of our hearts also which we have built, so that He may cast out from us the tables of the money-lenders and the sellers of oxen and doves,[64] so that our minds may not concentrate on the dealings of greed, and so that the slow manner of

oxen may not become installed in our thoughts; for *where there are no oxen, the cribs are clean.*[65] Nor let us sell our innocence, the fruit of God's grace, lest we make our *house of prayer a den of thieves.*[66]

Once our senses have been cleansed of all that gives rise to wickedness, our Lord Jesus Christ will gladly walk in them; in them, as in the five porticoes,[67] will stroll Wisdom, God's strength, *who healeth all our diseases.*[68] For in our souls, too, as in the porch by that healing pond of old, lie many sick and lame. If our souls hear the word of God, it will drive out the leprosy of greed, the cancer of envy, the blindness of dissipation, the madness of anger, and the paralysis of luxury, through the healing of His command; and when we are restored not only to the health of innocence but also to the strength of patience, it will bid us there and then not only to rise from our bed of weakness but also to take it up,[69] so that we may bear in strength what supported us in weakness.

This miracle is surely fulfilled also in the spiritual sphere of our weakness or health. Our flesh was the bed to which we entrusted ourselves as we lay enchained in vices and feeble in virtues. But then our inner self is reformed to goodness and purity of mind by the word of God and through the grace of Jesus Christ. So we become healthy, and take up that flesh like the bed in the Bible; we support it under the dominance of the spirit, and it attends us where we wish to go. In our sickness we awaited the help of another, and were always forestalled by the speed of those who entered the pool first, because there was no one to give us a hand or to make us whole. But then He who is greater than His envoys and angels (for He is the Lord of both prophets and angels) came, and in pity took in hand all our weakness. He took it up and healed it, and *filled our hungry souls with good things*, and bade us go into that house, which, as I have said, is *not made with hands*, in which there will be *the voice of rejoicing and salvation*.[70] There, too, will be Christ as Dwelling and Kingdom and King for all His people, as Paul attests, for *we shall be always with the Lord*,[71] to whom be honour, glory, and power forever.

LETTER 33

To Alethius[1]

Paulinus greets his blessed brother Alethius, rightly revered and most beloved.

1. *Thanks be to God, who has manifested the odour*[2] of His grace to me in your person, through the eloquence of your letter. It came by the hand of Victor, my dearest brother in God, who serves as a soldier for God by performing the duty of ministering to the love between brothers; for he offers his services as courier unwearied by yearly return journeys between distant points on the earth, and with spiritual love bestows physical labour on his most punctilious kindnesses on behalf of those who visit each other in turn by letter. So it was through this brother, my fellow servant in the Lord whom we both love (for it is his boast that you greet him with the same fervent affection with which he is grafted to me), that I received your letter, dear brother whom I religiously revere. It was a gift as sweet as it was unexpected, and in it the goodly treasure of your heart[3] became clear to me, so that I rightly rejoiced on perceiving the blessing of your service; for by observing from your most chaste eloquence how much assistance is afforded me by the Lord through you, I gained insight into the nature of your inner person.

2. However, in the task which you thought you should impose on me, you showed a flattering estimate of my poverty and indeed that pious confidence which belongs to

the purest charity. So far as I can see, you were impelled
and convinced by report of the Lord's work to believe that
in addition to the Lord's doing (it is He who has deigned
to instill in me anxiety for my redemption) I had also
abundance of genius and eloquence. But your hope, deceived in its great faith by groundless beliefs, has deluded
your well-intentioned desire. For where can I obtain the
amount of water to slake your thirst, or a drink worthy of
your lips? Where can I obtain the number of loaves you
demand?[4]

But you bring this wrong upon yourself, if you hunger
the longer,[5] for in your desire for the Gospel-food of light
and life during the deep darkness of this world, you beat at
the indigent storehouse of a poor and sleepy friend, and in
your thirst for rivers of living water,[6] you scrape a course
run dry and try to extract moisture from a pumice-stone.
For my inner fountain is either nonexistent because my inspiration is dried up, or it is sour because of the bile of
wickedness. I pray that your prayers and letters, bestowed
upon me more frequently, may cause that fount to bubble
forth and grow sweet through the wood of your faith[7] and
the sweetness of your eloquence, so that the rock of my
heart may be struck, as with the rod of the prophet,[8] by
the word of God which you as a good servant have rev-
erently uttered. . . .[9]

LETTER 34[1]

On the Alms Table[2]

1. Dearest brethren, it is not for nothing that a manger is set before beasts of burden, nor is it there merely to look upon; for it is a form of table devised by human reason for living creatures however blind to reason, so that the four-footed beasts may obtain food by this means. But if those who have gone to the trouble of erecting the manger neglect to put fodder in it, the beasts will be prone to fall ill and waste away in an empty stable. Hunger feeds on animals which get no food. Their masters will suffer a total loss commensurate with their carelessness or greed, for they worked hard only to provide the manger and did not trouble to replenish it. And so they will have no further use either for the dead beasts or for the manger, deservedly incurring two heavy losses because they were niggardly in providing the single necessary cost of a useful outlay.

Let this afford us an example, dearest brethren. We, too, ought to ensure that we do not run the risk of expending our souls and losing our salvation by ignoring the table which the Lord has placed in church for the poor, by gazing at it with haughty eyes and passing it with empty hands. I pray that this disease may not afflict your minds. For cancerous greed readily creeps into a heart not fortified by the bowels of mercy, and having gained access to the soul binds it with viperous coils, if the hostile serpent finds it naked of good works and full of the substance of

captivity, which is barren wealth. So let us not allow the
Lord's table to be left empty behind us without provision
for the needy, standing there visible but without resource,
lest the groans which our indifference has wrung from the
poor rebound upon us. For Scripture says: *He that de-
spiseth the poor provoketh his Maker*[3]—in other words, the
common Creator of all, whose joy at the refreshment of
the poor is matched by His sorrow at their need.

2. We must, therefore, rouse ourselves from the sleep of
sloth, and to shake off our sluggish indifference or to burst
the bonds of greed we must look carefully at all the words,
commands, promises, works, and advice of our Saviour
who is God. We must ask ourselves why and at whose
prompting this table has been set up in the hall of the
Lord's house in the sight of all His people. Above all, we
must reflect for whose advantage it is set there, gleaming
and conspicuous, what grace it bears, and for what harvest.
Consult the very oracles of truth, and the prophet will
answer you: *He that hath mercy on the poor lendeth to
the Lord.*[4] So this is the table of the heavenly Banker, which
exhibits the treasure of life, and applies God's capital to the
purchase of the pearl.[5] He who lends to the Lord's poor
awaits from the Lord the reward of eternal life.

The blessed Apostle Paul, though bearing the anxieties
of all the churches, shows in his teaching that his zeal for
the poor is not his least concern. He says that the apostles
were instructed: *Only that we should be mindful of the
poor, which same thing also was I careful to do.*[6] And in
another passage he cries: *We brought nothing into this
world, and certainly we can carry nothing out.*[7] And again:
What hast thou that thou hast not received?[8] So, dearest
brethren, let us not be niggardly as if dispensing our own,

but let us lend what has been entrusted to us. As Paul says: *A dispensation is committed to me*.[9] Money is not lasting, and must be enjoyed in common, for there is no eternal possession of private property. If you acknowledge that it is only yours for a time on earth, you will be able to make it yours eternally in heaven. If you recall from the Gospel[10] those who obtained the lord's talents, and what repayment the father of the household made to each on his return, you will realise how much more useful it is to invest your money for large returns at the bank of the Lord rather than to let it lie criminally idle out of barrenness of faith.[11] For the one talent was preserved without return to the investor, and at great loss to the useless servant, for it increased his punishment and nothing else.

3. Make haste, then, rather to deserve those words of the Lord, that you may be told: *Well done, good servant, enter thou into the joy of thy Lord*, and not: *Out of thy own mouth I judge thee, thou wicked and idle servant*.[12] The words that follow in Luke are known to you. The unprofitable servant was cast into the exterior darkness, and his talent was given to the one who was rich because the money entrusted to him had multiplied. *For to every one that hath*, says Scripture, *shall be given, but from him that hath not that also which he hath shall be taken away*.[13]

Let us remember the widow as well.[14] In her care for the poor she disregarded herself, and mindful only of the life to come she disbursed the entire substance of her livelihood, as the Judge Himself attests. For whereas others contributed out of their surpassing abundance, says Christ, the widow (who was probably in greater need than many of the poor, for all she had was the two mites, but her inner riches outstripped those of all the wealthy) trained her gaze

solely on the wealth of her eternal reward. In her greed for
the heavenly treasure, she accordingly renounced all the
possessions which are the gift of earth and which return to
it. She gave up what she had in order to possess what she
had not seen. She relinquished things doomed to crumble
to win those that are immortal. Though penniless, she did
not despise the precept which God disposed and ordered
for His reception when He would come,[15] and accordingly
the Bursar Himself remembered her, the very Judge of the
world anticipated His decision, and proclaimed in the
Gospel her whom He is to crown at the Judgment.

4. So let us loan the Lord His own gifts, for without
His gift we possess nothing, and without His nod we do
not even exist. We ought particularly to reflect on what we
have to call our own, since by that higher and special debt
we do not belong to ourselves—not only because God made
us, but also because He redeemed us. Yet we must be
thankful that we were bought at a great price, for this was
the blood of the Lord Himself, and it is this price which
makes us no longer cheap and easily bought. The freedom
which is cheaper than slavery means that one is free of
justice, because such freedom entails being a slave to sin
and a prisoner of death. So let us restore to the Lord His
gifts, give them to Him who receives them in the person of
each of His poor; let us give them, I say, and (in His
words) obtain them back from Him with rejoicing.[16] He
is pleased by that violence with which we bring force to
bear on His kingdom when we break down the gates of
heaven by good works. For our Lord, who alone is good
since He alone is God,[17] longs to receive not out of covetous
greed but out of generous love. For what can He fail to
have who has bestowed all things? What can He fail to

have when He possesses the very possessors, since all men of wealth are in His hands? It is His boundless justice and His goodness alike which long for gifts to be returned to Him from those which He has imparted. He wishes to obtain the material objects of His kindness towards you, because He is good, and to confer a reward which you may deserve to receive, because He is just.

5. Accordingly the treasures of His blessings lie accessible and the riches of His goodness are to hand, so that each of us does not have to wait to receive them, but of his own accord may lay hold of all that he wishes. This is why the good Lord, the holy Father, created us, to be good for our own profit. What external good could He require[18] when He is utterly and wholly Goodness and Blessedness? So, dearest brethren, so far as in Him lies, *He will have all men to be saved*,[19] for He loves in every man His own creation, and He is exceedingly generous to you from His riches, if only you yourself are not niggardly and greedy with the things which God has made yours. He hopes that these may not cause your death, but be the means of your return to life. How abounding is God's goodness! He desires a loan from the riches which He has bestowed, wishing to become a debtor of His own gifts that He may repay your loan with manifold interest.

6. So, brother, hasten to attach to yourself a Debtor who brings such wealth, that He may call you friend, not slave,[20] and having found you faithful in your earthly moneys may enrich you from His heavenly treasures. Do not fear, hesitate, hold back. Show violence to God, storm the kingdom of heaven.[21] He who forbids us to touch the possessions of others rejoices when His own are seized. He who condemns the rapacity inspired by greed praises the

plundering committed by faith. Your guests have for long
been standing before your door, waiting for the com-
mencement and the president of the meal. You are delaying them; make anxious haste, that they may not too long
remain fasting, and that their Creator who made them poor
for your profit may not be roused by the wrong they
suffer.

The almighty Lord, dearly beloved, could have made
all men equally rich so that none had need of a neighbour.
But the merciful and pitying Lord devised a design in His
infinite goodness to make trial of your purpose in their
regard. He made one man wretched so that he might look
to the man of pity; He made him penniless to make trial of
the wealthy. The right object of your wealth is the poverty
of your brother, if *you have understanding concerning the
needy and the poor.*[22] You are not to keep to yourself alone
what you have received, for God has in this world bestowed on you the poor man's share as well, so that He
may be in debt to you for whatever you offer in spon-
taneous love to the needy from His gifts, and so that He
may in turn enrich you from the poor man's portion on the
day of eternity. It is through the poor that Christ receives
from you on earth, and on their behalf that He shall repay
you in the next world.

We have the example of the rich man in the Gospel[23]
lying in hell, and Lazarus no longer begging but in Abraham's bosom, abounding in refreshing life while Dives
burned in the punishment of his need. This teaches us that
the conditions of men here and in the next life are inter-
changed; that the poor must there be repaid what seems to
be denied them here, and conversely that the rich who
provided no resource for the poor in this world will get no

part in the happiness of the poor, but in just retribution will be allotted unceasing beggary and heavy punishment for their injustice to the poor.

7. Therefore, in Scripture's words, *walk in the light as sons of the light while you have the light.*[24] As a Christian, while there is yet time to regain your senses and take thought for the future, act in such a way that you may deserve to hear the Lord say: *Well done, good servant, because thou hast been faithful over a few things, I will place thee over many things.*[25] So acknowledge and ponder this saying, brother, and do not neglect the grace offered to you. Do not go down empty-handed into the house of Christ, *which is the church of the living God.*[26] If you give only a little from your abundant store, you lay up a great addition to your remaining wealth. Crowds await you and hang on your arrival, looking round when they catch sight of you. The prayers of all the poor and the supplications of the sick are conferred on you. Be sure that they are not forced to withhold such devoted affection, transforming their prayers into complaints, and that through your lack of compassion the groans wrung from them in their extremity by the need of their pitiable condition do not strike and attract the notice of the *Father of orphans, the Judge of widows,*[27] and the God who suffers with His poor.

8. If you love yourself, beware of loving yourself alone, for this is love of iniquity, and *he that loveth iniquity hateth his own soul,*[28] as Scripture says. *The love of our neighbour is the fulfilment of the Law,*[29] for all men are related by natural brotherhood. So show as much care for the poor as for yourself, that you may imitate him who imitated Christ, by seeking what is profitable to others

rather than to yourself[30] so that God may more closely care for you. You must see how great a crime it is to separate yourself through pride or greed from him whom God has joined to you in His creation. Refresh that soul in need and you will have no fear from the anger to come on an evil day. In the words of Scripture: *Blessed is he that understandeth concerning the needy and poor; the Lord will deliver him in the evil day.*[31]

So work and cultivate this area of your soil, my brother, that it may bring forth for you an abundant harvest, full of ears of corn, bringing you the large interest of fruit sprouting a hundredfold[32] from the multiplied seed. It is a holy and salutary greed zealously to aspire to such ownership or business, for such avidity, which deserves the kingdom of heaven and longs for eternal good, is the root of all that is good. So, as I have already said, you must desire such riches, and enter into the inheritance which the Creditor pays you even to a hundredfold, so that you may enrich your heirs as well as yourselves with eternal possessions. For that is truly a great and precious possession which does not burden its owner with worldly treasure, but enriches him with an eternal yield, which flows with milk and honey, and provides its farmers with the nectar of those sweet liquids by pouring it out in abundant rivers rather than squeezing it from hives and cattle.

9. Dearly beloved, you must take thought now, not only to seek eternal blessings, but also to merit avoiding countless ills, by showing concern now and by diligently performing just works. You require great assistance and protection; we need the defence of numerous and unceasing prayers, for our foe is unresting.[33] Sleeplessly plotting our death, he lays siege to all our paths, and carefully

searches out the departures and approaches of all. He attaches himself as inseparable companion to the footsteps of each of us, and puts barriers before our exits and between our feet, so that the careless man trips over potholes even on level ground. So Scripture says: *There are ways which seem level to men, but the ends thereof lead to hell.*[34] But if you walk untroubled on the level and fall down the slippery slope through not taking precautions, the devil straightway rushes on you and holds you down where you have fallen, not leaving you unless he breaks and devours you. So keep guard in all circumstances; as you proceed, keep an eye all about you. The devil threatens from every side, *like a lion prepared for the prey.*[35] Do not trust the very earth you tread. You must walk over it on tiptoe, or better with feet shod, for it carries out the decrees of the Creator, and recognising that sin of our first parent in the flesh of all mankind, it sprouts with thorns and thistles[36] and snakes and wild beasts.

We have many other crosses to bear in this world, and countless dangers—the sickness of diseases, the fires of fever, and darts of pain assault our souls, the torches of lusts are kindled, hidden nets lie stretched before us everywhere, drawn swords bristle around us on all sides. Our lives are spent amidst ambush and fighting, and we walk on "fires lurking in deceitful ashes."[37]

10. So before you incur any sickness from such great hardships, whether impelled by chance or by your deserts, hasten to become accepted and dear to the Physician, that you may have the remedy of salvation at hand in the hour of need.[38] It is one thing to pray alone on your own behalf, and another when a crowd shows anxiety for you before God. You cease to speak, and at once they cry out on your

behalf. They see you and smile at you, seek you out and hail you. Unmindful of their need and frailty, they are refreshed in body by your health, and invigorated in mind by seeing you. For you are their fertile land, their fruitful farm, and in turn they are for you a rich and precious possession. They rate you higher than their children. Each of them is more exercised for you than for himself, and prays for your salvation at the same time as or before he prays for his own. They do not neglect themselves, but each loves himself by attaching his love to your person, and prays for your life as part of his own; for your life is the harvest he reaps, your riches are his wealth, the riches of his poverty. They pray for you in all the churches, they cry their thanks to you in all the streets, they are roused to bless the Lord, enunciate your name, and with their hands to direct kisses toward your absent person in each and every place. They perpetually keep their gaze on you, always seeing you because they embrace you in mind, which gives us sight of those away from us. For you are inscribed and implanted in their hearts because of your abundant kindness to them. They fear no hunger, since they are assured of your food; they do not fear for the winter, because you anticipate it and shut it out with provision of clothing. *Blessed is that man whom when his Lord shall come He shall find so doing!*[39]

LETTER 35

To Delphinus[1]

Paulinus greets his most blessed and revered father Delphinus, always most dear to him.

Your letter expressed your holy love in few words, but was full of great affection for me. I have taken it to my whole heart, where I pined for it. Yet *all things have their season*,[2] and since this is a time of mourning it seems also a time for saying little.

But I earnestly confess that I am grieved not so much at my brother's bodily death[3] as at his spiritual indifference. He was more mindful of the anxieties which he had to abandon here than of the cures to which he could look forward in heaven; he advanced the secondary things and relegated the primary. On his own behalf he ought to have given thought to the higher matters, yet without neglecting on his sons' behalf the temporal ones.

So I beg you, in your fatherly affection and sympathy for this grief of mine, to be pleased to remember that my brother, too, was by God's grace begotten as your spiritual son.[4] Remember that it is accordingly your special care to ensure that we do not perplex your paternal love, which took pride in us, your sons, by wasting the substance of our inherited portion.[5] May your prayers be so answered that a drop of cool water, dripping if only from the little finger of your holy person, may sprinkle his soul. I myself hasten back to you while there is still time, crying out:

Father, I have sinned against heaven and before thee; I am not worthy to be called thy son.[6] As I confess my sin, may God's mercy at your intercession come to my aid. May I not consume my eternal Father's substance, which my sins daily squander; may I not be overwhelmed through being ashamed to return; may I not linger in a distant land, be kept under restraint, and eat the lowly food of swine which is against the Law.[7]

LETTER 36

To Amandus[1]

Paulinus greets the holy Amandus, truly respected and dearly loved.

1. In those few words from a holy man, I tasted the full sweetness of your lips. A drop of honey has the same savour as an entire honeycomb; so, if only a single word falls from your tongue, it conveys all the flavour of your holy soul. What comes *from a good treasure*[2] is genuine and precious. A pearl is not cheap for being tiny; it is all the more valuable because its great value lies in its tiny shape, so that, as the authority of the Gospel attests,[3] a man must cast away all his patrimony to attain and purchase it. So, too, the grain of mustard seed, which seems smallest as a seed, emerges as the greatest of herbs.[4] The word of this seed is implanted in you, and thrives in your heart, so that you tread the path of the Lord with burning heart.[5] This is why even a few words from you contain the sweetness and strength of the heavenly word; and your words attend on me, so that I, too, am seasoned with the salt of your wisdom.[6]

2. So in this letter I shall imitate your thrift of expression without being able to aspire to the fulness of your meaning, and shall say in reply only this: As I write, my fresh grief at being sundered from my brother causes me deep anxiety. I know that he has been taken only from this world and only for a time, and that I must soon join him

in the next world. The more genuine reason why I mourn his death is the realisation that all his acts and arrangements up to his death were in accordance with my sins rather than with my prayers, so that he preferred to pass over to his Lord as a debtor rather than as a free man.

So I make this earnest request. You are pleased to be my brother in the Lord. So, like a brother lending aid to your loving brothers, by the merits of your faith gather this further reward; share my suffering endured on his behalf, combine with me in the toil of prayer, that the pitying and merciful God *who creates all things in heaven, in earth, in the sea and in the deeps*[7] may through your prayers refresh his soul with the drops of His mercy. For as a fire kindled by God *shall burn even to the lowest hell,*[8] so, too, the dew of His kindness will surely reach the lowest regions, so that as we sweat in the glowing darkness we may be refreshed by the dewy light of his dutiful love.

3. Pray also for me, that I may not die in my sins. Pray that the Lord may give me notice of my death,[9] that I may know my failings and hasten to fulfil what remains to be done. Pray that I may not be removed in the midst of my days[10] as I weave a spider's web of useless works. Rather may my days be lived to the full,[11] so that I die at a hundred and yet be still a boy, *in malice as children and in sense perfect.*[12] And when I die, may I leave behind me repentance salutary by its good example to those who survive me. Let not the mourning for me extend beyond seven days,[13] provided that I be in harmony with the Spirit and the Word of God, which war with us on the path of this life,[14] being the foe of us sinners.

For the Spirit *convicts the world of sin,*[15] and, as the Lord attests in His Gospel, the words of God will accuse us if we do not obey Him, and will hand us over to the Word our Judge.[16] He will demand an account of His talent up to the last farthing;[17] and unless *the exercise of godliness, which is profitable to all things*,[18] brings interest sufficient to redouble His capital, the portion of those of idle faith will be set with the unbelievers.[19] For he who is a Christian only in empty name, wielding a faith dead without works,[20] is almost the equivalent of one without faith. He who grieves for all time, because he did not have the fear of the Lord and so did not possess the source of wisdom, is a fool.[21] And *he has become the tail*,[22] for he who *loveth iniquity and hateth his own soul*[23] does not dwell in the heart of the house; he is committed to the gaoler of the prison below, and *cast into exterior darkness*[24] because he has lived the life of the outer man. So he must be mourned unceasingly, for he shall die unceasingly, condemned to eternal fire.

4. Let us therefore *have peace with the Lord*[25]—not the peace of this world[26] which befriends sin and is at odds with God, but the peace of Christ, which plants us with God and fashions us in accordance with Christ if our souls cling to the word of God, so that we may be made one with God through the intervention of the Mediator, who is our Peace. For *He hath made both one*,[27] combining in Himself the warring natures of God and man; and in us, too, He *makes both one*,[28] for He makes the flesh harmonise with the spiritual soul. Then He shall abide amongst us as fire, invited by the harmony of the two elements within us, or, if we include the spirit, of the three,[29] so that He may make in our hearts a dwelling place pleasing to Him[30] as to the Father and the Spirit, and in turn lead us to His abode with the words: *Enter ye into the joy of thy Lord*.[31]

LETTER 37

To Victricius[1]

Paulinus greets his loving brother Victricius.

1. *As cold water to a thirsty soul and good tidings from a far country,*[2] so did the eloquence of your holy person refresh and renew me. I received it in a letter brief in words but abounding in love by the hand of that most dear messenger, our son Candidianus.[3] I congratulated him on his service, because relying not on strength but on faith, his willing spirit forced the beast of his weak flesh actively to walk hard ways to deliver the words of your holy lips.[4] And doubtless by means of your prayers he found strength, and obtained the wings of a dove or the feet of a hind[5] to fulfil his duty of charity; and then, his small frame being transformed into a giant's, *he hath rejoiced to run the way.*[6] He filled my soul with blessed pleasure, bringing me letters *more to be desired than gold and most precious stones, and sweeter than honey and the honeycomb.*[7] Through these the holy and sweet breath of your blessed person with its spiritual sweetness transformed my mind embittered by sin into the sweetness of joy, like the waters of Mara which Moses' hand transformed by means of the wood of divine mystery.[8]

The source of my bitterness and grief was your failure to make the short journey from Rome to Nola as I had hoped after you had covered such tracts of territory to reach the capital. I admit that I was not only depressed but

also confounded at losing this blessing, for nothing made
my sins clearer to me (and of course to others) more than
their jealous refusal to let me see the light of your face
when you were so near. Would not God's hand, which
had guided you so far, have been sufficient to bring you
here? But my sins threw up a great wall before my longings and kept us apart. *Woe is me, because I am a sinner
with unclean lips*[9] for presuming to say that you were near
me or I near you. Even if you had come at all, I should still
have been equally distant from your holy person, since the
great inequality of our virtues and the gap between our
merits could not have been bridged or joined by travel.

2. Yet the harvest of your holiness could have been increased by a dutiful deed, and your reward in heaven
would have grown from so devoted a labour, if you had
fulfilled the injunction of the saving Lord to visit my
weakness[10] with the physical presence of your countenance
and hand, for *they that are in health need not a physician,
but they that are ill.*[11] For I would not have you so confident about me, blessed brother in the Lord, as to think that
all the fainting sicknesses of my soul, by which I have
sinned and still sin before the Lord, are now cured; even
though the highest Anointer, who to achieve a cure for
my salvation devises various sweet compounds of saving
unguents and virtues, has made a healing potion for my life
not only by pouring forth His spirit but also by taking on
our human form. As Scripture says: *He became sin for us
through the likeness of sinful flesh* (for He truly took our
flesh) *so that He might condemn sin by means of sin.*[12] In
other words, He being free of sin aimed to condemn the
root of our sin by means of the matter previously sinning,
and by *blotting out that which was against us, the hand-*

writing of that mortal decree, by means of the blood of His passion, He also *killed the enmities in himself*[13] by which we were cut off from God by the interposition of our sins. And He triumphed over hostile powers by His flesh, giving us an example for living and for conquering in ourselves the hidden enemies of the spirit, in the spiritual and hidden battle which is waged between the law of the spirit and that law of the flesh which strives to make us captive to the law of sin.

3. But pray to the Lord, and prevail on Him that *He may take hold of arms and shield and rise up to help us, and say to our soul: I am thy salvation*,[14] so that our way may not be dark and slippery, the shadow of death may not cover us, and our enemy may not say: *I have prevailed against them*.[15] But if you draw the bow of prayer on my behalf, I shall not *be turned aside as a crooked bow*.[16] *Let God arise* amongst us *that our enemies may be scattered*, for the Lord has arisen *by reason of the misery of the needy and the groans of the poor*, of whom we form a part, that He might *turn back our evils upon our enemies* and *save sinners of whom I am the chief*.[17]

Indeed, I am the lowest of Christ's servants, unable to do the things I ought to do;[18] for over and above what the law prescribes I ought to add some voluntary service out of love, as the master himself did, whose imitator you are. For Paul could have got enough to live on by preaching the Gospel, but he refused to adopt this possible course, and by not abusing the opportunity, he found the chance to increase his reward from Christ by preaching the Gospel at no one's expense.[19]

4. But your holiness has won the rich fame of Christian poverty not only by abstention from what is permissible

and by withholding yourself from visible advantages, but also, I am told, by reason of the crowd of your enemies and the endurance of trials, because *unjust witnesses have risen up against thee, and iniquity hath lied to itself.*[20] But one could not find a knot in a bulrush, or a black spot in light; for your lamp was not hidden under a bushel, but shines out prominently and brightly on its holy candlestick, that *it may shine to all that are in the house,*[21] and act as kindling for firing many lamps for the Lord.

So your candlestick has remained unshaken and unwavering because the hands which sought to bring it down were human hands. You did not deserve to have your candlestick brought crashing down by the hand of Him who *holdeth seven stars and walketh in the midst of the seven golden candlesticks, having in His mouth a sharp two-edged sword.*[22] With this he armed the right hand of your soul, so that with the torch of both Testaments you might victoriously extinguish the white-hot darts of the enemy, so that *a thousand might fall at thy side and ten thousand at thy right hand*[23] without drawing near to you. You will be guarded by God's truth whose shield cannot be overcome, so that the bows of those who are said to have whetted the swords of their tongues[24] against you are weakened. But the blows they inflict are feeble *as the arrows of children,*[25] and they could find no opening for a wound in your body guarded by the powerful arms of God. For the Lord is your protector and the light of your heart,[26] who has instructed you in the spirit of truth, so that according to the teaching of Paul you may be master of the Gentiles in faith and truth,[27] not puffing yourself on your knowledge *nor declaring the mystery of Christ in*

*loftiness of speech, but judging yourself to know nothing
amongst men but Christ Jesus, and Him crucified.*[28]

5. I confidently assume, then, that your faith and avowal
attests the coeternal Trinity of one divinity, substance,
action, and dominion, and that you believe that the Father
is God, the Son is God, and the Holy Spirit is God *that is
and that was and that is to come,*[29] who sent you as He sent
Moses and the apostles to tell the good news of the Lord to
mankind, as you teach in accordance with God's instruction.[30] You draw together the unity of the Trinity without
confusion of Persons, and distinguish the threefold form of
the Unity without separation in such a way that no Person
merges with another, and the one God shines out in each of
the Three. And the Son is as great as the Father and the
Holy Spirit, but each is distinguished by His own name
and keeps indivisible harmony in equality of strength and
glory.

6. But I am equally sure that you also proclaim the Son
of God in such a way that you have no shame in confessing Him also the Son of man, as truly human in our nature
as He is truly God in His; but that He is the Son of God
before all ages, for He is the Word of God, Himself God,
who was with God in the beginning, equally God, equally
omnipotent, sharing the work of the Father. For *all things
were made by Him, and without Him was made nothing.*[31]
And this Word, by the mystery of boundless love, *became flesh and dwelt amongst us;*[32] became not just the
flesh of our bodies, but wholly man by taking both our
body and soul, that is, our rational soul which has by God's
natural creation an engrafted intelligence.

Otherwise we shall go astray in the darkness of Apollinaris,[33] if we were to say that the humanity assumed by God had a soul empty of the human mind, like that of cattle or beasts of burden. That humanity which the Son of God assumed He must have assumed wholly, with that truth which He personifies and with which He created man, so that He might renew His work by saving it totally. For our salvation is nothing if not total. Indeed, the Son of God assumed the form not of man but of some beast of irrational creation, if His soul did not contain the right intelligence peculiar to the humanity He had assumed, and if, contrary to the nature of the human race, this Man who is truly the firstborn of all creation took on the form of human perfection and yet was so far deprived of native intelligence that His mind is said to have come from His divine and not His human spirit.

Such are the views of those in whose hearts this poison is generated, so that even the truth is counterfeited. But near you and in you is the Word of truth and the truth of God. You are not deprived of the Holy Spirit, either. For you proclaim that the Lord Jesus, Son of God and Himself God, abides as King of kings in the glory of God the Father and at the right hand of His power; and you confess and believe and proclaim that He will come after the resurrection of the dead to judge the living and the dead.

7. Remember me, and boast as Paul did, for this short trial has ensured you abundant glory forever, and has stored up for you the crown of justice which you will receive from the Lord's hand.[34] God has allowed war to be stirred up against you to provide opportunity for victory, so that following Paul your mentor you, too, can boast in your sufferings[35] and speak with opened mouth over your enemies. You can tell how you toiled *in long-suffering, in*

the Holy Ghost, in charity unfeigned, in the word of truth, in the power of God; by the armour of justice on the right hand and on the left; by honour and dishonour; by evil report and good report; as deceiver and yet true; as unknown and yet known; as chastised and not killed; as sorrowful yet always rejoicing; as needy yet enriching many.[36] For this very trial endured by your holy person led *to the furtherance of the gospel*[37] for many, for you caused confusion to none. The grace of Christ and the truth of your faith shone out not only in the guidance of your teaching but also in the virtue of *your conversation, which is in heaven.*[38] *For the kingdom of God is not in speech, but in power,*[39] as Paul says. Why then should investigation be made in your case when the surpassing quality of the word shines out in you? Who could doubt that faith in the truth dwells in the spirit of one whose life shows clearly the power of his faith?

LETTER 38

To Aper[1]

Paulinus greets his holy brother Aper, rightly revered and dearly loved.

1. *I rejoiced at the things*[2] you wrote to me because of your faith which, as your lips have attested, is born in your heart. If the Lord's grace enables me to share this great inspiration, I hope that we shall together enter the house of the Lord, that we shall behold together in their true appearance the things we have perceived by our common hope and faith. Then with harmonious joy we shall sing a hymn, so that we may say to the Lord our God: We believed that we were ashes and dust.[3] But *if our feet are now established in the courts of Jerusalem,*[4] we believe that by our action and works we cease to be dust and ashes. So in a spirit of humility we recall and confess to the Lord that we are dust;[5] and through Him, because we are won back through grace, we deserve to cease to be what the condemnation of sin makes us.

Blessed art thou, brother, and it shall be well with thee, for flesh and blood hath not revealed it to thee[6] but the spirit of the heavenly Father. For in very holy words at the close of your letter to me you maintained that you hold with unshakeable faith and proclaim openly that Christ Jesus crucified is the Son of God and Himself God, to whom *every knee bows of those that are on earth, in heaven, and under the earth,* and *every tongue confesses*

that He is at the right hand of the strength and *in the glory
of God the Father.*[7] You have embraced Him as our Lord
and God, for *no other shall be accounted of in comparison
of Him,*[8] in the entire mystery of His hidden love. You
believe the truth and proclaim your belief that He is Lord
and God, Son of God, before all ages; *made of the seed of
David*[9] in this world, He now lives forever to provide hope
of immortality for men after the resurrection of the dead.

After this, will you say that you are a novice and a child
before God? I do believe that you are become to some
extent a child, but a child in wickedness; I learn from your
profession of faith that in sense you are perfect.[10] For ap-
prehension of the truth, which you embraced in your brief
words, is the fulness of wisdom. So the master of the
Gentiles himself, the vessel of election and the vessel of
God, who claims that Christ speaks in him and that he has
the spirit of God,[11] does not glory *in loftiness of speech*[12]
or in knowledge of the Law. He bears witness that he has
renounced and counted as dung all the glory with which
the wisdom of the Jews or the philosophers is puffed up, so
that he may gain Christ,[13] and that by the loss of that
knowledge he may achieve the gain of this ignorance. So
he says: *I know nothing but Jesus Christ, and Him crucified.*[14]

And since the fulness and perfection of all wisdom and
knowledge[15] are embraced in Him, he speaks as though re-
viling this world and despising its literature and the whole
of its wisdom, with a spirit rising above the world's emptiness. *Where is the scribe? Where is the disputer of this
world? Hath not God made foolish the wisdom of this
world?*[16] And he reveals the reason underlying the error
by which the world's wisdom has deserved such destruc-

tion that for God it is foolishness. The wisdom of God appeared as foolishness in the eyes of the world, because of its pride in the wisdom which it regarded as its own, though no one possesses anything which has not been given to him.[17] So according to God's justice the roles of foolishness and wisdom are reversed; they who think themselves wise, not through God's gift but as if by their own merit, are condemned as foolish.

2. So I congratulate your loving person all the more, because you have rejected the wisdom which is disapproved by God, and have preferred to associate with Christ's little ones[18] rather than with the worldly-wise. Because of this decision you are now deserving to receive from the Lord the additional grace of being hated by all men, as you thought it right to mention in your honourable boast. This would not happen if you had not begun to be a true imitator of Christ. This world would not hate you if it did not realise that you are now a stranger and an enemy to it. Rejoice and be glad, for the virtue of perfection is at work already, even in your beginnings. The extent of your courageous belief in Christ is clear, for you have already been granted the privilege of suffering for Him.

Take note of the words of the Lord Himself and you will realise how blessed you are. *Be not surprised*, He says, *if the world hate you, for it hath hated Me before you. For if you had been of the world, the world would certainly love its own.*[19] And again: *The servant is not greater than his lord.*[20] *If they have called the father of the house Beelzebub, how much more will they so address his servants?*[21] In the light of this, see if we the servants can refuse to suffer for the Lord's sake what the Lord has already endured for us His servants. What a blessed in-justice to give offence in Christ's company! We ought rather to fear the love of those whom we please if Christ is not with us. *Have I not hated them,* said the Psalmist, *that hated Thee?* And then he added: *I have hated them with a perfect hatred.*[22] What traffic could we have with the friendship of such men, when their lot is separate from ours?

3. You are right to boast, most reverent brother, and gladly say that you are convinced that you are a Christian because those who loved you have begun to hate you, and those who feared you have begun to despise you. You are well aware that if you were without Christ they would love and reverence you as they used to do. *So be glad and rejoice, for your reward is very great in heaven;*[23] for it is not you they hate but Him who has begun to exist in you. He achieves in you the humility which they despise and the chastity which they loathe. Be glad to realise that you share this blessing with the prophets and apostles. For the prophet says: *They have detracted me because I followed goodness.*[24] And Paul says: *We are made the offscouring of all;* and again he witnesses that *we are made a spectacle in this world to all angels and men.*[25]

From the beginning of the world Christ suffers in all His own, for He is *the beginning and the end,*[26] who is cloaked in the Law and revealed in the Gospel, a Lord ever *wonderful* and suffering and triumphant *in His saints.*[27] In Abel He was killed by His brother, in Noe he was laughed at by His son, in Abraham He wandered abroad, in Isaac He was sacrificed, in Jacob He was a servant, in Joseph He was sold, in Moses He was exposed and made to flee,[28] in the persons of his prophets He was stoned and lacerated,[29] in His apostles He was storm-tossed on land and sea,[30] and on the many different crosses of the blessed martyrs He was often executed. So, too, He now also bears our weaknesses and our sickness,[31] for He is the Man who was always set in the snare for us, and who knows how to endure the weakness which we cannot bear and know not how to bear without Him. He, I say, now also bears the weight of the world for us and in us, and destroys it by bearing it, and achieves strength in weakness. It is He who suffers the taunts which you endure; it is against Him that the world directs the hatred which you experience.

But thanks be to Him, because He *overcomes when He is judged,*[32] and as you remember from Scripture, the Lord *maketh us to triumph*[33] under the appearance of slavery. He gained for His servants the grace of freedom, achieving this by that mystery of His love by which *He took the form of a servant* and for us deigned to *humble Himself even to the death of the cross.*[34] He did this so that through the lowliness which all could see He might secretly achieve for us that hidden eminence amongst the dwellers of heaven. Only realise from what we first fell, and you will become aware that by the design of God's wisdom and love we are being refashioned for life. In Adam we fell through pride, and in Christ we are humbled so that we may dissolve the sin of that ancient crime by obedience to the opposite virtue. So we who by proud conduct have sinned, win approval by humble service.

4. Therefore let us rejoice and glory in Him, who made us both His battle and His victory when He said: *Have confidence, for I have overcome the world.*[35] Similar are the words of the prophet in the Book of Kings to king Josaphat, when the king was frightened by the great bur-

den of war and the huge crowd of the enemy: *Thus saith the Lord: Fear ye not and be not dismayed at the appearance of the multitude, for the battle is not yours but the Lord's.*[36] Moses, too, had already spoken in similar vein: *You shall hold your peace, and the Lord will fight for you.*[37] Therefore *they that trust in their own strength* or wisdom *and glory in the multitude of their riches*[38] can sharpen the weapons of their teeth and the arrows of their words against us as they will, and with their vipers' tongues they can spit forth the poison of their evil store, because they are answered by the Lord speaking on our behalf: *I have kept silence; will I be silent forever?*[39]

As Scripture says, *let us hedge in our ears with thorns,*[40] that is, with the word of God and faith in the Word, which protect our lives' harvest with the most secure protection of innocence and patience. These are like thief-resistant thorns which oppose the devil as by his wiles he seeks access to our hearts, and which prick the vitals of those who hate the King. These vitals are those who love Christ's enemies, the Christians' detractors who are pricked when they consider our life of constancy. So let us say nothing to these men, but speak to the Lord with the silence of humility and the voice of patience. Then He who is unconquered will fight for us and conquer in us. Then *the prince* of this darkness *shall be cast out.*[41] He is not, to be sure, expelled from the world, but from the individual, for when faith enters us we shut him out and provide a place for Christ. Christ's dwelling in us expels sin, and spells exile for the serpent who is dislodged.

5. In enduring such treatment, the prophet teaches us what we ought to do. He says: *When they were troublesome to me, I clothed myself with haircloth and humbled*

my soul with fasting.[42] So we may bring low our detractors by precisely that facet of humility by which they are enraged; and they, continuing to cleave to that sin of ancient pride, are disconcerted before the Lord all the more as we glory in Him by whom they are disconcerted in our persons. For *God loveth a workman that needeth not be ashamed,* just as He loves *a cheerful giver.*[43] Therefore, steady in our faith in the truth and in performing righteousness, we rebut the hatred or rebukes of such men by our manner of life better than by words, for *he who hates discipline will cast Thy words behind him,*[44] and, as you recall from Scripture, he that rebukes folly wins himself abuse.[45]

6. Let the orators keep their literature,[46] the philosophers their wisdom, rich men their wealth, and kings their kingdoms. Christ is our glory, property, and kingdom. Our wisdom lies *in the foolishness of our preaching,* our strength in the weakness of the flesh, our glory in the stumbling block of the cross,[47] by which *the world is killed to me and I to the world,* so *that I may live to God,* and *now not I, but Christ in me, with whom we are buried together.*[48] In Him we are now hidden from the eyes of this world, so that we may be revealed with Him for the confounding of the world. Then the world, remembering the accusations it now levels at us, will say: "Are these the men whose *life we esteemed madness? How have they been numbered among the children of God?*"[49]

My most beloved brother, allow them meantime to enjoy their glory and their life, let them gain their fruits, for *as the green herbs they shall quickly fall* and their *days pass away like a shadow;*[50] for their hope is confined to the period of this life, for they have neither faith in the truth nor the will to believe. They concentrate only on the things before their eyes, and serve avarice and lust rather than believe in God. Both these forms of greed are brought to an end by fear of the Lord strengthened by faith in Christ; through Christ we learn to acknowledge the truth, whether by despising temporal goods or seeking eternal ones. But they are strangers to Him, and because Christ is also the Truth[51] they must inevitably cling to the blindness of their unhappy mistakes, believing that frailty contains firmness and that what is firm is frail. So they deride what is true as if it were false, and admire the false as if it were true.

If they desired understanding as a basis for right conduct they would raise their eyes, *which they have set bowing down to earth*,[52] to the salvation of righteousness, and if they raised themselves however slightly from the ground, they would be readily enlightened by those individual conversions which they disparage as pointless and stupid. For as Scripture says: *The Lord looseth them that are fettered; the Lord enlighteneth the blind.*[53] And again: *The Law of the Lord is unspotted, converting souls; the testimony of the Lord is faithful, giving wisdom to little ones.*[54] For it is God's task to change men, since He alone can renew those whom He made. This work Christ, the Wisdom of God, has long been performing throughout the whole world, visiting all regions with His flying word and *conveying Himself into chosen souls,* so that *in every nation He may have the chief rule,*[55] as He said through His prophet.

7. Because the day of examination now draws nearer every day, and every hour draws us to the judgment, the good Lord is busy, making haste to snatch us from the anger which is to come, and to withdraw us from the em-

brace of what Scripture calls the wicked generation of vipers.[56] This is why every day and in every place the number of miracles and signs is multiplying, so that He may do His utmost to save all men.[57] In isolated individuals He reveals what is of service to all, if men are so disposed. The model of the few is enough for the instruction of all, before whom it is set for a double purpose, to be an example to believers and a witness to the obstinate.

So if those men have any human wisdom, they who inwardly disown Him whom they ostensibly put first, they would marvel at and praise God in you. They would consider this most blessed change in your mind and life not as a mistake of your stupidity but as the truth[58] of God's wisdom. For the more they recall that you were more wise and learned than all your contemporaries, the clearer ought the working of God's power appear to them, since the wise man cannot be diverted from the progress or the condition of his belief except by the very highest wisdom. That wisdom is God in Christ, the Virtue of virtues and the Mind of minds, the Lord of majesty, the raised Arm which, as Scripture says, *has scattered the proud in the conceit of their heart, has put down the mighty from their seat, and has exalted the humble.* By this Arm, which is Christ, *the hungry are filled with good things and the rich are sent empty away.*[59] I see that this is being achieved in you also. For if you examine yourself, you will find there both what God casts down and what He raises up.

8. The proud man in you has been destroyed, and you have been given the role of the humble man. You have been thrust down from the seat of wicked power to be placed on the throne of peace and justice. You have been stripped of the rich man's life to become rich as a poor

man, and emptied of the superfluous repletion of a swollen belly to thirst for justice and be filled with the true blessings of religious poverty. Where now is the figure you once cut as a formidable attorney before tribunals, or as a judge sitting on them?[60] Where now is that fat bull's neck of yours, which you falsely aver is with you still, but which you more truly possessed then? How has it become so obedient and thin under the yoke of Christ since the groaning of your conversion began, and God was as pleased with you *as with a young calf?*[61] You have lost your bull's neck and are become as tame as the ox that *knoweth his owner.*[62] Blessed are the eyes of those who see these wonders of God performed in you, and equally and utterly wretched are those who have eyes and do not see.

9. *Who would give me wings like a dove's and I would fly to you and be at rest*[63] before your eyes, conversing with you! *With the voice of joy and praise*[64] I would feast there, seeing you thus changed, seeing a lion become a calf, seeing Christ in a boar,[65] seeing after the present reversal of your ferocity or strength that you are a boar to the world but a lamb to God. For now you are a boar from the corn-field, not from the wood,[66] enriched with the goodly fruits of training, and your pasture is amongst the harvest of virtues. You are armed with the teeth of both Testaments to break the net of the hunter Nemrod;[67] all the weapons which you haughtily wielded on behalf of the world you now with humility turn against the world. Now you are truly wise, truly eloquent, and truly powerful, for you are stupid and dumb in the eyes of the world so that with eloquence and wisdom you may serve God, the Creator of your tongue and your mind, with His own gifts.

10. Now that you are an attorney better equipped in

God's law, you must make a submission on your own behalf. As a juster judge you must judge yourself and pass sentence on your own case. Thus you may deserve to be acquitted and make yourself worthy not merely of pardon but also of glory. You must accuse yourself and sanctify yourself by condemnation, in awareness that holiness and innocence reside in the will of God and not of men.

So, as your letter says, you visit cities infrequently, and have grown to love the intimate remoteness of the silent countryside.[68] It is not that you put leisure before activity, and you do not withdraw yourself from what is useful to the Church, but you avoid the noisy councils and the bustle of the churches which almost rival the crowds of the forum. But I think that you are laying the foundation of greater services to the Church by wisely deciding to devote yourself wholly to religious instruction. By concentrating on spiritual studies, to which solitude is conducive, you are fashioning and strengthening Christ within you every day, so that you may become a more useful servant and a more learned teacher, and make yourself worthier of the position in which God's will has placed you; and becoming equally efficacious by deed and by word, you may achieve harmony of tongue and mind, and make yourself a true exemplar of the apostles' teaching as a writer and a teacher of the Lord's commands.[69] Only in this way will it be clear that you are a priest not by human choice but by the decision of God.

11. I believe that this is now being proved by both your faith and your life, and I ask and earnestly beg that you always include me in your prayers, and whenever opportunity offers to seek to reach me with another letter. I ask this favour of you not because I am keen to receive a kind-

ness, but because I wish to refresh my mind. So I may simultaneously obtain the consolation of love and joy, when by reading your letter I shall see that you are mindful of me in your holy traffic with God, and attentive to yourself in the progress of your spiritual knowledge and in the understanding of your heart which yearns for God.

Then you will assess yourself not by the word of strength which is the proclamation of Christ, but by the strength of the Word Itself, that is, by maintaining equally in words and life that you believe that Christ Jesus crucified is our Lord and God, because we ought *to bear the image of the heavenly man* with the same feeling *as we have borne the image of the earthly*.[70] Otherwise, who will give us what is ours if we have not been equally faithful to what is ours as to what is not?[71] For we were born to be good and to serve our Creator. If we live in opposition to His commands because of the failure of our will, we shall be opposing not only our own life but also our nature; and it is for this that men are compared with beasts *who have no understanding*.[72]

But God's goodness makes this compact with us: Pardoning us for our past wickedness, He is content that we should for our own sakes be slaves to Him such as we were previously, to our detriment, to the devil. As Paul says: *As we have yielded our members to serve iniquity, so let us now yield them to serve justice*.[73] He means that we should have the same feeling of delight in the Lord as we had in sin. Let us strive for the kingdom of God as we strove for position in the world. In short, let us attend to heavenly goods as carefully as we attended to earthly ones.

LETTER 39

To Aper and Amanda[1]

The sinners Paulinus and Therasia greet their holy, rightly revered, and most beloved brethren Aper and Amanda.

1. Let others draw revenues from the regular payments of their ancestral estates. Your love in Christ is our property, and so our revenues are drawn from your dutiful affection, and are assessed by the kindness of your letters. Thanks be to the Lord our God, who has repaid us with blessings that live in return for those which are transient and dead, and has in your persons bestowed on us a most fruitful farm. In matters of the world, a farm is more valuable when it responds with abundant produce to the greedy prayers of its farmer, or when it charms with its beauty the eyes of its self-indulgent owner. It is the same with our spiritual estate, with, that is to say, our holy brethren whom Christ's love has joined to and bestowed on us as a permanent possession. He is accounted the richer soil who shows greater concern for us and brings us a larger harvest by provision of the blessings which bring salvation.

So see how considerable are the possessions that we own in you, for apart from the abundance of love which you return to us, you bestow other gifts by your resources of eloquence and intellect, and these we cannot reciprocate. For your kind and eloquent letters, the generous revenue you pay us by annual provision,[2] reveal how extensive a property we have in you, and how fertile is your soil for God. You already bring forth fruit thirtyfold by the continence exercised towards each other; by the daily increase in your common faith you approach sixtyfold; and you give promise of a hundredfold from the children of your virginity.[3]

2. You write that you are hindered from achieving your vocation through looking after your possessions and your sons. They make it essential for you to devote your attention to worldly matters when you long for heavenly ones. But I believe that this is God's design to provide you with a manifold opportunity to practise your faith and perfect your virtue. Since the entire possession of this world has been established for man and is clearly subject to him,[4] no one could doubt that throughout the world and in every aspect of nature advantages lie ready for the human race, so that from them we can not only obtain benefits of the flesh, but also, and to a far greater degree, garner those of the spirit. This is why Wisdom, who created all things and who *ordereth all things sweetly*, says through Solomon that *husbandry was ordained by the Most High*,[5] so that you should cultivate it with spiritual as well as bodily effort.

Wisdom in fact teaches all the country lore that can be applied to the schooling of the soul, when It directs Its disciples to the ant and the bee, both country creatures; for the ant takes prior thought for life's sustenance, and the bee makes honey from the flowers.[6] Again, how much has the Lord taught us in the Gospel by rustic similes! He takes as symbols of our final days the fig tree and the countryside growing white when the harvest is near;[7] and He reminds us that we must learn from the fields what our inner selves must avoid, lest the enemy sow jealous deceit in our faith like cockle amongst the wheat.[8] So He called us His field, and showed Himself the Sower of our life in us, and illustrated the differences between souls by reference to various qualities of soil.[9] Let us ensure that the field is not barren; let us strain our energies according to the Lord's law, and cultivate ourselves to the fertility which we owe to God and which is useful for ourselves.

3. So when you are in the country taking a look at your estate, realise that you yourself are Christ's field, and examine yourself as you would your farm. Show to the Lord God your heart, cultivated and as presentable as you expect your land to be kept by your bailiff. Realise that what displeases or pleases you on your estate is what pleases or displeases Christ in your soul. If your soul lies unkempt and foul with sins which are like brambles, and if it is not watered by the rain of the prophets or apostles, then grace abandons it and it will be condemned to become a parched and desolate waste.

But if it looks after itself, and cultivates itself with regular prayer, and is enriched by the Holy Scriptures, and presses the plough of the cross deep into its heart, and digs out its thorns with the mattock of fear of God, and burns out its faults by the glowing word of God which also enlightens its thoughts, then the Father of the house cannot but take delight from strolling in your heart and wandering through all quarters of your soul. He will take joy in His field for your sake, and will say to you, if you show yourself a careful cultivator of your soil: *Well done, good servant; enter thou into the joy of thy Lord; because thou hast been faithful over a few things, I will place thee over many things.*[10]

4. But here am I doing things the wrong way round, the weak giving advice to the strong. What account can I render of myself, when I am as poor as you think, not in earthly so much as spiritual possessions, and humble not in inner virtue but in poverty of virtue? I am that indigent garden which you describe so vividly and so copiously, and which can scarcely bear and maintain a single cabbage; in the prophet's words, I have less flavour than a half-cooked beet.[11] I must ensure that in my house that single cabbage is not left unsalted. Yet it has some excuse for not being salted, for my impoverished need or culpable stinginess has deprived it of salt; it is I who have boiled away and am more guilty of losing my savour, for the salt of the apostles[12] has melted away through the stupidity arising from freely willed sins, and my spiritual seasoning has vanished at the sight of my faults. Unless I am renewed by your prayers, even that one cabbage will not continue to grow in me; I shall be wholly wasteland, empty even of that insipid vegetable.

5. So pray that the destructive worm does not ravage the seeds of my soul, that the devouring locust does not consume my mind's crop, that the lazy bruchus does not settle on my heart, and that the mildew, the final companion of these insects, does not devour the inmost entrails of my vitals.[13] For evil beasts oppress the inner man and savage birds continually menace me in the hope of bearing off the seed of the word. But I thank God that I have not fallen by the wayside from the hand of the sower, but have been sown on the very road—in other words, set in the womb of my Catholic mother. Yet to avoid being cast out from there as an abortion, I need God's help, that He may give me understanding on the path on which He has com-

manded and ordained[14] that we enter, and that He may *fix His eyes on me that I may not become like the horse and mule, who have no understanding.*[15]

6. But let me get back to my rural discussion, for our God and *Father is the Husbandman,* the God of our salvation is *the true Vine,*[16] and the Holy Spirit waters our souls. So ensure by your prayers that the highest Father of the household and the heavenly Husbandman and the careful Gardener attend, haunt, and mark out the garden of my soul like the one in which He taught, prayed, and rose again.[17] May He strengthen in me the bond of His love, that I may live as a branch which cleaves to Him. May He order His clouds to rain on me, and remove from my heart debased feelings of carnal reflexions, so that He may dispel the creatures hostile to a good harvest, and so that the words of the prophet may not come true in me: *That which the palmer-worm hath left, the locust hath eaten; and that which the locust hath left, the bruchus hath eaten; and that which the bruchus hath left, the mildew hath destroyed.*[18] For in my body reside those principal passions— hope, fear, joy, grief—which give rise to as many vices, and which most greatly disturb the human race. Two of them, mental grief and joy, are concerned with the present; the others, fear and hope, with the future.[19] So we must ensure that whilst we are avoiding one of the vices to which these emotions give rise, we do not fall into the opposite one.

7. So we must understand by "worm," "locust," "bruchus," and "mildew" those impulses of our feelings. Some of them cling but briefly to our hearts, but others gradually grow, and if not discarded they enter our marrow and absorb all the sap of our souls. For notice how these monstrous vices in our hearts correspond with each

other as do the harmful creatures in the crop. For example, if I harbour a forbidden desire and then dismiss the thought, this is the worm sitting on a leaf and then shaken off. If I dismiss the thought but it returns, and once I start to dislodge it it repeatedly returns, this is the locust flying away and coming back. If it begins to settle, and spends longer in eating than flying off, we can say it is the bruchus. But if the bruchus does not fly away enough but settles for longer, it will not be dislodged, and mildew forms. It gets a deep hold and is never dislodged from the grain or soul, or at any rate only with difficulty.

8. But I fear that I weary you with too much talk, and have settled on you more infuriatingly than locust or bruchus. Shake me off, then, as if I were a worm. Cast this poor paper far away that you may not be infected with the mildew of my foolishness, through too long an exposure to my words, in case your gleaming heart loses its shine, and your keen mind its edge. But pardon this sin of mine, by which I weary you so oppressively only because it is the licence of my love which leads me to overtax your patience. I am sure that your heart is so full of affection for me that you do not take offence, even if I do something wrong and manage to offend—if in fact you could ever take offence at me, however justified you would be in doing so.

LETTER 40

To Sanctus and Amandus[1]

Meropius Paulinus and Therasia greet their brothers in the divine Christ, Sanctus and Amandus.

1. There is a time for all and *a time for everything*,[2] provided it be under heaven; for above the heavens there is no time. There is no time in immortality, which the Creator has conferred even on His creatures in heaven. But He alone possesses eternity as His right, and dwells in unapproachable light. For true immortality exists only in Him; only He is what He is. In His own words: *I am who am.*[3] All else exists only in Him.

So there is a time for everything under heaven. A time for leisure, a time for business; a time for silence, a time for conversation; a time for fasting and a time for feasting. Hitherto it has been for me a time for fasting from your words, and now the time is come for feasting on them. For you have fed me on your letter, so sweet in God's word and smeared with the oil of gladness. With that oil I joyfully anointed my head,[4] for the wasted labour of the olive[5] is not manifested in you, in whom dwells *charity from a pure heart and a good conscience and an unfeigned faith.*[6] Yet no man with a mighty hunger can be filled with a single loaf, and I confess that I am not yet satisfied. Rather I am roused to longing for further word from you by this one letter. For I reckon only one, since so far I have received only one, which has caused *my soul to be filled as with marrow and fatness.*[7]

2. But if in the course of my duties there has been a varied timetable, so that there is *a time to keep silence and a time to speak,*[8] my time has not been likewise divided between love and neglect. For it is a long time, as you, dear Sanctus, undoubtedly realise, since I began to love you; and I have loved you continually, though not with the love of Christ, but with the friendship of human intimacy, which has flattery on the lips but no roots in the heart.[9] For the friendship not built in Christ is not founded on a rock. So from time to time it is troubled by a slight breeze, and is loosed; it bears a short-lived bloom through some transient attraction, but then *it quickly withers away as grass, and like the flower of the field quickly falls.*[10]

But the Lord's love abides forever. It binds us to each other both for life and for death, because the love of Christ is *strong as death.*[11] Just as the decree of death cannot be resolved, so the bond of love witnesses that it has the same power as death. As the prophet says: *Who is the man that shall live and not see death?*[12] So, too, Paul cries out: *Who shall separate us from the love of Christ?*[13] So, blessed Sanctus, that love will bear a more abundant harvest to you, for you were wounded by the arrows of this love before me, and you *prevented me with the blessing of sweetness*[14] through the chaste and faith-inspired eloquence of your letter, in which your tongue dripped honey and milk[15] from the word of the Lord.

3. In fact I had previously written to your loving person, but when I got from you a reply short by comparison with my letter, I retired again into a long silence, believing

that my obligations had been met. But Christ was keeping
keener vigil in your heart; your wisdom flourished again
before mine to rouse me to maintain my love so that it
should not sleep the death of forgetfulness. Because I had
showered you with unkindness, you submerged me with
kindness. For you increased my wealth by the loving
service of your affection, by which you adopted brother
Amandus, the blessed servant of the Lord, as your comrade
in approaching me. You have also provided me with a protector in him, for I am sure that he has become not only
your partner in corresponding with me, but also your associate in praying for me.

This spiritual brotherhood of yours demands that you
have not only one spirit of faith in and proclamation of
Christ, but also a single love and labour in liberating your
neighbours. So you will reap together a generous reward
from the Highest who pays recompense; you will be raised
aloft on His towers, because *a brother that is helped by a
brother*[16] shall be exalted, if only you remember always to
pray and be solicitous for me. For the rest, be careful not
to burden me with words that cause me happiness, lest you
set before yourselves as well a stumbling block by *calling
the bitter sweet*.[17] For you have read that *praise becometh
the upright*[18] and the truly holy; it does not become sinners
steeped *in the gall of bitterness*, who are tied by *bonds of
iniquity* still thick enough to ensure *grief and unhappiness
on our ways*.[19]

4. Yet we ought to feel grief in our minds for the additional reason that *God does not despise an afflicted and
humbled heart*.[20] Who *will give me a heart of flesh*,[21] that
my hard emotions may be softened and that I may feel the
arrows of the Lord piercing my flesh with holy fear, that

roused by the pain of my wounds I may *weep before the Lord that made us?*[22] May Jeremias lend me the fount of tears with which he lamented his times and his people.[23] May David, too, pour over me the streams from his eyes with which he washed his bed, wetting with his willing tears not only his cheeks but also the entire couch on which he lay.[24]

For my iniquities are gone over my head, and they are multiplied over the hairs of my head,[25] for the works of wickedness counted in me are more numerous than those of righteousness. So *my sores are putrefied and corrupted, because of my foolishness,* and *my bones have grown old because I was silent*[26] before God. I added *iniquity on iniquity,* and after I had *set my eyes bowing down to the earth,* it was only late and with difficulty that *I lifted them to the mountains* of God, *from whence help came to me from the Lord.*[27] He alone is able to *heal all my diseases* and *to deliver me from the body of this death;*[28] for I who was bound through Adam am loosed through Christ, if only I can *bear the image of the heavenly man as I have borne the image of the earthly*[29]—in other words, if only on behalf of my own salvation I can serve justice and truth as faithfully as I have assiduously served injustice and inhumanity in the interests of my death. Paul demands of us what is human; as we *have yielded our members to serve iniquity,* to achieve death and chaos, so we must now *yield them to serve justice*[30] to achieve life and glory. For I am saddled with the fruit of my former works, of which I am now ashamed.

5. But thanks be to the Wisdom of God, Christ who is God. Whilst abiding in Himself He renews all things, and *ordereth all things sweetly,*[31] so that *there is a time for*

everything; a time to kill and a time to heal, a time to laugh and a time to weep, a time to build and a time to destroy.[32] I pray that the time for killing, destroying, and laughing may have passed, and that the time for healing, building, and weeping has come. *Behold, now is the acceptable time; behold, now is the day of salvation.*[33] *The night is passed, and the day is at hand. Let us cast off the works of darkness, and lay hold of the arms of light. Let us walk in the light like sons of the day.*[34] *For lo, our enemies have prepared arrows in the quiver to shoot in the dark;*[35] for they will not be able to shoot with arrows those standing in the light, but will be sighted before they kill, and easily evaded by careful precaution.

Now the meaning of the two times can be reconciled in this action, so that the times which were previously kept separate may work simultaneously in us. For we are killed as we are given life, or given life as we are killed through Him who said: *I will kill and I will make to live.*[36] For unless Christ kills us we shall not live, and of Him Scripture says: *The Lord killeth and maketh alive,*[37] since if He does not destroy our sins He will not give life to our souls. So the prophet says to Him: *I rose up and am still with Thee, if Thou shouldst kill the wicked, O God.*[38] We shall rise, forsaking the muddy filth and the shadow of death, and abide everlastingly with Him, if He kills the sinner in us and creates the righteous man; for *the cup* of our frailty *is in the hand of the Lord*, and with it *He putteth one down and another He lifteth up.*[39]

Unless the outer man is put down, the inner is not lifted up. So it is that the times for killing and healing, destroying and building, merge at once into the one work, when the life of sin is destroyed in us so that the life of justice can be built up. For our new selves cannot be built unless our old selves are destroyed; we cannot love Christ unless we begin to hate mammon.[40] Nor shall we be able to rejoice in the life to come if we do not mourn in this life, for *they that sow in tears shall reap in joy*.[41]

6. So now the words of the troubled, grieving pauper in the Psalms are apposite to my case, for now *my days are* virtually *vanished like smoke*,[42] and not yet is my wickedness weakened. The course of time has extended my days and made them old; old age not merely sprinkles but dyes my hair with grey. Yet here I still creep along in my first attempts at the spiritual life, still a child with senses undeveloped, even now scarcely a beginner in speaking the word of God. Like a newborn soul with its first cries I seek to loosen my tongue, dumb and unschooled in the sacred writings. Once I was fluent in the fictitious literature of men, but now I stutter in the proclamation of the truth. I am wise in foolishness but foolish in wisdom, strong in vices but still a weakling in virtues, a novice in the will for justice which struggles to birth but a pensioner in a sin-consumed life.

As you know, Sanctus, my blessed brother, for a long time I wallowed in this world and grew old amongst my enemies. I pray that I have grown old towards them, so that now in retirement, having abandoned the broad road, I may have *my youth renewed like the eagle's*[43] in Christ, so I may be stripped of the old man's debility and *put on the new man who is created according to God*.[44] But I cannot yet *be like even to a pelican in the wilderness;* when will I be made *like a night raven in the house?*[45] Shall I ever be roused to such keenness and exaltation of mind as to attain the speed and promptness of the spirit, and be permitted to say, borne to the heights of the virtues by lofty faith:[46] *I have watched, and become as a sparrow all alone on the housetop?*[47]

If you are so disposed, let us examine here the meaning behind the arrangement of these different species of birds in the prophet's words, placed as they are immediately after the mention of the troubled pauper, who is the repentant man reduced to poverty of hope by some sin. (You will, I imagine, bear with my stupid chattering, for it is you who have incited it to win your contempt.) I have been told by a holy man,[48] one most learned and dear to me whose wide knowledge has been won by travel as well as reading, that the pelican is a bird commonly found in Egypt or in neighbouring regions. It wanders in the wilderness close to the Nile, and feeds on snakes after battering them into submission.[49] So it fights to conquer, and if defeated it dies; but if it wins it both escapes death and gains sustenance.

But my friend claimed that the correct form of the other bird is not *nycticorax* but *nycticora*. His argument for this seemed sound enough, for he said that the bird mentioned in that passage of Scripture is what we call the night owl, because it whistles by night from hidden places, and in flight it can see even in that pitch-darkness which causes all living creatures to grope. So it is called *nycticora* more accurately than *nycticorax*, for *nycticorax* means "night raven," whereas *nycticora* means "having night vision," being derived from χόρη, the Greek for the pupil of the eye. Now obviously the night owl has no connexion with the raven; moreover, as I have said, it is certain that like some other night birds it sees better in the dark and is

blind in the light, and that during the day it endures darkness and obtains light from the night.[50]

7. Blessed brothers, see how apposite this bird is to the
doleful pauper, who represents the repentant man. He is
beggared of the wealth of grace; in mind fully aware of
his sad faults he mourns the loss of his glory; his pitiable
troubles make him woebegone; groaning he strives to recover the life of his soul from the death of his flesh, and by
expenditure of prayers and lamentation he solicitously and
tearfully seeks the approval which will heal the wound to
his salvation.

How aptly is the poor sinner of this kind called an
Egyptian or nocturnal bird! For to lament and to confess his sins he seeks solitary retirement from the general
congregation of the church, and sadly shuts himself inside
the prison of his cell, departing in flight from this world
that he may remain in the loneliness of lamentation. There
he strives to grapple with the longings of the flesh, and
fight it out against his sins which must be worn down in
spiritual conflict. In this sense he is certainly *like to a
pelican in the wilderness,*[51] both in his dwelling and in his
struggle, and he emulates the snake-hating bird by warring
on the devil himself and on the princes of darkness, by laying assault to sins and the thoughts of the flesh. And if he
prevails in this contest, he will survive over his enemies and
live; from his victory he obtains his food, for he who is victorious over sin and the devil obtains the life that he deserves.

Every day, through the hazards run by our inner selves,
we feel the serpent with his whole army of spiritual
wickedness creeping to achieve our destruction by various

wiles. But thanks be to God for giving us the victory through Jesus Christ our Lord, so that *we may walk upon the asp and the basilisk, and trample underfoot the lion and the dragon.*[52] So let us fight[53] against such wiles which are the rulers of darkness—in other words, those men whose strength lies in sin, whom Paul calls darkness, and with whom we must wrestle and struggle for our salvation.[54] Pray that I may follow the example of that lonely bird, whilst I dwell in the wilderness of this world, and destroy these snakes. Once they are ground underfoot and consumed after victory, the cloud of darkness will be dissipated; our inner being will be illuminated and will then become *like a night raven in the house,*[55] that is, in the house of the Lord.

So the inward man may direct the sharp gaze of a purified[56] mind amidst the darkness of this world, and may say, with the prophet enlightened by similar vision: *For darkness shall not be dark to me, and night shall be light as the day.*[57] This happens when the two elements of man are in harmony, so that even the flesh denies its earthly nature and joins the soul in concord and spiritual feeling. Then *night shall be light as the day*, when the flesh is also made spiritual like the soul.

8. If by your prayers I am granted the power of both imitating the pelican of the desert by treading underfoot the hostile serpent, and of seeing with the night owl's vision amidst the darkness of this world, then at the end my feet shall be established upon the heights of perfected virtue, and by prayerful vigils and meditation on God's law I shall become *as a sparrow all alone on the housetop.*[58] With body and soul in harmony with God's will I shall justly say: *I am alone until I pass.*[59] What sparrow is this

which represents perfected man, if it is not the sparrow which *hath found herself a house, and with the turtle hath made Thy altars, O Lord of hosts, her nest?*[60] Perhaps this is one of the two sparrows *not one of which falls on the ground without the will of the Father.*[61] For the highest Sparrow fell in the flesh, yet He also rose again. He fell with the free assent of will, *becoming obedient* to His Father *even to the death of the cross.*[62] This Sparrow is the Wisdom who gladly appears in the ways to those who seek Him, who now meets them at the gates, now encounters them in the streets, and now aloft on walls or towers[63] solicits them to be His lovers, and invites them to His high dwelling that He may fulfil His word; for *when lifted up He draws all things to Himself.*[64]

Who will give me wings of silver like a dove, so that *through the pure words of the Lord, like silver tried by the fire,* I may wing *to the prize of supernal vocation,*[65] following the unique Sparrow fluttering above me which is the only Son of God? *He dwelleth on high, and looketh down on the low things; He that descended into the lower parts of the earth is the same also that ascended above all the heavens, leading captivity captive that He might fill all things.*[66] If I have the strength to follow this Sparrow with straight emulation, walking in those same footsteps in which *the beautiful feet of them that preached the Gospel*[67] trod, then I shall be set on high and shall be able to say: *I have watched, and am become as a sparrow all alone on the housetop.*[68]

9. Yet even when transported to the heights we must remember this utterance of the Lord: *He that is on the housetop, let him not come down to his house to take his baggage.*[69] In other words, we must not return to ourselves

and take up again the works of the flesh which have been
left like baggage in the lower regions. For Jesus says: *No
man putting his hand to the plough and looking back is fit
for the kingdom of God.*[70] Even if we are on the housetop,
in other words, if we have ceased to find rest in the flesh
and have soared above our earthly nature, we must follow
the example of birds and fear to fly down to the regions
below. For Scripture says that not in vain are nets spread
for birds.[71] We know that when fowlers set traps for un-
suspecting birds, they lay the snares on the ground.
Usually food is scattered about, and this or blinded decoys
beguile the birds into coming down, and entangle the
gullible creatures in the snares hidden in the treacherous
turf.[72] But when evil-spirited fowlers try to entice us with
similar guile by brandishing the attractions of this world,
we must be armed with faith and enlightened by truth, and
say: *In the Lord I put my trust. How do you say to my
soul: Get thee away from hence to the mountain like a
sparrow? Depart from me, all ye workers of iniquity.*[73] So
let us pray to the Lord, who *enlighteneth every man that
cometh into this world.*[74] I think that the words *every man*
are used because no one is a man unless he recognises God
and further deserves to be recognised by Him. Those who
do not recognise Him are *compared to beasts and become
like to them.*[75]

So we, who by His great mercy and not through our
works have been transformed from wickedness and justified by faith, must *run to the odour of His ointments,*[76] so
that we may draw from His name the odour of life. So
we may be made *the good odour of Christ unto God*[77]
when we have been given to drink (in Scripture's words)
of the wine of perfumes from the chalice of salvation.[78]

Ecclesiasticus says[79] that in this chalice the Lord Himself like a perfumer mixes perfumes of sweetness, *dividing to everyone according as He will,*[80] so that all things may be fulfilled in all men, and so that He may *manifest the odour of His knowledge in us,* for *His name is as oil poured out.*[81] May *our conversation be in heaven,*[82] so that this name may be invoked upon us perpetually, and named amongst us. For in this way we shall be made *as a sparrow all alone on the housetop* if our knowledge and our search is directed *not to the things that are upon the earth, but to the things that are above, where Christ is sitting at the right hand of the Father.*[83] There with eyes innumerable He surveys our deeds and watches this contest in which *we walk in the flesh but do not war according to the flesh.*[84]

10. *For our wrestling is not against flesh and blood,* but against foes unseen and *against the spirits of wickedness in the high places;*[85] not that wicked spirits dwell in heaven, but they war on those who dwell in heavenly intercourse. *So let us put on the armour of light;*[86] let us *through our God go over the wall*[87] which lies between God and ourselves. Let us not fear our enemy, so violent in his spiritual nature, because of the weakness of our flesh, because *power is made perfect in infirmity.*[88]

No man is powerful by his own strength; it is the Lord who makes his enemy weak. The Lord of hosts, King of glory, confounds the foe on our behalf. His manner of fighting is such that it was not divine strength but human weakness that on the cross of Christ conquered that foe. So let us walk after Jesus in His triumph. Let *His truth compass us with the shield* of faith, so that we are *not afraid of the terror of the night* or *of the arrow that flieth*

*in the day. A thousand shall fall at our side, and ten
thousand at our right hand.*[89] This is achieved not by our
strength but by Christ's. We fight His fight, and conquer
by His crown, for we are members of His body if only
we mortify our members on this earth that they may become the armour of justice.

I pray that thus armed I may in my struggle afford a
sight joyful to Christ, to His angels, and to you, and that
I may fly clear of the fowlers' snare, and sing in chattering
thanksgiving: *Our soul hath been delivered as a sparrow
out of the snare of the fowlers; the snare is broken, and we
are delivered, because our help is in the name of the Lord*[90]
Jesus Christ. For *no other name has been given to men
under heaven by which we are to be saved.*[91] Let us
triumph in this name, confess to the Lord His mercies, and
glory not in our praise but in His;[92] for, as the prophet
says, whatever good we have is from Him, and all that is
best is His: for *He made us, and not we ourselves.*[93] So He
says: *What hast thou,* man, *that thou hast not received?
And if thou hast received it, why dost thou glory as if
thou hadst not received it?*[94] With these words He warns
than *he that glorieth must glory in the Lord.*[95]

So now my distress becomes mild when I seem to be the
object of praise, for I am unaware of the blessing that is
mine; indeed I appear to acknowledge the praise when a
man assaults my modesty, because I know that it is not
myself but the gifts and works of God's goodness which
are being praised. Whatever good is seen or believed in me
belongs to Him *who is the one Good, and of whose fulness we all receive,*[96] being sprinkled according to the extent of our merit or faith. For the dew from Him is our

health, and *we rejoice in its showers*.[97] So the mistake through which you praise me will not harm you. Moreover, your devoted faith stores for you an abundant reward, for in your belief that I, wicked in mind and debased through the evil generation of this world, have become good, you show trust in the almighty Lord, who is capable of making the wicked just, of bringing life to the dead, of enlightening the darkness, and of whitening what is crimson.[98]

11. So pray anxiously that by this great work or gift of God I may gain a worthy heart, and that I who have been granted contempt for my inheritance may be granted also contempt for myself. It is a narrow path on which I tread, walking dangerously as on a tightrope. Unless my mental steps are unerringly poised and deviate neither to right nor left, the enemy will easily drive me to the destruction lying on either side. This is why Wisdom in the person of Solomon proclaims to us: *Go not aside from the Lord, lest you fall*.[99] For the Lord Jesus is Himself *the Way, the Truth, and the Life*.[100] He says: *With all watchfulness keep thy heart*.[101] For the very paths of the virtues can cause us to slip down into sins, and, as I have said, unless we organise and balance in fixed positions the forces of the mind, our very humility will give birth to pride; the glory of our devotion will fade if self-gratification creeps in because our poverty is praised. What good will it do to go without riches if I remain rich in sins?

So I beg you not to flatter me because of that saying of the Lord: *Sell what you possess*, for the remaining injunction is more important: *And come, follow Me*.[102] It is easy to appreciate the magnitude of the task in following Christ, since man strives to imitate God. But you also know the saying: *God hath spoken once, and two things have I heard.*[103] The words: *Go and sell all thou hast,* like almost the whole of Divine Scripture, have a double import. For we possess not merely external goods like money and estates, but also the inner wealth of our minds, which is in truth our substance. To sell this inner wealth—in other words, to cede possession of our minds—is the greater victory, accordingly as it is fundamentally more difficult to prise away what is innate than what merely lies before us, to root out what is implanted rather than to reject external attachments. He who renounces his character, withdrawing from himself his being, changes and overcomes himself, and so fulfils that most potent of God's words: *He that shall lose his life for Me shall find it.*[104]

Let us remember these words of the Lord, and pour out our souls to Him. He will nourish us, cherish our life concealed in Him, and reveal Himself with glory if only we pray for that soul at the opportune time, which means here and now in this world. For *who will confess to Him in hell?*[105] In this world we die to sin that we may not live for punishment in the next. For what is called the second death[106] is nothing other than a life of punishment.

12. Let us beware, then, of hell below, where eternal fire will torture body and soul. As the sinner's soul dies, his senses survive and his corrupt substance endures. As Scripture says: *The dead shall rise again incorruptible,*[107] in immortality not of glory but of punishment. *Unhappy man that I am, who shall deliver me from the body of this death?*[108] *The Lord strong and mighty, the Lord mighty in battle,* who *hath burst iron bars and humbled the oppressor,* that He might *lift me up from the gates of death,* and I

*might declare His wondrous works in the gates of the
daughter of Sion.*[109] *May the Lord bless you out of Sion,
and may you see the good things of Jerusalem all the days
of your lives,* so that *our portion may be* jointly *in the
land of the living.*[110]

LETTER 41

To Sanctus[1]

1. On the back of your letter I read a register of letters which you have informed me are mine.[2] So little indeed do I think of all of them that I would not have recognised them as my own had I not trusted your letter. This action has given me greater proof of your love, for I realised that you know me better than I know myself.

I am thankful at having received the hymns which I sought.[3] This gift of yours, brother Sanctus,[4] warned me to prepare my torch diligently whilst there is still time, so that I may not be shut out with the foolish virgins through failing to meet the Bridegroom with the wise ones.[5] You must pray that my soul be both virgin and fruitful—virgin without barrenness and fruitful without corruption. For through this mystery he who did not bestow his seed on Israel was cursed in the Law;[6] yet, in the Gospel it is the wise virgin who, having first obtained her oil, awaits the arrival of the bridegroom with wakeful vigil and wick well oiled, and at his coming fires the torch which the oozing wood does not allow to die out.

2. So I pray that my mind may be fruitful for God, and through good works bear the fruits of life; and that my spirit be virgin, despoiled by no attractions of this world and remaining unstained by any vice. For the foolish virgins seem to me to be the souls barren of virtues, and the wise virgins those uncorrupted by vices. And the

218

virgins of each kind number five in order that we may understand that they represent the purity or corruption of the human senses,[7] for we are all endowed with the five senses by which we attain life or death. It is these which the prophet means when he sadly says: *Death is come up through your windows.*[8] Let us block them up with fear of God, that we may be both deaf and blind to all the shapes and voices of this world. Let us *hedge in our ears with thorns against a wicked tongue*[9] and enticing melodies. *Let us turn away our eyes that they may not behold vanity.*[10] Let us stop up our nostrils that we may get no whiff of the corruption of the world's death. Let no taste entice us to gluttony, so that disease steals over us and weakens the strength of our self-discipline with the food of lusts. Let us not caress the flesh with soft garments, so that our limbs may not be evilly titillated by luxurious coverings and long for[11] the touch of the flesh and forbidden embraces.

If we avoid such things, each of us will keep his senses chaste and steeped in the oil of the faith's teaching; all five virgins will remain wise, and wait quietly in confident expectation, the oil stored in their lamps. Then they will have no difficulty in preparing the torches to meet the Bridegroom, when they have been roused at the first hubbub of His coming. This parable applies to the great nations of the Church, which contain not only virgins (however great their number) but also the married and the widows, whose ways of life and rewards are different.[12] So I think that the only possible interpretation of the five foolish and five wise maidens is that both wise and foolish are present throughout the divergent community of the whole people, and that the number five is contained in each individual, as I have explained above.

To recapitulate, each has within himself the foolish or the wise virgins according to the nature of his senses. If they are provident, their virginity is wise; but if they are sluggish, it is foolish. Though most unlike each other, foolish and wise are equally termed virgins, because virgins are fruitlessly barren in the flesh but fruitfully chaste in the spirit; so the wise maintain a virginity not barren because they are wise, while that of the foolish is not fruitful because they are foolish. The foolish virgins seem to me to represent *the wisdom of this world, which is foolishness with God,* and *the wisdom of the flesh,*[13] which is in truth the foolish virgin because it is not joined to the Law, or *subject to the law* and wisdom *of God.*[14] And its lamp is easily extinguished because being empty of the Holy Spirit it has not the oil of truth. It is the Spirit which enlightens the inner eye and fattens the head of the soul, which is our faith. And the oil which fattens it is the application of heavenly teaching.

3. So *the oil of the sinner will not fatten my head,* and *dying flies will not spoil the sweetness of the ointment.*[15] I pray that Christ may ever be my head, and that oil be never lacking to it, for *His name is as oil poured out.*[16] Then, when I am perfected in all my senses, I shall be the wise virgins, if only there abides in me God's Wisdom, by which virginity was made fruitful even in the flesh.[17]

But I weary you overmuch, and take many liberties with the patience of your love. I must hearken to the words of Solomon speaking with the wisdom of God, and make my words tread more thriftily even to my dearest friends, in case they hate me through satiety.[18] Yet I know that a man cannot hate his own entrails, and so you cannot hate my lowly person, for you have made me a part of yourselves. May the peace, charity, grace, and humility of Christ the highest Lord abound in you, my blessed brothers, deservedly revered and greatly loved.

LETTER 42

To Florentius[1]

Paulinus greets his most blessed and rightly revered father Florentius.

1. I rejoice in the Lord that the letter writen by your holy person has visited me and first established the liaison between us, for previously I had not the favour of your acquaintance, and now by God's sudden kindness I have gained full assurance in your friendship as if it were of long standing. As Scripture says: *A new friend is as new wine; it shall grow old and thou shalt drink it with pleasure.*[2] In fact your holy person bettered that statement of the prophet, for you have begun to love me with such perfect affection at the very outset of this friendship that you have given me the sweetness of long-established love. So I do not need to long for increase of love, since I experience it full-grown because of these generous beginnings, so that I can compare the richness of your soul with the sources of great rivers, bursting out of their mother the earth in full spate through huge openings, which are at once rivers at their very rising.

So blessed be the Lord who has submerged my sins with such grace, so that He enriched me even with your love though I was unworthy of your acquaintance. At a time when I had as yet not tasted the lesser good, not having made your bodily acquaintance, He allowed you to present me with a gift the greater as the human spirit is greater than the flesh. Therefore my heart rejoices, and I say with mouth filled with joy: *The Lord hath done great things with us, for you have prevented me with blessings of sweetness*, by your holy eloquence which is *tried like refined silver*.[3] You visited me, as I have said, and roused me from my idle inactivity, in which ignorance caused me not to sleep but to be silent, so that I might observe your love. So *blessed be the name of the Lord*, and may He rejoice through this additional work[4] of His devotion, by which He has preferred to show me the complexion of your mind in which you have been fashioned more handsomely by Christ, rather than acquaint me with your physical features. For words reveal the man, and *out of the abundance of the heart the mouth speaketh*.[5]

2. So your words, seasoned with the salt of the apostles, tasted of that grace[6] which has been given to you; and from the drops from your lips I have tasted the sweetness of the Lord[7] in you. You were appointed and set over your people, chosen from the sheep to be shepherd of the flock, to rule the sheep of the pasture of Him who laid down His life for His sheep.[8] He will rule us forever as Lamb and as Shepherd, for out of wolves He has made us sheep, and He is now the Shepherd guarding the sheep on behalf of which He went as a Lamb to the sacrifice.[9] So our Lord and our God, *who was seen on earth and conversed with men*[10] on our behalf, is both Sheep and Shepherd among us, because He controls us within by means of the hidden stick and rod of salvation;[11] so that even *if we walk in the shadow of death, we fear no evils, because God is with us*[12]—the great Emmanuel, Lord of majesty and Son of a maidservant,[13] the first of these by His nature and the second by what He became. He is both man's Creator and

his Redeemer; God of God, Man for the sake of man, Son of God before all ages, Son of man for the world's sake. He took the form of a slave to win the freedom of slaves. *He became poor to enrich the poor through His poverty, for He is rich unto all* with all blessings, *who is filled all in all, the Fulness of the Godhead, the Hope of all the ends of the earth and in the sea afar off*, our saving God, *our Mediator between men and God, the Man Christ Jesus, who is in the glory of God the Father*,[14] God blessed above all forever.

3. God deigned to appoint you to the role of His apostles, so that deploying their skill you might become a fisher of men,[15] and with the net of the saving word draw from the bitter, deep waves of this world a haul which God can invest with life rather than destruction. This is precisely your daily work, for He has made you a helper in His building and in His husbandry.[16] Now He has deigned to instil into your soul, so lofty in its humility of heart, a love for my lowly person, for there is no doubt at all that you have deserved to become a shepherd because you are as gentle as a sheep and blameless as a lamb. It is God, I say, who has condescended to make you love me, not treating me harshly as I deserve, but through the riches of His goodness He has increased both the aid lent to me through the patronage of your prayers and the reward owed to you through your great love even for an insignificant neighbour.[17]

I pray that He may make you ever mindful of me, that He may intermingle with all your prayers and offerings an anxiety for my salvation, for I fear that this great imparting of your affection, of which I boast in the Lord, may be a stumbling block to me if I conceal those plundering beasts which are my unsubdued senses with the clothing of sheep.[18] So pray, until you gain your prayer, that my heart may be spotless[19] in God's sight, that I may not mingle with or be drawn away with those *who speak peace with their neighbour, but evils are in their hearts*,[20] but that harmoniously with tongue and mind I may *believe unto justice, and with the mouth make confession unto life*.[21] In this way your devoted love for me will be fruitfully returned to you, if your prayers on my behalf are so effective that I am transformed from my earthly appearance into your likeness, so that as genuinely as you *I bear the image of the heavenly man*.[22]

4. Then truly your love will make me happy, if you ensure that I am not unlike your loving self. Yet I do not go so far in my apparently arrogant aspirations as to hope to attain the peak of your merit; but my aspiration is that enclosed within the bounds of salvation, adapting myself to the shape of your faith, I may take the straight path and follow the steps of truth. I pray that Christ the Rock,[23] the Head[24] and Foundation[25] of His body, may be my End as He is the Beginning.[26] That Rock serves us in the desert of this world with unfailing waters,[27] and refreshes us with a sweet draught when we thirst for justice, so that we are not consumed with the heat of bodily desires. This is the Rock on which the firmly built house does not fall.[28] This is the Rock which flowed with water and blood when His side was pierced with a lance,[29] so that He poured forth for us two streams equally saving, the water of grace and the blood of the Sacrament—in other words, both the source of our salvation and its price.

5. Yet what have I, wretched sinner, come to or rather descended to? In addressing you with a stream of words so

that in saying your prayers you may regard me as a deserving case in the light of or rather in the face of my sins, I impose on myself by my garrulity a burden as great as that which I hope your prayers will diminish. I seem to have forgotten the words of Scripture: *Because of thy multitude of words thou shalt not escape sin.*[30] What am I to do? With what words shall I ask to be cleansed? By what means can you defend me when with full knowledge and forethought I have sinned against the prophet's injunction, harming myself with the sin of garrulity and wearying your holy person? I shall certainly be stuck with this charge, and even your prayers will not be able to protect me, unless you yourself first absolve me of the guilt of this injustice and offer to God on my behalf a victim to placate Him, even as the blessed Job was ordered to do on behalf of his loquacious friends.[31] Indeed, all I ask of you for myself is the presumption that my multitude of words may go unpunished through your indulgence, for I am certain that your love for me is equalled by your patience.

LETTER 43

To Desiderius[1]

The sinners Paulinus and Therasia greet the holy Desiderius, deservedly revered brother and longed for more than all else,[2] in Christ the Lord.

1. Some time ago I entrusted to brother Victor[3] a short letter for you. I wanted this to be conveyed to your holy person so that it might attest that its messenger had not been detained at Nola of his own accord. The reason for its brevity was that Victor, a short time after his arrival, made such haste to return to you from here, and insisted with such obstinacy on making his way back, that he scarcely gave me the chance of writing even a short letter to you. Meanwhile, however, sudden obstacles dragged him back as he was setting out, for winter blocked his route and he was afraid to make the journey. So hindered and recalled by these obstacles, he yielded to necessity and consented to the long delay which my affection had unsuccessfully solicited.

During the period of waiting, he also fell ill, and indeed was in such straits that he was rescued from death's door, so that more time was spent in recovering his health than the period in which he endured the illness. Subsequently, since the feast of the apostles was approaching, I thought it unkind to send him away. So my wish added this short period to the long delays conceded to the pressing circumstances I have mentioned. My motive was that after he had

joined with me in my vow and my annual pilgrimage, and
had attended the solemn celebration of the apostles,[4] he
should report these additional activities on his return to
you.

2. The correspondence which Victor carries for that
blessed man of God, our brother Severus, was written at
different times, as the variation in the text will show, this
being the result of the pressing circumstances of Victor's
haste. For the shorter part was extorted when our messenger was in a hurry and waiting impatiently to leave. On
the other hand, the more extended sections I wrote when
I began to be sure that his stay would be long, and my
mind could relax and take its leisure. Our brother Severus
had asked in his letter that I should send Victor back, and
he had laid down the time, demanding that he return for
the wine harvest.[5] I could not follow his instructions in
this matter, but I did try to obey him in one way, at any
rate. I ensured that he would welcome Victor on his return at the time of year requested if not in the year he anticipated.

If Severus is unwilling to attribute Victor's delay to the
pressing circumstances explained earlier, he must debit his
stay here to my fault. But the credit for Victor's return,
however late, he must accord to his own prayers. For
when Victor in his illness was wholly despaired of,
Severus' faith gave me hope for his recovery, whereas my
own merits made me despair of it. I saw that Victor's
innocence was being afflicted by what I merited, so that
my wickedness could be punished in him. God's justice
was taking vengeance on Victor because of his error in
loving a sinner. And that love exacted its punishment from

me, for I endured in affliction of heart and sympathy of
mind the suffering which my dear friend sustained in body.

3. I come now to the request you yourself made through
Victor. You are looking for welling streams of sweet water
in a brackish brook⁶ run dry. So I return your query which
your own grace must explain, for I confess that I have not
dared even to touch with my finger the weighty problems
of such great terms and mysteries.⁷ I have read that *wisdom
will not enter into a malicious soul*,⁸ and so conscious of
my wickedness I could not be confident of a divine revelation because in my dark heart I have not obtained the light
of wisdom.

But you are a blessed man, a pure vessel fit to receive
God, and if you have received the understanding endowed
by that blessing with which the patriarch,⁹ blind in body
but enlightened in soul, addressed his sons with prophetic
spirit, you must write back and expound to me the secrets
of the kingdom, the mysteries which lay hidden from all
ages and were revealed for later generations in Christ Jesus,
in whom merge the diverse figures of all holy men. He is
prefigured in the patriarchs, He speaks in the prophets, He
is at work in the apostles, and He is *filled all in all, because
in Him it hath pleased the Father that all fulness should
dwell*, for *He is the beginning and the end*¹⁰ of all things.
But if you have not yet received this understanding (perhaps because you have postponed making this request of
the Lord specially for yourself, believing that what has
been given to me, your neighbour, is already available to
you in your store), you must ask and you will receive according to your faith and disposition. The more chaste you
are in body, the more lively will be your faculties; the

purer you are in heart, the more capable will you be of receiving Christ, who is possessed by the humble and beheld by the clean of heart.[11]

4. To mitigate your annoyance at being deceived by my poverty, you ought to regard yourself as having experienced at my hands what the Lord Himself encountered in the fig tree. He approached it when hungry, and finding it figless smote it with His words,[12] so that since it had been barren for the Lord's blessing it should be withered by His curse. But I beseech you, my brother, not to smite me with similar words though you find me like that barren tree, in case I wither completely and, naked of the fruit I should bear, am robbed even of the covering of leaves which are the foliage of grace.

However, second thoughts occur to me. The merciful and pitying Lord desires no man to die, and He did not condemn His creation in that tree, but cursed the flaw in it which was hostile to His planting. So I beg you rather to curse my barrenness, so that no fruit may ever grow from it but instead fruit may spring up for God from my real self. The death of my barrenness is in my interest, so that the fertility of the Lord's planting may take fresh root in me. Once the flaw which makes me fruitless is dead, I can take fresh life for my Cultivator by the return of my good will, so that when the Lord hungers for my life He may find me extending to Him on fertile branches the fruits I owe Him.

5. Now in the matter of this tree Mark has added a point of some importance. He is in harmony with the other evangelists in saying that the tree is cursed and made to wither, but his words go deeper in one respect. After saying that the Lord found no fruit on the tree, he added

words which seem to exculpate the tree: *For it was not the time for it to bear fruit*.[13] If this is the case, the tree seems to have been cursed unjustifiably. If the reason for its not having hanging fruit was that it was as yet the wrong time of the year, it was not barren from some disease but unripe because of the season.

However, we can adapt Paul's words about the cattle to this matter of the tree, and say: *Doth God take care for a tree?*[14] The passage was written preeminently for us, in whom God always wants to find His food, for in us He has His land and His vineyard. He fans us on His threshing floor, cleanses the wheat in us, casts out the chaff, and burns the cockle.[15] So in the passage on the tree He was thirsting for man's salvation and seeking from man the fruit owed to Him. But even when *He came unto His own, His own received Him not*.[16] The barren synagogue of the unfaithful Jews did not yield Him the due fruit of faith which He had sown in them through the Law and the prophets. He came to their tree seeking from the sons of His plantation sweet food from the long-awaited seed. But the synagogue withdrew the fruits of filial devotion and gave Him gall as food.[17] They offered Him thorns when He asked for grapes,[18] and gave parching vinegar to drink[19] to the very Planter of the good vine, who is Himself the true Vine[20] and the Cluster of sweetness. Hence *their table became a snare before them, and their grapes bitter, and their wine the incurable anger of dragons*.[21]

6. But you, my brother, must entreat the Lord that my vine come not from the vineyard of such as these, for the stock of those who came from the vineyard of the Lord of hosts[22] deteriorated into the vineyard of the Sodomites. We would indeed have been *like to Sodom and Gomorrha*[23] in

the totality of our wickedness if the Lord had not left to us a nursery for our life amongst the vines of the apostles which spring from the roots of the patriarchs. The Lord intended that from this nursery the salvation of the Gentiles would sprout forth, and that in it the blessed seed would take firm hold. But because *it is the last hour and the axe is now laid to the roots of the trees*[24] and threatens with deserved destruction those which are withered and barren,[25] I beg you to pray for indulgence and a respite for me, so that if my death is postponed I may perhaps obtain the sap of fruitfulness from the tending of your love and the cultivation of my own troubled heart.

So the fear of God may prick my heart, and due repentance may enrich my stock with the manure of humility. Then I shall be roused to anxious watchfulness, and will stand ready and trembling at every hour[26] in the absence of the Lord, so that I may be easy at His coming, and that always and every day Christ may find me fertile for Him. I pray, then, that I may never show myself unripe for the performance of His will. But if He should ask His peace of me in time of anger, may my mind not be unprepared for reconciliation through bitter wrath. May I not wait for *the sun to go down on my anger*,[27] lest my life end if night closes on the day before peace quenches rage.

7. You must consider my words about anger to apply to every kind of sin. For this, I think, is what is meant by the Lord's seeking fruit on that tree before the due season. He who *knoweth the secrets of the heart*[28] and has insight into men's thoughts did not fail to see what was clear to human eyes. His senses were not inferior to those of men. He did not fail to recognise the season of the year which was obvious even to children, nor did He demand in spring

the fruits of autumn. No, the Craftsman of our salvation, the Creator, whose life and entire works on earth provided an exemplar for our behaviour and manners, gave visible form to His secret plans, and by use of the irrational objects of creation delineated the outline of His economy to souls endowed with reason, so that He could school us in all things conducive to our salvation by the written account of His actions and the proofs of His words. When He showed us through the evangelist that He had sought fruit from a tree before its due time, He wanted us to realise that man owes fruit to God at all times.[29] For the good Lord, who prepares mortal man for immortality, wants man to clothe himself in the robe of eternity now, even in this world. This is so that the Lord may obtain fruit not merely in season, but rather that at all times man may be ripe for that One with whom or in whom he will eternally abide.

LETTER 44

To Aper and Amanda[1]

The sinners Paulinus and Therasia greet their holy, rightly revered, and dearly beloved brethren Aper and Amanda.

1. O that someone would give me literary resources like yours, so that I could adequately reply to your letter![2] Interwoven with the diverse blooms of spiritual graces, eloquent with the language not of secular learning but of God, it flowed with the milk of God's love and the honey of wisdom as though coming from the land of promise. You have *sucked honey and oil* of wisdom *out of the firm Rock* which is Christ the Lord.[3] He is the Foundation of the eternal house on which you have begun to erect the building of salvation by works that live. No wood, hay, or straw do you strain to build upon it, but gold, silver, and precious stones.[4] For your heart has ceased to be hard, parched, and fickle. Laying aside these faults with the old man, you have become the moist wood which flourishes because of the running waters near by, and will bring forth its fruit in due season, and will never be robbed of the glory of its foliage.[5] Your thoughts are as gold *tried by the fire*, your words as silver *refined seven times*, all gleaming with spiritual grace and uttering *the pure words of the Lord*[6] from a pure heart and a tongue which mirrors your heart. You keep the good, strong treasure in its earthenware vessel of a faith not frail, for your mind is the vessel of the grace entrusted to you; and it is strengthened

by the primacy of the spirit[7] within its bodily frailty, and provides solid protection for God's gift.

But how shall I, *who am poor and sorrowful*,[8] obey Wisdom, who ordered me to take food at the table of the powerful only on condition that I recognise my obligation to provide a similar meal?[9] For you have become "the table of the powerful" so far as I am concerned; you have set before me rich food, which has enticed me in my hunger to feast without reluctance on all the delicacies of your words, as on the dainties of a gourmet's table, so various to the taste and to the eye. Mindful more of my gluttony than of my poverty, I dared to eat the food which I cannot rival at my own board.

What then shall I do? From whom shall I seek the gift or loan either of the furniture with which to emulate in worthy splendour the rich man's dining room, or of the outlay to enable me in my poverty to match the rich man's meal? Who will help me to meet this necessary debt but You, Lord Jesus? For You always commit yourself to all Your poor who lend to You, and You promise that You will make repayment on behalf of those who have now no means of making recompense.[10] Help me now, and from Your riches meet my debt to Your Aper, because I am poor. *Fill up plentifully his streams and multiply your generations in him, so that he may spring up in Your house as a fruitful olive tree, flourish like a palm tree and multiply like the cedar of Libanus.*[11]

2. But let me return to your letter at which *I rejoice as one that hath found great spoil.*[12] Though I cannot make similar recompense by my own words, I shall do what famished persons do. After they have digested a richly served meal and begun again to feel the hunger of poverty,

they console themselves in their hunger by present recollection of past feasting and feast their empty hearts by
thinking of the dinner now gone. So the text of this letter
will recall your words, and so renew my pleasure without
conferring any on you. I shall speak not of my prayer for
you but of its fulfilment by experience. For your letter has
depicted for me the appearance of your heart—that letter
of goodly hope, of unfeigned faith, of pure love. What
most holy affection it breathes forth! How sweet and
abundant is Christ's fragrance in it! What riches of a pure
heart well forth from it! How it savours of your thirst, the
longing and fainting of your soul for the courts of the
Lord! What thanks it gives to God, what favours it suc-
ceeds in begging from Him![13] As I read it, what a vision it
affords me of divine graces flowering in you, and virtues
already effective!

3. In your letter *the little sons* or even the young men
of Babylon are dashed against the rock.[14] They represent
the vices of worldly turmoil and pride, with which our
faith joins battle and will quite easily prevail provided that
it foresees the weakness of our adolescence and runs
aground on to Christ at the outset. In your letter the cedars
of Libanus have been laid upon the earth, and built into the
structure of the ark with the binding joints of charity;[15]
and now they cleave with their indestructible timber
through the waves of this world.[16] In that letter also Christ
is aroused to guide your righteous course to His own steadfastness; He seems to be calming the winds and the seas
for you,[17] for He now sails in the vessel of your body, and
His pillow is on your heart. For *the sparrow has found
itself a house there*,[18] and has in you *a place whereon to lay
his head*.[19]

In your letter, too, your wife, who does not lead her husband to effeminacy or greed, but brings you back to self-discipline and courage to become the bones of her husband,[20] is worthy of admiration because of her great emulation of God's marriage with the Church.[21] She is restored and reinstated into unity with you, for Christ's love joins you with spiritual bonds which are all the stronger for being more chaste. You have passed from your own bodies into Christ's.

4. The Lord has blessed you, for He *who alone doth wonderful things hath made both one, establishing the two in Himself.*[22] He transforms not only souls[23] but also feelings, changing the transient into the eternal. See how you remain the married couple you were, yet not coupled as you were. You are yourselves yet not yourselves. Now you know each other, as you know Christ, apart from the flesh.[24]

This is the change of the right hand of the Most High which contains itself yet makes all things new, which *turneth the sea into dry land,*[25] reducing the stream of vices to the solid land of self-control. Blessed is Amanda amongst women,[26] faithful and most acceptable to the Lord by reason of that further dedication with which on your behalf she has confronted worldly needs as a tower founded on unbudging rock confronts storms. Established on that rock, on which a house once built shall not fall,[27] with the steady immobility of her unremitting mind, she has become your *tower of strength against the face of the enemy;*[28] she breaks the force of the worldly waves and whirlpools by interposing her holy slavery, so that you may be shielded from the sea and preserve your mind unshaken like a ship safe in the harbour of the Church, plying the oars of salvation which are persistent meditation on studies and works of godliness.

For *bodily exercise*, says Scripture, *is profitable to little, whereas godliness is profitable to all things.*[29] This godliness made you submit to Christ, for you preferred even to *lie abject in the house of the Lord rather than be* prominent *in the tabernacles of sinners,*[30] and bound your fellow servant Amanda to physical labours on behalf of your soul out of spiritual love for you, so that she might make her service the price of your freedom.

In the transactions of the world she serves not the world but Christ,[31] for whose sake she endures the world that you may avoid enduring it. Truly she has become the help to you that God's work and word prescribes.[32] To you she turns, hanging on your nod, standing where you stand, walking in your footsteps, enlivened by your spirit. She suffers need on behalf of your life, that she may be refashioned by it. She takes charge of secular business so that you may forget it; she handles it so that you may handle God's. She gives the appearance of having possessions so that you may be possessed not by the world but by Christ. No discordant will severs her from your committed life; more remarkable, harmonious faith keeps her apart from your work but joins her to you in will. Uncaptured in mind, she carries out the tasks of captivity with freedom of spirit. *She has strengthened her hands for works of virtue; she has girded her loins with strength and stretched out her arms to useful tasks. She has not eaten the bread of idleness but is* for you *become like a ship which brings merchandise from afar.*[33]

She makes the necessary division; through her own person she *renders to Caesar the things that are Caesar's,* so that through you she may *provide God with the things that are God's*.[34] For when, as Scripture says, she has paid *tribute to whom tribute is due*, then she *opens her hands to the needy*.[35] By proffering the fruits of her work to the poor, she pays spiritual taxes and devotes the revenue from her possessions to your salary as a soldier; for she is more greedy for the loss which brings salvation than for the gain which brings death. She is the kind of person in whom *the heart of her husband trusteth*. As Scripture says, *she renders her husband good and not evil all the days of her life*,[36] so you have no worry about the secular matters of your house, but are free to devote your strenuous efforts to the business of your heavenly home. *You shall not be confounded when you speak to your enemies in the gate*,[37] for the wise woman who has been given to you is more precious than precious stones and *makes you honourable at the gates*[38] of the Church.

Scripture further says: *She has made a double cloak for her husband*.[39] It must surely be clear to you that your wife also weaves a double cloak for you, and fine linen or purple covering for herself.[40] Her faith redoubles your grace, since *a woman is a goodly crown to her husband*,[41] and your distinction is in turn her purple. For under the guidance of the Lord's grace you have both been simply clad in the unity of faith, and now you clothe each other further with works of spiritual virtues. You are her head in Christ, and she is your foundation.[42] By her work your foot stands on the Lord's path; and she will share your head because you are one framework of faith united in the body of the Lord. For though her preoccupations are different from yours, she keeps unaffected her mind in compliance and harmony with yours, agreeing with your decision to follow your vocation. While you with faith and skill fulfil the stewardship entrusted to you by multiplying your master's talents, she, too, does not bury in the ground the treasure[43] which she toils to wrest from worldly harvests. She makes loans rather through your good works than through the grasping profit which leads to perdition.

So *the fruit of her hands will be given to her* and her husband shall be praised at the gates[44] of the Daughter of Sion. He shall be praised in the Lord, who prepares for your joint harvest the crops which you have sown by performing in the same work different labours with equal earnestness. So on the great day together you may *come with joyfulness carrying your sheaves*,[45] she who ministers to the seed and you who sow the seed of the ministry. She will not lose her share in your reward because of the exemplary scale of values by which she sought not her inclination but your salvation. This very action gives sufficient proof of the judgment of her faith; she well shows how she, too, prefers to despise the world and not enjoy it, for she put your spiritual welfare first, preferring you before herself, not this world before Christ.

5. *May the Lord add blessings on you and your children*.[46] For when the parents deserve the mercy of the Lord, He will (in Scripture's words) raise up their sons, and they will be enriched by the blessings of the Lord.[47] I hope that just as your wife is *as a fruitful vine on the sides of thy house* abounding with the fruits of devoted regard for you, so that *a thousand fall at thy side and ten thousand at thy right hand*, so also your sons will deserve *to sit round the table* of the Lord with you *like olive plants*.[48]

I believe that they are now fed by the food of God's wisdom and your good life like the young of eagles,[49] so that they are already learning to eat and with greed of the spirit devour the flesh pillaged by their parents' plundering, the enmities of the flesh which war on the spirit. They learn also to strengthen the beating of their wings and to mount up to the heights of the virtues. May they be reared like the sons of the prophets, who turned away from the noisy life of the city to order their minds in the peace of silence, and erected secret dwelling places for themselves near the course of the Jordan.[50] May they be consecrated like the sons of Aaron—not those who kindled an alien fire before the Lord and were consumed by the divine flames which they did not possess;[51] but like Eleazar and Ithamar may they deserve to be unbroken successors of their father's priesthood,[52] because they are heirs who do not fall below him in sanctity.

6. I believe that "an alien fire" is kindled when a person lights the flame of a bodily or worldly desire in the shrine of his heart and dares to approach the altar of the Lord. For His altar allows only the kindling of that fire of which He says: *I am come to cast fire on the earth, and what will I, if it now be kindled?*[53] Lord Jesus, always kindle us with this fire, that our senses may be enlightened and our vices burnt out, for only the fire which You send will resist eternal fire. But if we keep our hearts burning on the way of the Lord,[54] we kindle not an alien fire but His. We are defended by this fire amongst the fires of the world, and like the boys in the furnace we shall be cooled with dew as fierce flames lick around us. In company with the Son of God we shall sing a hymn to the Lord amidst the refreshing fires.[55] For Christ has said that where even two or three are in harmony, He will always be amongst them.[56]

So I am sure that He is lodging in the very midst of your

house where parents and children form a single group of many souls. In this gathering I beg you to include me (for I am with you in spirit and absent only in body), so that you may water the thirsty garden of my soul with words and prayer. I cannot cultivate it with my own hands, for I am weak, or with hirelings, for I am poor. I cannot find a way of seeking your way, for I am unable to dig and ashamed to beg.[57] So I need more urgently the help of your prayers, for who will hire useless labourers or pay those who do not seek work? Yet sometimes those who have poor uncultivated fields abandon hope of a harvest by the resources of their own hands and turn to God's help. And often they obtain a result that accords with their faith, for their devotion makes good their lack of industry, and pious prayers help those who have lost the farmer's skill.

7. Both of you pray, then, that the almighty Lord who has set rivers in the wilderness may transform my barrenness into water springs,[58] that He may shatter and disperse my hardness of heart, and that He may turn this rock also into a pool of water.[59] May He sprinkle me with the dew in which He steeped the mystical fleece of Gideon on the floor.[60] For His dew is my healing. Pray, I say, that He may deign to enter my garden, and to order the north wind to rise and the south wind to come,[61] so that my seeds may flourish under the impulse of those breezes of life.

But even if He enters His vineyard and finds my tree without fruit, may He refrain from cutting it down. May He in His mercy postpone that course, and trust the Farmer who stays the execution by promising that fruit will be produced from the barren fig tree by His tending.[62] For the Lord Himself, who makes intercession for our sins[63] and *calleth those things that are not as those that are*,[64] is able to make even of this needy and barren person a fruitful tree. He can enrich my empty soul with the fertilising word, which is like the bag of dung. For it is written that by His grace *the wilderness shall grow fat*.[65] The bag of dung which makes a barren tree fertile seems to me to represent especially that spiritual humility[66] by which we afflict our hearts with repentance for past stupidity, purge ourselves of what is empty, and receive the sap of virtue by which we who were barren of righteous works are made fruitful.

It is good, then, that we should dig deep into ourselves, and humble our souls by the fasting by which we abstain from the works of darkness. So through this fertilising humility, cheap in the sight of the world but dear to God, our souls may be raised through Him who *raises up the needy from the earth and lifts up the poor from the dunghill*.[67] The grace of God be with you both.

LETTER 45

To Augustine[1]

The sinners Paulinus and Therasia greet the saintly and most blessed servant of the Lord, whom they especially love, revere, and long for, their father, brother, and teacher, Bishop Augustine.

1. *Thy word is a lamp to my feet and a light to my paths.*[2] So whenever I receive a letter from your most blessed and holy person, I feel the darkness of my foolishness being dissipated. It is as if a light-bearing salve were being poured into the eyes of my mind,[3] and I see more clearly once the darkness of ignorance is dispelled and the mist of doubt removed. I have experienced this benefaction of yours on numerous other occasions when you have sent me letters, but never more so than on receiving this latest one, brought by our brother Quintus[4] the deacon, a man blessed in the Lord, a messenger as welcome to me as he is worthy.

It was some time after reaching Rome that he passed on to me your verbal blessing. I had come to Rome, as I do regularly after the Lord's Pasch,[5] to venerate the apostles and martyrs. However, I expunged from my mind the time which he had spent at Rome when I was unaware of his presence; and then he seemed to have left your gaze so very recently that I could believe that he had come from you directly when I saw him and he proffered to me that full savour of your sweetness[6] in your words redolent of the purity of heavenly perfume.

However, I must confess to the revered and loving friend that you are that I could not read your letter the minute I got it at Rome. For the tumult there was such that I could not carefully scrutinise and enjoy your gift as I wished—that is to say, by reading through to the end once I had begun. So the certain expectation of a feast in store allowed me, as often occurs, to curb the hunger of my mind though it was greedy. The sure hope of obtaining my fill (for the loaves that I longed for were in my hand, in the form of the letter which I was soon to devour, and which later tasted most sweet to mouth and stomach when I devoured it) allowed me easily to postpone my gluttony, which gaped openmouthed at the honeycomb of your letter, until I could set out from Rome and devote a whole day to the task. This I did at Formiae,[7] where we took a day to rest from our journey, so that I feasted on the spiritual delicacies of your letter, free from all distasteful duties and the stifling atmosphere of the Roman crowds.

2. How then am I, a lowly man of earth, to reply to the wisdom granted you from above? This world does not embrace it, and no one has it save he who is wise in the wisdom of God and eloquent in the word of God. So because I know for certain that Christ speaks in you,[8] *in God will I praise your speech and I shall not be afraid of the terror of the night*.[9] With the spirit of truth you have taught me how to exercise salutary control over the mind in the frail affairs of men; you witnessed the restraint with which Melania, blessed mother and grandmother that she is, mourned the death in the flesh of her only son.[10] Her grief

was silent, but her sorrow did not restrain a mother's tears.
You had deeper insight into her controlled yet grievous
tears, for your spirit is closer or more like to hers. From
your position of equal eminence, and because you have a
heart like hers, you had a clearer view of that maternal
heart of Melania, a woman perfect in Christ yet retaining
unaffected the courage of her manly spirit. You saw that
she wept first from natural affection, but then from pain
for a more important reason. It was not so much the human
loss of her only son, after the completion of his mortal
span in this world, as the fact that she thought he had been
summoned early, so to speak, while still preoccupied by
worldly foolishness, because he had not yet dropped the
desire for senatorial distinction.[11] He had not been taken
up to heaven, as the saintly greed of her prayers had demanded, to pass from the glory of human intercourse to
that of the resurrection and to share with his mother rest
and glory, as he would if he had followed his mother's example in his life in this world, and put sackcloth before the
toga and monastic life before the Senate.

3. Yet this same man, as I think I have already mentioned to your holy person, died rich through works which
showed that he inwardly put first the nobility espoused by
his mother's humility, even if he did not show it by his
garments. For he was so gentle in his manners and so
humble of heart as the Lord's word recommends,[12] that we
may confidently believe that he has entered into the rest
of the Lord. *For there are remnants for the peaceable man,
and the meek shall possess the land* if they *please the Lord
in the land of the living.*[13] Publicola at any rate fulfilled the
injunction of Matthew both through the meekness of

silence and a sense of religious duty shown by striking
works.

So though he was the colleague in rank and distinction
of the notables of this world, he did not seek to boast of
nor to *mind the high things* of this earth, but to *consent to
the humble* as a perfect imitator of Christ, and to continue
to *show mercy and lend all the day long.*[14] So *his seed was
made mighty upon earth* among those who *are exceedingly
exalted as the strong gods of the earth,*[15] so that his holy
merit is reflected also in the great blessings visited on his
family and house.[16] Scripture says: *The generation of the
righteous shall be blessed; glory* which does not fade *and
wealth* which does not disappear *shall be in his house,*[17] the
house built in heaven, not by manual labour but by the
holiness of his good works.

But I refrain from recounting further the memory of a
man as beloved by me as he was devoted to Christ, for I
recall that in my previous letter I wrote at length about
him. Moreover, in regard to Melania, the blessed mother of
this son, the root which is the equal of the holy branches,[18]
I can make no better or more pious a statement than your
holy person has so generously proclaimed and maintained.
For I, a sinner with impure lips,[19] could have made no
worthy comment since I am remote from the merits of her
faith and the virtue of her soul; whereas you, the famed
man of Christ, the teacher of Israel in the true Church,
were provided by God's grace, which guides things for the
better, as a more worthy eulogist of that soul so virile in
Christ. For, as I have said, with a spirit closer to hers you
beheld her mind strengthened with divine virtue, and with
a worthier eloquence you praised her combination of devotion and virtue.

4. You have graciously asked me what the activity of the blessed will be in the next world, after the resurrection of the body. But I consult you as a mentor and spiritual physician on the condition of my life here and now,[20] so that you may teach me to do what God wills, to walk in your steps after Christ, and first to die the death which the Gospel demands. By this we anticipate the dissolution of our flesh with a voluntary departure, retiring from the life of this world (which is so full of temptations, or, as you once expressed it in a letter to me, one long temptation) not by death but by deliberate decision.

So I pray that my paths may follow your steps in such a way that with your example I may loose my feet of their old sandals, break my bonds, and in freedom take joy in hastening along the way, so that I can attain that death to this world which you have embraced. You live for God because Christ lives in you. His life and death are seen in your body, heart, and lips; for your heart is ignorant of worldly things and your lips make no mention of the works of men, but the word of Christ abounds in your heart,[21] and the spirit of truth pours forth from your tongue, gladdening the city of God with the force of the celestial waters.[22]

5. Now what virtue fulfils this death in us except charity, which is *as strong as death?*[23] For charity so expunges and blots out the world from our eyes that it achieves the effect of death through our love for Christ. When we turn to Him, we turn away from this world; when we live in Him, we are *dead from the elements of this world.*[24] We do not fight the fight as men who live in the sight and enjoyment of those elements, for Christ's death is our portion, and we do not partake of His resurrec-

tion from the dead in glory unless we imitate His death on the cross by mortifying our bodily limbs and senses.[25]

As a result we live not by our will but by His, for His wish is our sanctification.[26] He died and rose again for us so that we should live not for ourselves but for Him;[27] for He died and rose again for us, and through His Spirit gave us the pledge of His promise,[28] just as He deposited in heaven the pledge of our life in the form of His body, which is a part of ours. So now *the Lord is my hope*, and *my substance*,[29] which was made by Him, is with Him and in Him and through Him, who took the form of my lowly body to fashion me to the body of His glory,[30] and to set me with Him in heaven. So, too, those who were worthy of eternal life have now for a long time been in the glory of His kingdom, so that, as Paul says,[31] they are with Him, abiding with Him. As the Lord Himself said to the Father: *I will that where I am, they also may be with Me.*[32] And you doubtless remember the words of the Psalm: *Blessed are they that dwell in Thy house; they shall praise Thee forever and ever.*[33]

6. I believe that this praise must be uttered by the voices of the saints in harmony, even though when they rise again their bodies are changed[34] and they become as the body of the Lord appeared after His Resurrection. In that Resurrection above all the living image of man's resurrection shone forth; for the Lord Himself appeared to all men as a mirror for their examination in that very body in which He had suffered and risen again. There is no doubt that after rising again in the same flesh with which He died and was buried, He approached men's eyes and ears frequently, and publicly performed all the tasks apposite to each of His limbs.

Moreover, if even the angels, who are created as pure spirit, are said to have tongues with which they certainly sing praises and render thanks unceasingly to their Creator, how much more so will men have them? True, their bodies after the resurrection will now be spiritual, yet the glorified flesh will retain all its limbs in all their shape and number. They will have tongues in their mouths, and when these speak they will give utterance to proclaim in words the praise of God or their own joyous feelings. Perhaps the Lord will also bestow on His saints in the world of His kingdom the additional grace and glory of singing with tongues and voices more powerful in accordance with their progress to a more blessed state by their blessed change of form. Since they will then be equipped with spiritual bodies, they may speak not human words but those angelic and heavenly ones which Paul[35] heard in Paradise. Perhaps he declared that those words could not be spoken by man because one of the rewards of the saints is the gift of new tongues. Men in this world cannot as yet employ these so that as immortal saints they may speak with tongues apposite to their glory.

Scripture says of the saints: *For they shall shout and sing a hymn.*[36] This will, of course, be in heaven, where they will be with their Lord, and *shall delight in abundance of peace.*[37] They will rejoice in sight of the throne, throwing before the feet of the Lamb offering-bowls and wreaths, and singing a new hymn to Him, joined with the choruses of Angels, Virtues, Dominations, and Thrones, so that with the Cherubim and Seraphim and the four beasts[38] they may sing in never-fading harmony: *Holy, holy, holy, Lord God of hosts,*[39] and the rest which you know.

7. So what I am saying is that I who am needy and poor,

your foolish little one whom you are accustomed to tolerate as a truly wise man does, am asking you to tell me your own knowledge or theory on this matter,[40] because I know that you are enlightened by the spirit of revelation from the very Leader and Fount of wise men. Just as you know the past and view the present, you should also assess the future. Express your views about these immortal voices of heavenly creatures as of those who dwell above the heavens in the sight of the Most High; decide by what kind of tongues their voices give utterance.

It is true that when Paul says: *If I speak with the tongues of angels,*[41] he is showing that angels have speech peculiar to their nature or (if you will pardon the word) to their race, and that this speech is higher than human sensation and speech accordingly as the created angels and their station transcend mortal dwellers and their earthly abode. Yet Paul may have used the phrase "tongues of angels" in distinguishing between voices and ways of speaking, just as when discoursing on the diversity of charisms he counts diverse kinds of tongues amongst graces bestowed, showing by this demonstration that individuals have certainly been given the power of speaking in the language of many races.[42]

But the voice of God, often issuing from a cloud to holy men, shows that there can be utterance without a tongue, the tongue being both the weak and the mighty member of the body.[43] It is in fact possible, because this member has been given by God the duty of speech, that He has termed the words and utterance of angels created without bodies their "tongues," just as Scripture usually assigns to God the limbs which correspond with the type of action He performs. Pray for me and instruct me.

8. Our most dear and sweet brother Quintus shows as much haste to return to you from here as he was tardy in coming to me from you. But this very note, containing more erasures than lines, tells of his insistence in demanding a letter; my pages show that the haste of the collector I have named is excessive. He came to ask for my reply on May 14, and got his dismissal before noon on the 15th.[44] You must decide whether I have praised or accused him by such testimony. Perhaps, or I should say undoubtedly, he will be judged worthy of praise rather than blame, for he has most rightly made haste to return to his light from this darkness. For by comparison with the light you are, I am darkness.

LETTER 46
To Rufinus[1]

Paulinus greets his brother Rufinus.

1. Even a short note from your loving self is a great refreshment to me, and I am renewed as a parched field by the dew in time of drought. So the letter, however brief, has given me new life because it is from you, brought by the servant of the sons we share. Yet I confess that I am also troubled by your information that you are still enduring Rome in the heat of anxiety and the uncertainty of delay.[2] The Lord grant that He give me joy with regard to your activity as soon as possible, so that my sympathy in your anxiety may be transformed to shared joy in your gladness, and I may still begin to hope for the reward of your presence here[3] once you begin to be definite on your decision or on God's will as it affects yourselves.

2. I was most pleased to receive your kindly advice, given with that affection with which you love me as yourself, that I should attend to Greek studies more closely. But I cannot do this unless the Lord chances to consent to my desire to enjoy your companionship over a reasonably long period. How can I improve in a language which I do not know if I am deprived of the means of learning it? I think that in the matter of translating Saint Clement[4] you have taken into account not only my general mental inadequacies but also the poverty of my ignorance; for I have rendered certain passages, where I could not understand or

translate the words, by taking or (to be more truthful) hazarding the general sense. So I need the mercy of God all the more to grant me fuller access to you, for this poor man considers it wealth to gather even the crumbs which fall from the rich man's table;[5] for the mouth of his famished heart is greedy for food.[6]

3. At the very moment of writing this, there has come to my notice a chapter of Genesis[7] which I chanced upon because it was part of the reading I set myself. In it Juda is blessed by Jacob. Since the Lord has granted me this most timely opportunity, I decided to knock on the door of your heart after the due time.[8] So if you love me, or rather because you have much love for me, I beg you to write to me about this. You know the meaning of these blessings of the patriarchs, and if you are aware of any deep significance which is worth my knowing, you would want me to grasp it. I am thinking particularly of the verse in which we read: *Tying his foal to the vineyard and the foal of his ass to the goat-hair covering.*[9] Whom do the foal, the ass, and the ass's foal represent? And why should this foal be tied to the vineyard, and the foal of the ass to the goat-hair covering?[10]

LETTER 47
To Rufinus[1]

Paulinus greets his brother Rufinus.

1. Though our son Cerealis has told me it is uncertain whether he will reach you in time on his return to Saint Peter's,[2] I have nonetheless decided that to fail to send you a letter by the hand of one equally dear to us both would be both reprehensible for me and melancholy for you. So I have preferred to risk the waste of a sheet of paper, should he fail to see you, rather than neglect an obligation, as I think would be the case if he did see you; so I have entrusted this letter not to chance but to faith. For I have faith in the Lord that my letter and our son are to make their way to you, since for those who desire good *all things will work together unto good,*[3] and since Cerealis sighs for you as you ought to be sighed for by one who understands how profitable to him is his fellowship with you. So I assume that his faith and devotion will ensure that his hunger will be *filled with good things,*[4] that he will reach you and stay with you, and that the saving protection which you both afford me before the Lord will be redoubled. You will be joined by a son, companion, disciple, and helper of outstanding goodness, and you yourself, who have been bestowed on him by the Lord to be his father and mentor in all that is good, will add to the effective power of prayers the strength of spiritual grace. But though your love makes me confident that when you

journey back to the east you will not be so hardhearted as to depart without visiting me, my sins make me afraid that the daughter of Babylon,[5] though so close to Nola, may distract your attention from me. So I commit to the Lord my longings and prayers that He may act according to my desires and not my merits, and guide your steps to me on the path of His peace; for those who do not walk that path are condemned *to a reprobate sense,*[6] much less do they deserve to long for you.

2. I have certainly never been forced through fear of a rebuff to desist from the incivility with which I beat on your door even at midnight,[7] and to feel a sense of shame and the need to limit my requests. So now I pass on to you this request preoccupying me, that you be kind enough to explain the blessings of the twelve patriarchs. You have made a beginning of it by sending some written pages explaining the prophecy concerning the person of Juda, with the threefold interpretation I asked for.[8] Now, I beg you, deign to explain the prophecy as applied to the other sons of Jacob. Thus I can through you become aware of the truth, and regard you as an authority of great grace and glory, if I can send back to my correspondents[9] a sublime reply from your spirit rather than a foolish one inspired by my own thought; for they think too highly of me because I received the grace to perform the work which I had to do.[10] May the grace of God remain with you as now forever, my loving brother in Christ.

LETTER 48

A Fragment[1]

. . . If today you were to look for bishops worthy of the Lord, however great the evils of our age you will find men who in spiritual progress are most worthy guardians of our faith and religion. There are Exuperius of Toulouse,[2] Simplicius at Vienne,[3] Amandus at Bordeaux,[4] Diogenianus at Albi, Dynamius at Angoulême, Venerandus at Auvergne,[5] Alethius at Cahors,[6] and now Pegasius at Périgeux. . . .[7]

LETTER 49

To Macarius[1]

Paulinus greets Macarius.

1. *It is honourable to confess the works of the Lord.*[2] This is my reason for writing this letter, because the affairs of Secundinianus, the paterfamilias whom I am introducing to your dear person through this letter, cannot be related without giving glory and praise to the Lord. As Christ Himself said in the Gospel: *My Father worketh until now, and I work.*[3] This is what He now does; the good Lord never ceases to arouse and truly to challenge our faith with clear proofs of His truth. So, as Scripture says, the divine Saviour shows Himself to us by different proofs,[4] and works on our behalf on land and sea. By the acts He performs in individuals, He tends the faith and salvation of many.

Observe how remarkable and praiseworthy a work the Lord Jesus and His holy angels performed in one old man, for I am taking up with you the case of the friend and brother I have mentioned, a man of faith in Christ. Last winter in Sardinia, in company with other shipowners he was compelled to make his ship available to take on grain to be transported to the granaries of the imperial treasury, and under pressure from the state authorities he ordered his laden vessel to set sail before the summer weather, not waiting for the time when the regular supplies were sent.[5]

He told me how immediately a storm arose on the sea

off Sardinia, hurling back from the course they had set and breaking on the shore a fleet of many ships which had rashly put out from the harbour. The crew of Secundinianus' ship tried to drop anchor in a Sardinian area which they call The Pillows,[6] to avoid being likewise dashed against the shore. But the force of the storm got the upper hand, and the sailors in panic cut the ropes and let down the small boat,[7] either to lend the ship greater steadiness by refloating[8] the anchors and embedding them more deeply,[9] or to remove themselves, if they could, from the peril in which the ship stood. But then the storm, so the story goes, snatched them, frail refuge of ship's boat and all, on to the rocks, and buried them in submerging waves. One old man, assigned to bailing out the water, had been left behind out of the whole crew. Either they had forgotten him in their panic, or they held his life unimportant. Meanwhile the ship, bereft of sailors and anchors, was carried out to sea.

2. The old man had not realised that he had been left behind. When he felt the ship being tossed and rolled, he came out of the ship's hold and saw a scene of complete desolation, "with sea and sky all around him."[10] His loneliness increased the poor man's fear and danger, and he spent six days and nights without food. *His tears were his bread day and night.*[11] Then, when he was more eager for death than life, when he longed for his torment to end with the flight of his soul from his body, the merciful and pitying Lord deigned to draw near and give him life with the food of the Word.

He himself relates and still weeps over the happy nature of his danger, and one cannot hear without inner tears and joy of the spirit how he was accosted by Christ's approach and strengthened by His exhortation, how on Christ's orders he chopped down the mast, on the removal of which the safety of the ship then depended.[12] In his solitary and weakened state he had not dared to take in hand a task which many men of great strength can scarcely accomplish without danger to themselves and the ship, but now at God's word he dared to do it. At only the second impact of the axe—and it was not so much a blow as a light touch, for his was an old man's hand—the mast leapt so far forward from the blow that it was hurled far from the ship into the sea, where it fell safely.

Then the Lord hailed him by the name Victor, and ordered him merely to go through the motions of doing the various jobs which the sea-swell and the ship's provision demanded, when a foremast[13] had to be fitted or the bilge water bailed out. And in the abundant and varied grace conferred by divine miracles on this old man, we must not I think leave unmentioned the gift of God which conferred on him the name by which he is known in his new life, by which he is enrolled both by men and by angels. For he who was called Valgius by the family name is now called Victor by the Lord; and he is victorious in the Lord who has conferred on him a name suited to the work He has performed in him. That is, he triumphed both at sea through Christ's help over storms and shipwreck, and recently on land through his grace over sin and the devil, so that he who was to be wholly made new in Christ continued neither with his old name nor in his old man.[14]

3. What wondrous protection, what unutterable devotion the Lord of salvation shows! With a gentle hand He first stroked the old man in case he should wake up in fear, then He roused him by tweaking his ear, in case he should

be inert through sleep and rise too slowly to perform the necessary tasks. As soon as Valgius made the slightest effort, he saw the work performed by the hands of angels just as he was beginning his attempt. He had scarcely laid hands on a rope to pull it when the foresail was already billowing out on its beams, or the ship was under sail. When water poured through the holed timbers and tried to sink the ship, the use of a small scoop a couple of times emptied the water and made the ship dry, so that he had nothing to do, and he stood astonished that his work had been performed for him without any effort on his part, and his tasks taken over by a hidden hand—if "hidden" is the right word for the hand which lent such obvious help. Even the workers were not withdrawn from the ingenuous sight of that most innocent old man, for on numerous occasions he saw armed soldiers from the army of heaven on watch on the ship, and performing all the sailors' duties.

Indeed, none but angels were suitable sailors for that ship, for its rudder was the Helmsman of the universe. Yes, the Lord Himself sat at the stern, now with his own shining countenance and gleaming hair, as described in the Apocalypse,[15] now in the revered appearance of His friend and confessor, my lord and our common patron Felix; in nautical parlance, He sat *ad temones*,[16] or rather He took the rudder's place, for the ship had lost it altogether together with the anchors and the sailors on that wreck-littered shore. How fortunate was its misfortune, since in place of all its lost crew and tackle it obtained either the Lord's martyr or the Lord of that martyr![17] The old man recounts with tears of joy how he used to throw himself at the feet now of the Lord Himself, now of the martyr steering for him; and in still more intimate fashion, at the invitation of the Lord he found a blessed cushion on which to lean his head, on His sacred bosom and lap which was wafted by divine fragrance.

4. Can we now doubt that the patriarchs open their hearts to faithful servants in Christ, since on this occasion God in His boundless goodness hugged this catechumen on His own lap or on that of His saint? For there was present also in the person of His saint He who as you know said to the Father: *The glory which Thou hast given to Me I have given to them, that they may be one as We also are one, I in them and Thou in Me.*[18] Again, to the apostles, in whom He addressed the whole of His body, He said: *Behold, I am with you all the days of My life, even to the consummation of the world.*[19] This His power proves every day through the hands of His apostles and martyrs working with outstanding virtues, so that we may believe that the Son of God, our Lord Jesus, reigning in heaven on the right hand of the Father[20] after His Resurrection from the dead, is *Lord of the living not of the dead.*[21]

So when he cherished the old sailor in the appearance of His holy confessor, He was present Himself in His saint, soothing the weary, downcast man with kindly words, and refreshing him with the Word as much as with food, for He is *the living Bread which came down from heaven to give food to all flesh.*[22] He loves His own creation in the shape of every man, and so far as in Him lies *will have every man to be saved;*[23] for He who gives life and is wholly Life *hath made not death, neither hath He pleasure in the destruction of the living.*[24] He prefers *mercy not sacrifice;*[25] He who made all men does not regard their persons, but judges in accordance with their merits, for *God is our Judge.*[26]

5. Accordingly, in God's eyes this sailor was no more contemptible because of the disaster of the shipwreck or because of his old age and need. He roused Christ and excited the bowels of God's mercy by all those attributes which had caused his comrades to despise him. For His eyes are always on the poor.[27] Assuredly *this poor man cried and the Lord heard him.*[28] Perhaps the Lord and the very cause of his danger dictated to him the words of the prophets so that he could pray and cry out: "*Save me, O Lord, for the waters are come in even unto my soul. I am come into the depth of the sea; let not the tempest of water drown me, nor the deep swallow me up.*[29] *Let Thy mercy speedily prevent me,*[30] before *I stick fast in the mire of the deep,* and *the pit shut her mouth on me.*[31] *Look Thou upon me, for I am alone and poor,* and *am become like to a pelican of the wilderness, like a night raven in the house,* and *as a sparrow alone on a housetop*[32] so am I in my ship.*"

The Lord heard and had mercy on him, and *sent angels to surround him and delivered him.*[33] He commanded the storm and stilled it into a breeze.[34] *He rebuked the sea,* and *its waves were still.*[35] He led him through many waters, and he *saw the works of the Lord and His wonders in the deep.*[36] *He fed him with the fat of wheat,* and when Christ spoke with him *he was filled with honey out of the rock.*[37] He who blessed the poor in spirit looked mercifully on that humble man; He who promised consolation to mourners spoke to him as he wept; He who gives fulness to those who hunger and thirst after justice, He who is Himself Bread and Justice and the Fountain of life, fed and watered this failing man from His own store.[38] He took pity on Valgius with the same devotion with which He pitied all who toss on the sea of this world, when He rendered to the Father the devotion which He extended *even to the death of the cross.*[39] For one man is part of the whole and the whole is the shape of the one Man and the cause which He espouses.

6. In short, Christ governed not only the ship but also Valgius for whose sake He guarded the ship. In him He performed the separate tasks of body and spirit. He bade him take untroubled rest at night, and to watch anxiously by day, and promised to keep guard as he slept and to aid him as he watched. You will surely perceive in these words that love of the Lord by which He ever fosters our hope without relaxing our anxiety, and lends aid to our weak flesh without our spirit ceasing to be willing.[40] So he allowed the exhausted old man to sleep but without relaxing his anxiety, however old and however wearied he was with the task of keeping watch, for He did not wish him to sink into sluggish slumber and to sleep in mind as well as in body.

It was for fear of this that one holy man said: *Enlighten my eyes, O Lord, that I never sleep in death.*[41] For mental torpor is a sickness close to death. And then the enemy will say: *I have prevailed against him,*[42] if sleep also overtakes the eyes of the mind. So we realise that before the old man stood He who said to His followers as their eyes kept closing: *Watch ye and pray that ye enter not into temptation;*[43] and again, as they kept watch, as He was confident that they were roused and lively, He told them: *Sleep ye now, and take your rest.*[44] In another passage He teaches us that these words have reference as much to steadfastness of faith as to physical sleep, when He says: *Have confidence, for I have overcome the world.*[45] For a man obtains true repose if, steadfast in faith and untroubled by any enemy

through the victory of Christ, he enjoys peace in harmonious love. *For He is our Rest*[46] who is our Peace, who keeps
watch for us that He may rest in us, and bids us watch
now to obtain eternal repose.

7. The Lord Himself deigned to perform in the single
person of this old man these services of love which He
wishes to be performed throughout the world. Mingling
sternness and sweet words, checking His kindness with the
rein of fear, He tweaked his ear to shake off torpid sleep,
and proffered His lap to provide repose forever.

The man was sundered from not only land but also
human intercourse for twenty-three days. He was the
plaything of all the winds, an exile from every land, a
visitor to various seas, cut off from the human race. I ask
you, exhausted as he was by hunger and age and fear,
could he ever have lasted out by his own resources amongst
the waves and beasts of the deep in the shifting shelter of
that vacillating ship? Who then can fail to realise that God
was within him? And which God do I mean? Surely the
God *who alone doth wonderful things, who calleth those
things that are not as those that are.*[47] By His help that ship,
cut off by the entire ocean, sailed to safety; by the help of
the Helmsman unseen, that apparently empty ship advanced with its heavy burden, enclosing in its hold a man
and its cargo of grain. It floated like the ark on the flood,
pregnant with the seeds of the world;[48] tossed on more
than one sea, it changed its course with the wild weather.

8. First it was driven towards Rome, and beheld the
lighthouse in the harbour of the capital;[49] next it skirted
Campania for a huge distance, and when the winds shifted
it flew over to the shores of Africa. Pulling back from
there it raced over to Sicily. Around Sicily the straits are

rough and high (they say that the number of islands causes this), and even with a helmsman journeys are hazardous for ships. Yet amidst these dangers and obstacles afforded by the islands the old man sailed by without effort on a direct route unscathed, so that the boat seemed endowed with divine powers, avoiding the hazards and seeking the right course of its own accord, as if it were wise with God-sent inspiration. So in a salutary, experienced manner it weaved its way past scenes of inevitable destruction.

Finally God showed pity, and on the twenty-third day it was to put an end to its wanderings and dangers on the shores of Lucania.[50] As it approached land the eternal Lord willed His unwearying goodness to perform its miracles to the very end of the voyage He had undertaken; so with the silent instigation of His inspiration, He induced some fishermen to put out from the shore in two skiffs and meet the ship. When they saw it from a distance they were terrified at first sight and fled; later they said that it seemed to them to be full of armed men and like a fast pirate vessel. But subsequently they were drawn back by the loud repeated shouts of that old man of ours. After taking stock of the situation, and under the guidance of the Lord, they realised that they had nothing to fear from the ship to which they had been summoned. When they drew near to it, they could scarcely believe the old man's word, or the evidence of their own eyes when they boarded her, that the vessel which to their distant gaze had been crowded should be empty of soldiers.

On board the old man welcomed them with a meal which the Lord had bidden him prepare the previous day, and he loaded them with the large reward of abundant food belonging to the sailors who had perished. Delighted with this payment, they offered the service of their small boats, and drew the ship with a towrope into their harbour as if it were the survivor of a grievous war and the recipient of a wreath after the contest, for it had survived the shipwreck and conquered winds and waves. How would those empty minds, which by the false worship of their own imaginings consecrated in fiction the construction of the ship of the ill-fated Argonauts, and which even today believe that they see the ship in heaven and count it amongst the companies of stars,[51] have reacted to the achievement of this ship? With equal madness they venerate the ship which conveyed the Epidaurian serpent, while the snake himself whose physical appearance they bore mocked at them.[52]

9. Let us, however, take no thought for what is false and foreign; let us not mingle the lies and poison of those who perish with the light of our truth. We have our own ships, so that we can more worthily cite examples which are true and our own. We have the ark of Noe, the ship to Tharsis, the ship of the man of Tarsus.[53] Now the ship from which the whale received the fleeing prophet to punish and to protect him can be compared to this ship of Secundinianus in the danger it sustained before the drawing of lots;[54] but the third ship which I exemplified accords with the one I am describing, because it had on board an apostle and martyr, and through him and in him entertained Christ, as when Christ entrusted to Paul the whole ship's complement when it was doomed to founder.[55]

10. So let us keep before our minds and inwardly look on that most noble vision of God's work. We see a single ship delivered from the wreck of many vessels and all their crews; and one old man roams over various seas—a solitary ship upon the ocean, a solitary figure sailing in her. She

will appear before our eyes as that ark of the flood which is the image of the Church, sailing securely over the whole world between the flood waters of heaven and of the deep, as the sea presented everywhere its single face extending over the submerged earth.

This ship represented the appearance of the ark in many ways, if in slighter measure. As the ark was filled with the seeds of all forms of life, so the ship was filled with various produce, for apart from the state cargo there was more on board representing the pay and possessions of the sailors. The ark took on a single household for the renewal of the human race; this ship took on a single man to gain the faith of many. To the ark a dove brought the branch of peace; to this ship the Lamb proffered peace. A bird entered the ark to figure the Holy Spirit; and Christ entered this ship under the image of His confessor.

Let us look back at Jonas' ship, too, and we shall see that it was preserved by a greater miracle and a more abundant gift of that same strength. For Jonas' ship was saved with the loss of one man, whereas this ship was preserved with the loss of all save one survivor. The ship in this case seems to have imitated the whale which devoured the prophet alive and did him no harm; for it bore him in the same manner enclosed in its belly over the depths of the sea, and set him on land safe and sound, just as the beast refrained from eating its booty, and dislodged him undigested from the cell of its spacious stomach with coughing spasms,[56] regurgitating him for God on whose order it had swallowed him. Once the mystery of the Passion which brings salvation had been unfolded, it vomited him forth on the third day to engender hope in the Resurrection.[57]

11. Happier was the crew of Paul's ship, which was en-

trusted to the Apostle, though not because of the crew's own merits; for that crew, too, deserved to be wrecked for having despised his advice when setting sail. But we can glory in the works of God no less in the case of this ship of Secundinianus, for though its crew had no spokesman like Paul, Paul's God was within its sole sailor as Helmsman. Through him the ship merited deliverance to ensure the salvation of one innocent man, whereas the ship which had first taken on board *the chosen vessel*[58] in chains, did not gain this privilege, but was condemned for its contempt and captivity of Paul since it was charged with imprisoning him.

But the crew of Paul's ship seems to have been delivered through the mystery of grace, so that they might emerge naked from the wreck of the condemned ship. The purpose was that they might be freed from the sin of that first ship which symbolises the flesh of Adam, purified by the waters through which they made their escape,[59] lightened of all the luggage which they had thrown into the sea, the type of worldly burdens, and stripped of the garment of the old man which is wet and weighed down with the waters of sin; and so an undamaged, sound ship could take them aboard, which showed itself full of the faith of the Church, and conveyed them safely to harbour and to Rome.

These events likewise are the medium of mystical tokens. For the change of ship represents renewal of life in Christ, and the harbour of salvation is the Church, and as Greece attests the name Rome means "strength."[60] So let us bless God, and exult in *our God, who dwelleth on high and looketh down on the low things, whose delight is not in the strength of the horse nor in the tents of a man, but in*

the humble and *them that fear Him*.[61] As He showed also
in the case of this old man, *He healeth all the broken of
heart and bindeth up their bruises*.[62]

12. But I chatter too much, my brother. I know it, but
I beg you to bear with me for a few words more, for I wish
to ask you if there is any worldly distinction which you
would prefer to have conferred on you more than the
kindness of God experienced by this old man. Do those
men seem to you[63] happier who are bright with purple,
who sip from jewelled cups, who swell within a toga, who
are adorned with embroidered tunic? who lord it over their
fellow mortals, many of them their betters, but who are
slaves to their desires and possessions? who show arrogance
to God because of God's gifts, who are poor in Christ but
rich in sin, barren in life but fruitful in death?

What disadvantage was it to the old man, I ask you, to
have been the one of least account among the sailors, the
one who bailed out the bilge water, who was considered a
helpless Sardinian idiot? For he was clothed in skins sewn
together[64] when the Lord of virtues, King of glory, enriched him with His words, enlightened him with His
appearance, and gave him rest in His bosom; and what certainly endeared him to the Lord was the fact that with his
goat-hair garment he was imitating the sheepskin of Elias
and the clothing of His precursor John.[65]

A great proportion of mankind accounts it such a privilege to see an earthly king at close quarters, and to be
sprayed with his words however condescending, that if
they cannot get it any other way they incur financial loss
to purchase it, and once they have obtained it they are
oblivious of both others and themselves. How much more
blessed than they in dignity is he whom the King of kings

honoured! How much more noble is the nobility of him
whom Christ acknowledged! How much greater[66] is the
wealth of him with whom were comparable the great
blessings of numerous saints; for like Israel he saw Christ,
like Moses he spoke face to face with the King of heaven,
and he rested in Christ's bosom with an intimacy almost
equal to John's when the apostle reclined on His breast.[67]
And finally he received a new name like those friends of
God with whom you are well acquainted amongst the
patriarchs and apostles.[68]

I asked you a moment ago whether you preferred to be
accorded the grace of Valgius rather than all the glory of
this world; I myself believe that the very *rulers of this
darkness*,[69] if they had the merit to see, would prefer the
most happy disaster of our impoverished old man to their
own wretched successes and joys which they must forever
bewail.

13. Perhaps you are asking by what merits this aged
sailor, who had lingered all his life in the darkness of
ignorance and was a stranger both to works of righteousness and to the knowledge of truth, appears to have obtained what is readily granted to but few labourers, even
though they bear the weight and heat of the whole day
from the morning watch even until night.[70] Paul will certainly give you your reply: *The graces and gifts of God
are without repentance*, and *it is not by works that all flesh
will be justified*.[71] There is a time for grace, and faith is
accounted for justification,[72] for every day children are
raised up for Abraham from stones.[73] *For now is the acceptable time, now is the day of salvation*[74] on which we
offer victims of peace and praise; and *an afflicted spirit is a
sacrifice to God*.[75] God's temple is in man,[76] salvation lies

in a heart that believes, the holy of holies is in a breast that is purified.

So God, *who does not despise an afflicted and humbled man*,[77] has Himself accepted our aged friend as *a sacrifice for an odour of sweetness*,[78] pleasing to Him because of his natural goodness. For through his innate simplicity he is said to have been always so pure of mind that he did not know how to sin. Though in extreme old age, he is still young in physique and a tiny boy in wickedness,[79] and is a child in mind as well as in grace. For, as I have said earlier, he has lately been reborn in Christ and dedicated to the Lord, through whom is life,[80] and through whom he has escaped the waters of death.

14. So welcome him with joy in the Lord as *the good odour of Christ*,[81] as a lamb born *in the month of the new corn*.[82] I who am the shepherd of a small flock[83] make this gift of one I greatly cherish. I pass him over to your affectionate person as a spiritual gift, a spotless lamb with snow-white wool newly brought forth by Mother Church. I believed that there was none more worthy of such a gift than you, for by the grace and action of God you had come to acknowledge and welcome Him. I seem to picture already the rejoicing and admiration and faith with which you will both hear of and look upon the man with whom, as you will recall, angels have voyaged, the man for whom a martyr steered the ship, who slept in Christ's lap, whose ear Christ pulled, to whom Christ gave a name. I freely admit to you that my loving heart was almost cruel to the old man in vehemently admiring and cherishing such notable works of God achieved in a man of our time. I have so incessantly fingered his ear that I have almost worn it away; I should have liked even to cut off a part of that

one ear, except that such a keepsake would have meant wounding him!

No other sentiment draws men to Jerusalem but the desire to see and touch the places where Christ was physically present, and to be able to say from their very own experience: *We have gone into His tabernacle, and have adored in the places where His feet stood.*[84] Though a deeper meaning may be read into this passage, we must not ignore the simple and literal sense when apposite. So if the desire is a truly religious one to see the places in which Christ walked, suffered, rose again, and ascended into heaven, and if there is a blessing in taking and keeping a pinch of dust from these places or a mere mote from the wood of the cross, just think how much greater and fuller is the grace of beholding an old man yet alive who is the walking proof of divine Truth! If the manger of His birth, the river of His baptism, the garden of His betrayal,[85] the palace of His condemnation, the column of His scourging, the thorns of His crowning, the wood of His crucifixion, the stone of His burial, the places of His resurrection and ascension are famed as recalling God's former presence, and if living proofs in lifeless objects demonstrate the ancient truth for today's belief, then with what reverence must this man be regarded, with whom God deigned to converse, before whom God's face was not concealed, to whom Christ revealed now His martyr and now His own person?

Valgius is the living earth on which we see impressed the traces of the Lord's body, if with the eye of faith and spiritual sight we scrutinise what Christ's bosom and Christ's hand have touched in him, if we frequently stroke with our hands the gray hair which often reclined on the

Lord's knee and grew warm in the Lord's embrace, if we repeatedly touch that tender ear which heavenly fingers pulled when the Lord played His joke.

15. My brother, you now have my gift. Take it in the spirit of charity, and if my offensive garrulity nauseates you, you must restrain your disgust through the grace of the Lord and the charm of this heavenly story. I am sure that you will seek and desire some means of demonstrating the love you bear for Christ towards this man. An opportunity lies open for you. You must direct the enthusiasm of your dutiful devotion and show all the love that your faith can muster towards Valgius' patron Secundinianus, to whom the almighty Christ has restored his ship safe and sound when he despaired of its safety.

You will be performing the work of Christ. Do not allow the envy of the devil, through the agency of a wicked man, to deprive or to continue to deprive Secundinianus of what God restored to him from the shipwreck. I hear that it was the agent[86] of a Christian, our brother Postumianus,[87] who seized and stripped the ship. It had run aground on the Bruttian shore[88] where the estate of the senator is washed by the waves, and the bailiff showed himself greedier than the sea, practising piracy[89] on land without a pirate ship. Even now it lies empty on that shore to bear witness to the loss of its cargo which was vainly preserved on the sea and lost on land. Numerous complaints have been lodged with the provincial judge about this act of brigandage, but our Pharaoh there has hardened his heart—perhaps so that there may be a miraculous outcome.[90] When the bailiff was summoned to court by officials, he first offered resistance, and later fled to Rome.

This is the emergency which has caused my dear Secundinianus to journey to Rome by land in company with his sole sailor. I do not doubt that our brother Postumianus will be stirred by your intervention, and by his own faith and righteousness. This is why we must interfere by such action. You will certainly act without my urging to defend and to excuse with equal effort before that excellent senator and Christian that guilty servant of his. So the pirate's reward may be the avoidance of punishment, and we shall be content to get back from him the gifts bestowed by God.

LETTER 50

To Augustine[1]

Paulinus greets Augustine.

1. I do not want you to have to write to me without receiving the pleasure of a letter, so I shall put forward some observations on the few topics which occur to me as the bearer of this letter is impatient to get to the ship. His haste makes me write at speed. If my queries are easily answered and seem opaque only to me, none of your wise sons who happen to be with you at the time of your reading my letter should laugh at my foolishness. Instead, with the kindness of brotherly charity, they must be indulgent and instruct me, so that I may become one of those with vision, who with minds enlightened by your teaching meditate on the wonders of the Lord's Law.[2]

2. Tell me, then, learned doctor of Israel, what is the meaning of the words in the fifteenth Psalm: *To the saints, who are in His land, He hath made wonderful all His desires amongst them. Their infirmities were multiplied, afterwards they made haste?*[3] What saints does the Psalmist mean, these saints on earth? Could they be the Jews who as sons of Abraham's flesh but not the sons of promise are cut off from the seed which was called in Isaac?[4] And so does he call them saints on earth because they are holy by physical descent, but earthly in their lives and thoughts —knowledgeable in earthly things,[5] ageing *in the oldness of the letter* rather than winning fresh birth *as a new crea-*

ture,[6] because they did not accept Him by whom *the former things have passed away and things are made new?*[7]

So perhaps he calls them saints in this Psalm just as in the Gospel He calls them the just, when he says: *I am not come to call the just, but sinners.*[8] By the just He means those who boast in the holiness of their race and in the letter of the Law,[9] those who are told: *Do not boast of Abraham as your father. For God is able from these stones to raise up sons of Abraham.*[10] These just men are typified in the Pharisee, who hymned his own works of justice in the temple, bringing them to the Lord's notice as if He were unaware of them.[11] He did not pray to have his prayer heard, but demanded, so to say, the reward due to his good works. Yes, his works were good, but still unwelcome to God because pride destroyed what justice had built. Nor did he make this demand silently, but in a loud voice, so that it became clear that he was not addressing the ears of God since he wished men to hear him as well. So since he was pleasing to himself he did not please God, for God has scattered the bones of men who are pleasing to themselves;[12] *they have been confounded*, says the Psalmist, *because God hath despised them*, but He does not despise a humble and afflicted heart.[13]

3. In brief, then, in the parable of the Gospel which compares the characters of the Pharisee and the publican, the Lord is clearly showing what He accepts and what He rejects in a man. As Scripture puts it: *God resisteth the proud but to the humble He giveth grace;*[14] so He proclaims that the publican left the temple more justified after confessing his sins than did the Pharisee after submitting his account for his just deeds. Now it was right that the one who praised himself left God's presence rejected, for

though he boasted of his knowledge of the Law by his very name, he had forgotten what the Lord says through His prophet: *Over whom shall I dwell but over him that is humble and silent and that trembleth at my words?*[15] But he that accuses himself with contrite heart is received and obtains pardon for the sins he confessed because of the grace of humility, and that holy Pharisee ("holy" in the sense that the Jews are holy) bears off the burden of his sins through boasting of his own holiness.

Surely those Jews of whom Paul speaks are in the image of the Pharisees: *Seeking to establish their own justice,* which comes from the Law, *they have not submitted themselves to the justice of God,*[16] which springs from the faith *which was reputed to Abraham our father unto justice,* and not from works.[17] For Abraham put his faith in God because of His omnipotence, and in God's eyes the truly just man is he *who lives by faith,*[18] who is a saint not on earth but in heaven because he walks *not according to the flesh but according to the spirit,*[19] whose *conversation is in heaven,*[20] who boasts not in the circumcision of the flesh but in that of the heart, which is performed not by the letter but invisibly by the spirit so that *his praise is not of men but of God.*[21]

4. Secondly, when the Psalmist in the same verse adds: *He hath made wonderful His desires amongst them,*[22] I think he means by this that for them first He lit the lamp of the Law and gave rules of living. For, as he says, *He has made His ways known to Moses and His wills to the children of Israel.*[23] Moreover, it was amongst them that He brought to pass the very mystery of His love, when He, God, was born in the flesh of a virgin amongst their race, and became Man of their flesh from the seed of David.

Amongst them, too, He demonstrated the strength of His healing which He performed in them and in their presence, for not merely was He disbelieved in these acts but even blasphemed by them when they said: "If this man was from God he would not heal on the Sabbath, and he casts out devils only in the name of Beëlzebub the prince of devils."[24] It was because of this attitude, blinded with stubborn irreverence, that *their infirmities were multiplied*[25] together with their darkness.

5. But what meaning have the words: *Afterwards they made haste?*[26] Does it mean "to repentance," as in the case of those in the Acts of the Apostles whose consciences were pricked by Peter's teaching and who believed in Him whom they had crucified?[27] For they hastened to be cleansed of so great a sin and hastened to the gift of grace. Or is the explanation that, because the soul's virtues are strengthened by faith in and love of God, and those impious men were bereft of both, *their weaknesses were multiplied* because their souls were seized by mortal illness arising from the wickedness of their crimes? For Christ is the Light and Life of those who believe, and health is beneath His wings.[28] So it is not surprising that the darkness and the infirmities are multiplied and bring death to those who have not accepted the Life and Light, and have not wished to linger under His wings. As He frequently attests with tears in His Gospel, He has often sought to gather them under His wings as a hen gathers her chicks, but they have refused.

So since their infirmities are multiplied, where have they hastened to? Perhaps to clamour for the crucifixion of the Lord, and by their wicked cries to extract it from an unwilling Pilate, so that they might *fill up the measure of their fathers*[29] and might themselves kill the Lord of prophets as their fathers killed the prophets themselves who announced that He was coming as Saviour of the world. That was how they *afterwards made haste*, for their feet were swift to shed blood. Affliction and failure attended their paths, and they did not know the path of peace which is Christ, who says: *I am the Way.*[30]

6. In the next Psalm I should like an explanation of the meaning of the words: *Their belly is filled from thy hidden stores. They are filled with pork* (or, as I am told is the version of some psalters: *They are filled with children*) *and they have left to their little ones what remained of their substance.*[31]

7. There is another Psalm which often causes me surprise when I consider that this is a son speaking to his Father. It is the fifty-eighth, where the Psalmist has been saying of the hostile Jews: *Behold, they shall speak with their mouth, and a sword is on their lips,*[32] but a little later he says: *Slay them not, lest at any time they forget Thy law. Scatter them by Thy power and bring them down, O Lord.*[33] This we observe is fulfilled in the case of the Jews even up to our day; for they have been brought low from their ancient fame, and they live without temple, without sacrifices, and without prophets, scattered through all nations. But we should not be surprised that Christ already, through His prophet, prayed for a reprieve from death for those for whom He prayed also at the very hour of His Passion, as they led Him to crucifixion. Then He said: *Father, forgive them, for they know not what they do.*[34]

But the following words of the Psalmist: *Lest at any time they forget Thy law*, which seems to imply that their life would be essential even without belief in the Gospel, I confess I find puzzling. How does a life of recalling and meditating on the Law help them to attain salvation which is won only by faith? But perhaps by such honouring of the Law, or of the race of Abraham, the letter of the ancient Law may survive even in the earthly portion of his bodily seed, which we are told is as numerous as grains of sand on the seashore,[35] and perhaps some men by a study of the Law may be enlightened to gain faith in Christ, who is the end of the Law[36] and the prophets, and shines forth prefigured and prophesied in all their books.

Alternatively the reason may be that from those impious men is to come forth the generation of the elect who will be chosen and signed, twelve thousand from each tribe.[37] The revelation of the blessed John bears to them this testimony from the mouth of the proclaiming angel, that they will be attached more intimately to the retinue of the eternal King, wholly spotless and having no part in the human condition. Of these thousands John specifically says: *These will follow the Lamb whithersoever He goeth, because they did not defile themselves with women; for they are virgins.*[38]

8. The sixty-sixth Psalm contains amongst other problems this verse which I find most difficult: *But God shall break the heads of his enemies, the hairy crowns of them that walk on in their sins.*[39] What does this mean, that "their hairy crowns" should "walk on in their sins"? The Psalmist did not say "the crowns of their heads," but "the crowns of their hair," yet hair possesses no feeling. Does he wish to show that man is filled with sins? Scripture says: *The whole heart is sad from the feet unto the head.*[40]

A little later in the Psalm there is the verse: . . . *the tongue of thy dogs be red with the same from thy ene-*

mies.[41] What does he mean by "the same"? Can "the hounds of God" here designate the Gentiles whom Christ Himself calls "dogs" in the Gospel?[42] Or perhaps he terms "hounds of God" those who can be reckoned as such, for there are some nominally Christian Gentiles whose fate is with the unbelievers, because their deeds deny the God whom they verbally worship.[43]

9. So far, then, some problems from the Psalms. Now let me mention a minor problem in Paul. In his letter to the Ephesians he repeats a point made in another letter about grades or ranks of position when the Holy Spirit of God creates different kinds of graces. *And He gave some apostles, and some prophets, and other some evangelists, and other some pastors and doctors for the perfecting of the saints,*[44] and so on. I should like you to specify for me the distinctions in this group of different titles, and tell me the peculiar duties and graces of each office. What is particular to apostles, to prophets, to evangelists, to pastors, to doctors? For I see that amongst all these different offices a similar, almost identical duty of teaching was carried out. I take it that "the prophets" whom Paul listed after the apostles are not those who came chronologically earlier than the apostles, but those who immediately succeeded them and were by grace given the power to interpret the Scriptures, to see into men's minds, and to foretell the future. Such a vision Agabus had; he foretold the impending famine, and the future sufferings of Saint Paul at Jerusalem he both revealed in words and indicated by gesticulating with Paul's girdle.[45] I particularly desire to know the distinction between pastors and doctors, because both these terms are normally applied to those with a position of authority in the Church.

10. Next, a remark of Paul's to Timothy: *I desire, therefore, first of all that supplications, prayers, intercessions and thanksgivings be made for all men.*[46] Please explain to me the difference between these various terms, because all that he bade Timothy do seems apposite to the duty of prayer.

11. Then again I have an enquiry and a request for your explanation of what he said to the Romans. I confess that I cannot see at all the meaning of Paul's comment on the Jews where he says: *As concerning the Gospel, indeed, they are enemies for your sake; but as touching the election they are most dear for the sake of the fathers.*[47] How can the Jews be enemies for the sake of us Gentiles who are believers—as if Gentiles could not have believed unless the Jews had refused to believe! Was God, the sole Creator of all, *who will have all men to be saved and to come to the knowledge of the truth,*[48] not able to win both Jew and Gentile without obtaining one in place of the other?

And then the *most dear for the sake of the fathers.* How and why are they "most dear" if they are unbelievers and obstinate enemies of God? *Have I not hated them, O God, who hated Thee?* says the Psalmist. *And shall I not pine away because of Thy enemies? I have hated them with a perfect hatred.*[49] I am quite sure it is the Father's voice speaking to His son through the prophet in that same Psalm, in which earlier he has spoken about the role of believers: *But to me Thy friends, O God, are made exceedingly honourable; their principality is exceedingly strengthened.*[50] Now if the Jews are *most dear for the sake of the fathers,* how does this help them to attain salvation, which is gained only by faith and the grace of Christ? What purpose is there in their being loved when they must be condemned because their lack of belief puts them at odds with the faith of their fathers, the patriarchs and prophets, and makes them hostile to Christ's Gospel? So if they are *most dear* to God, how will they perish? And if they do not believe, how will they fail to perish? Yet, if they are loved *for the sake of the fathers* without merit of their own, how can they fail also to obtain salvation *for the sake of the fathers?* However, even if Noe, Daniel, and Job are in their midst they will not succeed in saving their impious sons, but they only shall be delivered.[51]

12. There is another still more obscure point which you must bring out of the depths for me, and guide into the shallows. I cannot understand at all the meaning of this passage in the letter to the Colossians: *Let no man seduce you, willing in humility and religion of angels, walking in the things he hath not seen, in vain puffed up by the sense of his flesh, and not holding the head.*[52] Which angels does he mean? If they are the hostile and wicked ones, what is their religion or what is their humility, and who is this seducing master who, under cover of some sort of angelic religion, teaches what he has not seen as if he had seen and understood it? I suppose the heretics are meant, for they follow and bring forth the teachings of the demonic angels; their devices are given life by the spirit of those demons, they fashion apparitions unseen as if they have seen them, and by baneful arguments instil them into hearts perversely credulous. These are the men who do not "hold the head" which is Christ the Fount of truth; all that opposes His teaching is mad. These are *the blind leading the blind,*[53] and I believe it is they to whom Scripture refers: *They have forsaken Me, the Fountain of living water, and have digged to themselves broken cisterns that hold no water.*[54]

13. Paul then adds in the next chapter: *Touch not, taste not, handle not. Which all are unto destruction by the very use, according to the precepts and the doctrines of men. Which things have indeed a shew of wisdom in superstition and humility in not sparing the body; not in any honour to the filling of the flesh.*[55] What are these elements, which in the words of the master of truth contain "a shew of wisdom," yet do not in his view have the truth of religion itself? Is he perhaps speaking of such men when he says, in his letter to Timothy: *Having an appearance of godliness, but denying the power thereof?*[56]

So I particularly ask that you should explain to me word by word these two chapters from the letter to the Colossians, because Paul has mingled the praiseworthy with the execrable. For what is so praiseworthy as "a shew of wisdom"? Yet what is so execrable as erroneous "superstition"? Then "humility," which is both pleasing to God and most praiseworthy in true religion, is attributed together with "a shew of wisdom" to those things the teaching and acts of which we are told not to touch or taste. For they cause our destruction, because they are not from God, and *all that is not of faith is sin.*[57] But God scatters the counsels of the wise, who are foolish in God's eyes because their wisdom is of the flesh which cannot be subject to God's law;[58] for *He knoweth the thoughts of men, that they are vain.*[59] I wish to know the nature of the "humility" and of the "shew of wisdom" which Paul says is present in the "superstition" which attends the teachings of men.

As for these words of his, *not sparing the body, not in any honour, to the filling of the flesh,* I certainly cannot understand them sufficiently because the one sentence seems to me to contain a large contradiction. *Not sparing the body* is a phrase he uses, I think, in reference to any feigned or useless abstinence such as heretics usually affect. The next words, *not in any honour*, are used because the heretics practise the appearance of holy deeds without faith in the truth; and so their action is without the honour or reward of any glory, for they *transform themselves into ministers of justice*[60] but finally incur a heavy blame for their wicked sinning. But his following words, *to the filling of the flesh*, seem to me to contradict his statement about not sparing the body; for he who does not spare the body seems to me to do so because he subdues his flesh by fasting. As Paul says: *I bruise my body, and bring it into subjection.*[61] But the filling of the flesh is foreign to such chastisement.

But perhaps Paul meant that taking care to fill the flesh, which is a most heinous thing for those who make claim to religious observance, is not sparing the flesh in the sense of that command to behave well which he enunciates elsewhere. There he says that *each one should know how to possess his vessel in honour,*[62] that he may *present his body as a living sacrifice pleasing God,*[63] not filling the flesh because when the body is satiated it kills the sobriety of the soul and is hostile to chastity.

14. It remains for me to furnish your blessed person with some Gospel difficulties—not the numerous problems which usually confront my leisure reading, for I have no time at the moment to look for scattered passages in various books, or to exercise my memory in recalling them, but I shall ask you some questions (only a few) which occur to me as I dictate this. The letter about the nature of the Resurrection, which you wrote while you were winter-

ing[64] at Carthage in reply to my second question, was not long but full of instruction in the faith; if you have it committed to paper, I beg you to send it—or at any rate to rewrite it for me as you can easily do. For if a written version has not survived—it was a short letter, and you may have scorned to include it amongst your books because it was hastily composed[65]—you must write it afresh to me in the same terms from the treasure-house of your heart.

Send this to me with the other replies[66] which I hope you will dispatch to me if Christ allows us both length of days. So your toil may bring forth fruit in me, if I obtain your answers on the chapters of Scripture about which I have consulted your divinely inspired vision, so that I may hear what God is saying in you or from your lips to me.

15. What I want you to make clear for me is how or by what means the Lord after His Resurrection first passed unrecognised and was later recognised, whether by the woman who first came to the tomb, or by the two men on the road, and later by His disciples.[67] For He rose with the same body with which He suffered; how did that same body not have the same appearance as before? Or, if it had, how did it go unrecognised by those who knew it? I believe myself that it is part of the mystery that He who went unrecognised to those who were walking on the road was revealed at the breaking of bread.[68] But I wish to understand the passage on your interpretation, not on mine.

16. Then there are His words to Mary: *Do not touch me, for I am not yet ascended to the Father*.[69] If she was not permitted to touch Him as He stood face to face, how could she touch Him after He ascended to the Father—except perhaps by growth in faith and the ascent of the

mind, in which God becomes either distant from or intimate with men? Again, she had doubted if it was Christ,
and thought He was a gardener, so perhaps the words *Do
not touch me* were what she deserved, for she was judged
unworthy to touch Christ with her hand because she had
not yet laid hold of Him with faith. She had not apprehended God, thinking He was a gardener, whereas she had
been told a little earlier by the angels: *Why seek you the
living with the dead?*[70] Hence she was told: *"Do not touch
Me, for I am not yet ascended to the Father* so far as you
are concerned, because to you I still seem only a man; later
you will touch Me, when by belief you ascend to identify
Me."

17. Another query. Tell me your view, so that I may
follow your thought, on those words of blessed Simeon
with which he blessed the infant Lord. He came into the
temple under the impulse of the spirit to look upon Christ
in accordance with the divine oracle, and took Him into
his arms, and said to Mary: *Behold this Child is set for the
fall and for the resurrection of many in Israel, and for a
sign which will be contradicted; and thine own soul a
sword shall pierce, that out of many hearts thoughts may
be revealed.*[71] Are we to believe that here he prophesied
about some suffering of Mary which has never been set
down? Or does this relate to her maternal feelings when
she later at the time of the Passion stood by the cross where
the child of her own womb was nailed, and was herself
pierced by the anguish of a mother's heart? Was the sword
which pierced her heart that sword formed by the cross,
which before her very eyes had transfixed her Son of the
flesh?

For I note that in the Psalms it is said of Joseph: *They*

humbled his feet in fetters, the iron pierced his soul,[72] just as Simeon said in the Gospel: *Thine own soul a sword shall pierce.* He said "soul," not "flesh," because devoted love resides within the soul and it is there that the sting of grief pricks like the sword. This is the case when the soul is wounded by some injury to its flesh, as when Joseph (whose sufferings, admittedly not mortal, were undeserved) was sold as a slave, and chained and gaoled as a convicted prisoner;[73] or when the soul is tortured by the grief or pain of inward love, as happened with Mary.

It was her maternal spirit above all that had drawn her to the cross of that Lord in whose person at that time she saw only the Son of her flesh; so that when she saw Him dead, she mourned Him with the weakness of a human being, and arranged Him for burial without thought of His coming Resurrection, because the punishment of the suffering before her eyes blinded her faith in the wonder which was to follow. Though the Lord consoled her, as she stood by His cross, by showing none of the frail fear of the dying, nonetheless as He willingly embraced death and turned His death to strength, He admonished her from the cross with the full power of a living Man and the steady purpose of One who was to rise again.

For He said, in reference to the blessed Apostle John: *Mother, behold thy son;* and then to John, who also stood there: *Behold thy mother.*[74] When He was doubtless already quitting the human frailty in which He had been born of a woman, to attain by the death of the cross the eternity of God so that He might dwell in the glory of God the Father, He delegated to a man His rights of human love. Being himself quite young, He chose a younger disciple so that He could appositely trust His virgin mother to a virgin apostle. In this one sentence He taught us two things. First, He bequeathed to us an example of dutiful love when He showed care for His mother, so that when He left her in the flesh He should not renounce His anxiety for her; though in fact He was not leaving her in the flesh, because after seeing Him die she was later to see Him restored to life. Secondly, by means of that utterance He carried out the secret design of the divine plan, for He demonstrated the mystery of His dutiful love which brings salvation, so that it might impinge on the faith of all men; He delegated to another His mother so that John might look upon her as his mother and console her in her turn, and on the other hand He gave her a new son in place of His own physical presence. I might even say that He begot a son for her, to show that she had no son past or present except Him who had been born of her virgin womb, for had He not been her only Son the Saviour would not have shown such concern that she was being left unsupported.

18. But let us get back to the words of Simeon, because I must confess that my understanding is clouded by that final sentence: *And thy own soul a spear or sword*[75] *shall pierce, that out of many hearts thoughts may be revealed.* If I take this literally, it is utterly obscure to me, because we nowhere read that the blessed Mary was killed, so it seems that the holy Simeon, by reference to the physical sword, foretold to her the suffering she was to experience. But what of the words he added, *that out of many hearts thoughts might be revealed?* Scripture says that *God is the searcher of hearts and reins.*[76] Paul says of the judgment to come that God will then make manifest *the concealed thoughts of hearts and the hidden things of darkness.*[77]

Likewise Paul gives a spiritual interpretation to the heavenly arms with which we must all arm our inner man, and gives the title *sword of the spirit*[78] to the word of God, concerning which he said to the Hebrews: *The word of God is living and effectual and more piercing than any two-edged sword, and reaching unto the division of the soul and the spirit,*[79] and the rest with which you are acquainted.

So it would not be surprising that the fiery force of this word, and the more penetrative point of this two-edged sword, pierced the soul of holy Joseph earlier and that of the blessed Mary subsequently. We know that the steel passed through neither of their bodies. And to make it clearer that the prophet uses the word steel to denote the sword of the Word, he says in the verse immediately following of the same Psalm: *The word of the Lord inflamed him.*[80] The Word of God is both fire and a sword, for the Word Himself who is God used both expressions of Himself: *I am come*, He says, *to cast fire on the earth. And what will I, but that it be kindled?*[81] Again He says elsewhere: *I came not to send peace but the sword.*[82] You see that He has described the single power of His teaching with the different names of "fire" and "sword"; otherwise how could the suffering or distress inflicted on Mary by the sword have been so influential?

So I am keen to know what connexion with Mary is denoted by the words *that out of many hearts thoughts might be revealed*, or where did it happen that as a result of a physical sword of steel, or a spiritual sword which was the Word of God piercing her soul, the thoughts of many hearts were revealed? So explain to me in particular these final words of Simeon, because I have no doubt that they are clear to your holy soul, which has deserved through the purity of its inner eye the illumination of the Holy Spirit, so that through that Spirit it can observe and examine even the lofty things of God. May God through your prayers have mercy on me and cause His countenance to shine on me[83] through the lamp of your word, holy lord and most blessed and loving brother in Christ the Lord. You are my master in the faith of the truth and my patron in the bowels of Christ's love.

LETTER 51

To Eucher and Galla[1]

Bishop Paulinus greets his holy and beloved children Eucher and Galla, who are truly worthy of praise and esteem.

1. The blessed Lord our God, who grants the wishes of those who long for them, and who in answering our prayers always grants us more than we pray for, has deigned to proffer me unexpectedly a chance as apposite as it was desired. The opportunity has come through three young men in religious life, my sons and fellow servants in the Lord, Gelasius, Augendus, and Tigridius. They were sent to my lowly self by my brother and fellow priest Honoratus,[2] a man deserving of praise and famed in Christ. The Lord inspired him to send these youths from his holy and most chaste community to give me new life, following the example of your own affection.[3] When I dutifully enquired, in accord with the love which your merits deserve, about your state of bodily health (I could, of course, be in no doubt about your religious state and your heavenly health), they gave me such a reply as to refresh my soul. They said they had left you through God's kindness in good health, and that you were carrying out the activities of your admirable calling, working at your studies and aiming at heaven with the same harmony with which you left behind worldly matters.

2. I remembered that those other sons of mine, whom

you had sent for my sake a year ago to visit my poor person, informed me of the location of your dwelling and of that of the venerable lord Honoratus. In other words, they told me that you had settled on the islands called Lerum and Lerinum,[4] which are as close to each other in name as in position, separated by a strait of sea.[5] So when these sons of ours said that they came from the isle called Lerinum, I recognised the name and readily remembered the name of the neighbouring island, where I knew that your holy selves were lodging, in retreat from the din of this world. I knew that the courtesy of a letter from me would please your loving hearts, and besides I owe you a debt for your spiritual favours, so I gladly seized this chance of my spiritual sons becoming bearers of my letter to your blessed and harmonious union. This charge they most readily accepted, as the sons or servants of obedience which they are, obeying or following God's teaching. So in these sparing words from my insignificant self receive the tokens of a love far from sparing, and preserve my letter as a pledge to your souls and as testimony of my affection and love for you.

3. I hope that by the mercy of Christ the Lord these words of mine find you in good health, and that if He grants you a suitable opportunity on future occasions you can stir yourself to reply. I am sure that in your affection you would also have written through these sons of mine, if you had been aware that they were setting out directly to me. When I asked them about this (I knew that you were neighbours), they said that they had set out from their monastery without your knowledge. However, charity, like *the kingdom of God, is not in speech but in power,*[6] for in the perfection and fulness of charity the

kingdom of God is embraced or obtained, and charity resides in the treasury of the heart and in the strength of faith. And therefore I long for a letter because of the intimate favour of your love. However, since I am sure of the most devoted affection of your hearts, I have no doubt that I am securely established in your thoughts even when you are silent; for we have become known to each other not by human friendship but by divine grace, and it is by the bowels of Christ's love that we are joined.[7] Therefore between our hearts there must inevitably abide that perennial harmony which was joined at Christ's instigation, for what force or forgetfulness can separate what God has joined together?

4. *May the Lord bless you out of Sion* with the blessing *by which the man is blessed that feareth the Lord.*[8] May he bless you who are man and wife forever, and not only you who are parents but also the holy God-sent offspring of your most eminent sanctity. *May you see the good things of Jerusalem,*[9] and may you deserve to dwell together *in the house of the Lord unto length of days.*[10] Holy children, worthy of true respect, I cherish you with heartfelt affection and constantly long for you.

NOTES

LIST OF ABBREVIATIONS

ACW	Ancient Christian Writers (Westminster, Md.-London 1946–)
Cavallera	F. Cavallera, *Saint Jérôme: Sa vie et son oeuvre.* 2 vols. (Louvain-Paris 1922)
CCL	Corpus christianorum, series latina (Turnhout-Paris 1953–)
CSEL	Corpus scriptorum ecclesiasticorum latinorum (Vienna 1866–)
DACL	Dictionnaire d'archéologie chrétienne et de liturgie (Paris 1907–53)
DHGE	Dictionnaire d'histoire et de géographie ecclésiastiques (Paris 1912–)
DTC	Dictionnaire de théologie catholique (Paris 1903–50)
Duchesne	L. Duchesne, *Les fastes épiscopaux de l'ancienne Gaule.* 3 vols. (2nd ed. Paris 1907–15)
Fabre *Chron.*	P. Fabre, *Essai sur la chronologie de l'oeuvre de saint Paulin de Nole* (Paris 1948)
Fabre *Paulin*	P. Fabre, *Saint Paulin de Nole et l'amitié chrétienne* (Paris 1949)
Goldschmidt	R. C. Goldschmidt, *Paulinus' Churches at Nola* (Amsterdam 1940)
Hartel	*Sancti Pontii Meropii Paulini Nolani epistulae,* ed. G. de Hartel (CSEL 29, 1894)
Jones	A. H. M. Jones, *The Later Roman Empire.* 3 vols. (Oxford 1964)
JTS	Journal of Theological Studies (London 1900–05; Oxford 1906–)
Lagrange	F. Lagrange, *Histoire de s. Paulin.* 2 vols. (2nd ed. Paris 1884)
MG	Patrologia graeca, ed. J. P. Migne (Paris 1857–66)
ML	Patrologia latina, ed. J. P. Migne (Paris 1844–55)
Quasten *Patr.*	J. Quasten, *Patrology.* 3 vols. thus far (West-

minster, Md.-Utrecht-Antwerp): 1 (1950) *The Beginnings of Patristic Literature;* 2 (1955) *The Ante-Nicene Literature after Irenaeus;* 3 (1960) *The Golden Age of Greek Patristic Literature from the Council of Nicaea to the Council of Chalcedon*

RB   Revue bénédictine (Maredsous 1884–   )

RE   A. Pauly-G. Wissowa-W. Kroll, *Realencyclopädie der klassischen Altertumswissenschaft* (Stuttgart 1893–   )

Reinelt   P. Reinelt, *Studien über die Briefe des heiligen Paulinus von Nola* (diss. Breslau 1904)

SC   Sources chrétiennes (Paris 1940–   )

LETTER 23

[1] This letter was probably written in 400. The dating rests on the reasonable assumption that it was sent at the same time as Letters 24 and 29 (cf. below, no. 1 to Letter 29). Letter 29.14 refers to the first arrival of Nicetas at Nola. Later a return visit "in the fourth year" is attested by Paulinus' *Carm.* 27.333 (*venisti tandem quarto mihi redditus anno*), and this poem can be dated to 403, as it is the ninth of the yearly *Natalicia* which began in 395 (cf. n. 1 to Letter 1 in ACW 35.211). Nicetas' first visit, then, and this group of letters can be ascribed to 400. Cf. Fabre *Chron.* 29 ff., 35 ff.

[2] This letter reflects the reconciliation effected between Severus and Paulinus after the period of strained relations. This explains the effusive and extended introduction here on the special intimacy of their Christian affection.

[3] Cf. Matt. 6.27.

[4] Ps. 144.3.

[5] Cf. Rom. 11.36.

[6] Ps. 24.8.

[7] Ps. 30.20.

[8] Gen. 27.27.

[9] Cf. Cant. 1.3.

[10] Gen. 27.28.

[11] Ps. 128.7.

[12] Cf. Luke 16.22.

[13] Matt. 12.34; Eccli. 13.20.

[14] Ps. 24.21, 25.5.

[15] Cf. Ps. 10.6; John 12.25.

[16] Cf. 1 Cor. 14.20.

[17] From 395 up to 400 Severus had sent a single letter a year. Now, in an effort to resolve the crisis affecting their friendship, he had sent two couriers with letters in a single year. Cf. Fabre *Chron.* 30 ff.

[18] Perhaps in the religious sense of "Christian faith," or, possibly, "your faithfulness to me," as Fabre (*Paulin* 301 n. 3) prefers.

[19] Cf. Ps. 38.4.

[20] Ps. 64.5.

[21] Matt. 10.41.

[22] This is the first extant reference to Victor the courier of Severus who became a great favourite of Paulinus and is repeatedly praised in later letters. This Victor had served in the army in Gaul (cf. Letter 25.1) before becoming the monastic comrade of Clarus and of Martin (cf. § 3 of this letter). He seems later (perhaps on the death of Martin in 397) to have joined the community of Severus at Primuliacum, and from 400 onwards made a yearly journey to Nola with letters.

[23] Luke 17.10.

[24] On Martin, cf. n. 80 to Letter 11 (= ACW 35.233). Clarus, the most illustrious of Martin's companions, is celebrated in the verses written by Paulinus to be inscribed on the new basilica at Primuliacum, where Clarus' bones were buried beneath the altar (cf. below, Letter 32.6).

[25] Luke 10.6.

[26] Matt. 11.29.

[27] I read, and translate, *quas a vobis geminas in litteris et palliis adferebat.* Fabre *Paulin* 301 defends the MSS reading *litteras* ("sa double lettre").

[28] The "burden" here refers to the acceptance of Christian kindnesses from others—a notion to which Paulinus obsessively returns. Cf., e.g., Letter 24.1.

[29] Ps. 108.18.

[30] Severus had sent a copy of his *Vita sancti Martini* to Paulinus in 397 (cf. n. 80 to Letter 11 [= ACW 35.233, where through a slip this prose work of Severus is incorrectly described as having been written in verse]). In that *Vita*, Severus recounts how Martin used to pour water over his followers' hands and feet (cf. § 25: *aquam manibus nostris ipse obtulit. Ad vesperum autem pedes ipse nobis abluit*).

[31] Cf. John 13.9.

[32] Cf. John 13.10.

[33] I read and translate *ungentis* (Roswyede) here.

[34] Ps. 50.10, 102.1.

[35] Ps. 44.8.

[36] Cf. Eccle. 10.1.

[37] Paulinus had senatorial rank by right of birth, as well as by tenure of office. Cf. n. 13 to Letter 5 (= ACW 35.219 f.).

[38] Ps. 105.20.

[39] Ezech. 4.12–15.

[40] Cf. 4 Kings 4.38 ff.

[41] 4 Kings 4.40.

[42] John 1.14.

[43] Ps. 30.13.

[44] Rom. 8.3.

[45] Ps. 59.10.

[46] Cf. John 6.48.

[47] Cf. Jer. 1.13.

[48] Luke 12.49.

[49] Ps. 11.7.

[50] Cf. Num. 13.24. One wonders if Venantius Fortunatus had read this passage. He uses the same image strikingly in his poem *Crux benedicta nitet* (2.1: "And between thine arms there hangs a vine, from which flows sweet wine with the redness of blood"). See my essay "Venantius Fortunatus" in *Spirituality through the Centuries* (London 1965) ch. 6.

[51] Perhaps an echo of Cicero, *Tusc.* 2.13: *cultura animi philosophia est.* But the statement here is deliberately reorientated towards the Christian view.

[52] Rom. 7.24 f.

[53] Cf. 3 Kings 17.16.

[54] Ps. 131.15.

[55] Cf. Rom. 7.3; 1 Cor. 7.39.

[56] Cf. 3 Kings 17.7 ff., 18.1.

[57] Ps. 33.7, 106.14.

[58] Ps. 50.9, 41.5, 118.176, 33.2.

[59] Ps. 39.3 f.

[60] Ps. 77.33; Luke 1.49.

[61] Ps. 35.9, 27.7.

[62] Gen. 27.28.

[63] Ps. 91.11, 4.9, 90.16.

[64] Ps. 39.13.

[65] Cf. Deut. 21.11 f.

[66] I.e., Samson. Cf. Judges 13.5; Num. 6.5.

[67] Judges 16.19. The influence of Ambrose in this discussion of Samson is marked. See especially his prologue to the second book of his *De Spiritu Sancto* (ML 16.774).

[68] Cf. Ambrose, *loc. cit.*: *utinam tam cautus ad servandam gra-*

tiam quam fortis ad superandam bestiam! Also, *Apol. David altera* 3.16 (ML 14.934): *Samson validus et fortis leonem suffocavit, sed amorem suum suffocare non potuit.*

[69] Gal. 1.16.

[70] Cf. Judges 16.21.

[71] Ps. 31.9.

[72] Cf. Ps. 48.13.

[73] I.e., Nabuchodonosor. Cf. Dan. 4.30.

[74] Ps. 1.1.

[75] Cf. Prov. 7.22 ff.

[76] Cf. Ps. 77.39.

[77] So Ambrose, *De Spiritu Sancto* 2, prol. (ML 16.774): *et fortasse hoc non solum virtutis miraculum sed etiam sapientiae mysterium prophetiae miraculum fuit.*

[78] Gal. 4.4.

[79] I read and translate: *suscipiendo virum* (*verbum* in the MSS and in Hartel).

[80] Eph. 2.14.

[81] This discussion of the parable of the Samaritan (cf. Luke 10.30–35) is likewise inspired by Ambrose. Cf. his *Expos. in Luc.* 7.71 ff. (ML 15.805). There, too, the Samaritan is Christ, the money paid over to the innkeeper represents the Old and New Testaments, and the innkeeper is Paul. Contrast Origen, *In Luc. hom.* 35 (MG 13.886), and Irenaeus, *Contra haer.* 3.17.3 (MG 7.930), where the two denarii represent the Father and the Son.

[82] I read *denarium* (genitive plural, as in Cicero, *De off.* 3.92, and elsewhere) *mercede* for the *denarii mercede* of the MSS and Hartel.

[83] Cf. Luke 10.35. Paulinus here supplements the allegorical interpretation he had read in Ambrose, and the addition is characteristic. Paul, as innkeeper, provides from his own store the emphasis on virginity (as at 1 Cor. 7.37 f.).

[84] Cf. Jer. 17.9.

[85] Ps. 21.23.

[86] Ps. 48.8; 1 John 2.2; Ps. 48.9.

[87] Rom. 7.14.

[88] Cf. 2 Cor. 5.21; Gal. 3.13.

[89] Ps. 48.8. The quotation here by Paulinus agrees with the Latin of the Vulgate (*Frater non redimit, redimet homo*), and the translation here given accords with Paulinus' interpretation

of the passage. The Challoner-Douay translation reads: "No brother *can* redeem, *nor* shall man redeem," which is in line with modern versions. But Jerome, *Ep.* 54.18, puts forward an interpretation similar to that of Paulinus.

[90] 2 Cor. 5.19.

[91] Col. 2.14.

[92] Cf. Gen. 3.13.

[93] Cf. Judges 14.8. Ambrose makes a similar comment in his prologue to his *De Spiritu Sancto* 2 (ML 16.775): *ideo in corpore eius, hoc est Ecclesiae, apes repertas quae condunt mella sapientiae.*

[94] Cf. Ambrose, *loc. cit.: qui populus feritatis erat ante, nunc Christi est.*

[95] Judges 14.14.

[96] Cf. Ambrose, *loc. cit.: hunc igitur leonem Samson quasi Iudaeus occidit.*

[97] Likewise in Ambrose: *fundari non potuisse coniugium, nisi occiso leone de tribu Iuda.* The symbolism becomes confused here in both Ambrose and Paulinus, because they revert to the view of those who make Samson the prefiguration of Christ.

[98] Gen. 49.9.

[99] Cf. John 10.18.

[100] Judges 14.14.

[101] Ps. 71.12.

[102] Gen. 3.19; Phil. 3.20.

[103] Gal. 6.1.

[104] Ps. 17.35.

[105] 1 Tim. 4.8.

[106] Ps. 114.7.

[107] Ps. 35.10.

[108] John 12.31.

[109] Cf. John 12.31.

[110] Cf. 1 Kings 1.11, etc.

[111] Cf. 2 Kings 14.26.

[112] Cf. Dan. 4.30.

[113] Judges 16.17.

[114] Wisd. 1.4.

[115] 2 Kings 14.26. The Vulgate gives the weight as "two hundred sicles, according to the common (*publico*) weight."

[116] Ps. 51.3.

[117] Matt. 11.8.

[118] Eph. 2.2.
[119] Cf. Phil. 3.19.
[120] Cf. Judges 16.12.
[121] Ps. 118.61.
[122] Ps. 37.5.
[123] Ps. 17.34.
[124] Rom. 8.9.
[125] Ps. 118.37.
[126] John 9.41.
[127] Cf. Gen. 3.7.
[128] 1 John 2.16.
[129] John 1.9.
[130] 1 John 2.15; 1 Cor. 7.31.
[131] Col. 3.1.
[132] Eccle. 1.14.
[133] Cf. Rom. 1.25.
[134] 2 Cor. 3.18.
[135] 2 Cor. 5.17.
[136] Ps. 111.4.
[137] John 4.24; 2 Cor. 3.17.
[138] Ps. 2.3.
[139] 2 Cor. 6.2.
[140] Cf. Matt. 17.5.

[141] Translating *opportune ad gratiae tempus et speciem libertatis tonsor in promptu est.* Hartel follows the Codex Parisin. 2122 s. X and the 1515 Paris *editio princeps* in reading *species* for *speciem* and *tonsori* for *tonsor.*

[142] 1 Cor. 11.3; Matt. 5.14; Eph. 1.22 f.

[143] Cf. 1 Cor. 11.3.

[144] Gal. 3.28.

[145] Cf. Luke 7.38. Paulinus here echoes Ambrose, *Expos. in Luc.* 6.19 f. (ML 15.1759): *Habeat plane capillos quibus Christi circumvolvat vestigia . . . ut extremo saltem rore divinae virtutis humescant . . . ut aliud nisi sapientiam loqui nesciat, ut aliud nisi justitiam diligere nesciat, ut aliud nisi castitatem libare nesciat, ut aliud nisi pudicitiam osculari nesciat.*

[146] Isa. 26.19. The Vulgate reading, "Thy dew is the dew of light," is an alternative rendering of the Hebrew.

[147] Ps. 44.14.

[148] 1 Cor. 11.10. There have been various attempts to elucidate

this notoriously difficult Pauline passage. Some patristic authorities regard "angels" here as meaning bishops; others suggest that the passage is urging women to be modest before their guardian angels. Paulinus' suggestion that the angels referred to are wicked ones is also popular, since it can claim scriptural warrant at Gen. 6.1 ff., and has also a Neoplatonist flavour which Paul may possibly have been exploiting when writing to sophisticated Greeks. For documentation of these varying views, see J. Hering, *La première épître de s. Paul aux Corinthiens* (2nd ed. Paris 1949) *ad loc.*

[149] I read *dissideant* for the unlikely *dissiliant* of the MSS and Hartel.

[150] Cf. 1 Cor. 11.5.

[151] Cf. Rom. 8.26; 1 Cor. 14.14 f.

[152] 1 Cor. 11.10.

[153] Cf. 1 Pet. 3.7. By "vessel" is meant womanly powers.

[154] This section on women in church is of great interest as reflecting the orthodox attitude of Western churchmen about 400 A.D. Paulinus' words were inspired by Ambrose; cf. n. 145 above.

[155] Luke 12.7.

[156] Cf. Cant. 5.11. The phrase *aurum cephas* means literally "gold stone," and Paulinus' interpretation seems to be correct. Cf. the note at ML 61.861. The Vulgate version, *aurum optimum*, elucidates the literal meaning. The exposition here is similar to that in Gregory of Nyssa, *In Cant. Cant. hom.* 13 (MG 44.1053 ff.).

[157] Apoc. 3.18.

[158] Wisd. 3.5.

[159] Ps. 4.7.

[160] Cf. Eph. 1.22.

[161] Cant. 4.1.

[162] Acts 10.38.

[163] Gen. 3.20; Cant. 1.1.

[164] 2 Cor. 3.6.

[165] I cannot translate Hartel's emendation here, *sed hoc . . . semini detur*, and I tentatively suggest: *sed hoc . . . serum indicetur*. Severus may have offered, as explanation of *bona ubera eius super vinum* (cf. Cant. 1.1), the suggestion that the newborn child first sucks from the mother's breast the thin, wheylike fluid (*serum*) and later the milk; this might symbolise the transition

from the Old Law to the New. For an alternative explanation, see Rosweyde's learned note at ML 61.861. He points out that milk and wine, representing the New and Old Testaments, were drunk by the newly baptised, and quotes Clement of Alexandria's *Paidagogus* in exemplification of this.

166 John 10.11; Ps. 8.3.

167 1 Cor. 3.2.

168 Cant. 5.11. For the Vulgate's *sicut elatae palmarum* ("as branches of palm trees"), *nigrae quasi corvus*, Paulinus has *abietes nigrae sicut corax*. The difference occurs because the Greek word ἐλάτη could bear the meaning of "palm bud" as well as of "fir."

169 Cf. Gen. 8.6 f.

170 Cf. 3 Kings 17.6, where, however, it is said "the ravens," not just one raven, brought food to Elias.

171 Cf. 3 Kings 5.8; 2 Par. 9.21.

172 1 Pet. 2.9.

173 Cf. Ps. 77.49.

174 Prov. 30.17.

175 Cf. 3 Kings 17.6; Ps. 146.9.

176 Cf. Cant. 1.4.

177 Ps. 17.12.

178 John 12.35.

179 For Paulinus the woman in Cant. 1.4, *nigra sed speciosa*, symbolises the Church, the spouse of Christ.

180 Ps. 91.13, 15.

181 Cf. 2 Cor. 6.7.

182 This image of the Church (in § 29), and of the saints here, as a ship with the Cross as yardarm is a commonplace in patristic writing. For a general treatment, cf. H. Rahner, *Greek Myths and Christian Mystery* (London 1962) ch. 7.

183 Isa. 11.1.

184 Cf. Letter 16.7 and n. 22 thereto (= ACW 35.159 and 246).

185 Cf. 3 Kings 5.5 ff., 10.22.

186 Cf. Matt. 12.42; Ps. 47.8.

187 Cf. Matt. 13.46.

188 Paulinus has in mind various scriptural passages such as Ps. 117.6: *dextera Domini fecit virtutem, dextera Domini exaltavit me.*

189 Cf. Matt. 25.33.

190 Cf. Matt. 10.30; Luke 12.7 ("Yea, the very hairs of your head are all numbered").

[191] Reading, with Sacchini, *dapes* for *opes*. The emendation is certain; see § 42 of this letter for a repetition of the *pedibus Christi . . . dapes Pharisaei* contrast.

[192] Ps. 50.19.

[193] Cf. Matt. 26.13, etc. Cf. also Ambrose, *Expos. in Luc.* 6.15.

[194] Cf. Rom. 9.24.

[195] Throughout this section, as Rosweyde has demonstrated (ML 61.863), Paulinus has had Ambrose's commentary on Luke at his elbow. I have quoted in later notes the more striking borrowings.

[196] Eph. 3.9.

[197] Cf. Gen. 9.27.

[198] Reading: *unde ipsius in Iohanne persona lex legis. . . .*

[199] John 1.30.

[200] In Matthew 26.7 the ointment is poured on Christ's head; in Luke 7.38 the ointment is applied to His feet. Ambrose, *Expos. in Luc.* 6.14 (ML 15.758), comments on this difference. Paulinus was following much early Latin tradition in believing that Matthew and Luke were describing the same incident. Greek tradition generally and much modern commentary see the accounts as being of two separate incidents.

[201] Reading *forte*, not the *fonte* of some MSS and in Hartel, which would ruin the point of the sentence.

[202] Ps. 140.5, 22.5.

[203] I prefer the reading *fragrantibus* to the *flagrantibus* of Hartel.

[204] Cant. 5.2.

[205] Cf. Phil. 2.15.

[206] Ps. 138.11.

[207] For the figurative representation of the Church as the moon in patristic literature, cf. H. Rahner, "Mysterium Lunae," *Zeitschr. für kath. Theol.* 63 (1939) 311 ff., 428 ff., and 64 (1940) 61 ff., 121 ff.; and, for briefer treatment, the same author's *Greek Myths and Christian Mystery* (London 1962) ch. 4.

[208] 2 Thess. 2.3.

[209] The price of betrayal was actually thirty silver denarii (cf. Matt. 26.15). The gold denarius was worth twenty-five times as much as a silver denarius.

[210] Cf. John 12.5.

[211] The thought is again from Ambrose, *Expos. in Luc.*

[212] Prov. 22.2; Wisd. 6.8.

[213] Matt. 10.8.

[214] Cf. Acts 3.6.

[215] 2 Cor. 4.10.

[216] Gal. 6.14.

[217] Similarly Ambrose: *non amanti divitias, non amanti honores saeculi, non amanti quae sua sunt sed quae Iesu Christi; non amanti quae videntur sed quae non videntur.*

[218] Ps. 115.16 f.

[219] Ps. 133.2.

[220] Cf. Eccli. 6.36.

[221] 1 Cor. 14.19. As Ducaeus suggests (ML 61.864), Paulinus' *in lege* ("in the Law") here for the Vulgate's *sensu meo* ("with my understanding") may reflect a Greek version which has διὰ τοῦ νόμου (or τῷ νόμῳ) instead of τῷ νοΐ μου.

[222] Ps. 83.11.

[223] John 3.8.

[224] Again here there is an extended verbal echo from Ambrose: *Quocumque vel in domum immundi, vel in domum Pharisaei audieris iustum venisse, contende praeripere hospitis gratiam, praeripere regnum caelorum. Ubicumque audieris Christi nomen, accurre; in cuiuscumque interiorem domum Christum intrasse cognoveris, et ipse festina. Cum repereris sapientiam, cum repereris iustitiam in alicuius penetralibus recumbentem, accurre ad pedes . . . noli fastidire pedes. Fimbriam illa tetigit et sanata est.*

[225] Cf. Acts 5.15.

[226] Cf. Ambrose, *Expos. in Luc.* 6.19 (ML 15.759): *expande capillos, sterne ante eum omnes tui corporis dignitates.*

[227] Ps. 112.5.

[228] Luke 7.44.

[229] Cf. Ambrose, *Expos. in Luc.* 6.18: *et fortasse ideo non lavit pedes suos Christus, ut eos lacrimis nos lavemus.*

[230] Luke 7.45.

[231] 1 Pet. 4.8.

[232] Cant. 1.1.

[233] Cf. Ps. 33.9.

[234] Cant. 2.5, 4.9.

[235] Cf. Isa. 6.6 f.

[236] Ps. 94.6.

[237] Luke 7.50.

[238] Luke 7.39.

[239] Cf. Gen. 18.2.
[240] Cf. Gen. 18.4.
[241] John 8.39.
[242] John 8.56.
[243] John 20.29.
[244] Cf. Matt. 3.9.
[245] Cf. Gen. 48.14.
[246] Rom. 11.17 f.
[247] Matt. 25.40.
[248] Ps. 45.2.
[249] Deut. 32.9; Ps. 118.57.
[250] John 8.12; Matt. 5.14.
[251] John 6.35; 1 Cor. 10.17.
[252] John 15.1; Jer. 2.21.
[253] Ps. 67.16 f., 75.5.
[254] 1 Cor. 10.4.
[255] Matt. 16.18.
[256] Ps. 81.6. Cf. John 1.12.
[257] Ps. 81.7.
[258] Reading *deficiendo* for the *deiciendo* of the MSS and Hartel.
[259] Isa. 14.12.
[260] I.e., Adam; cf. Gen. 3.
[261] It will be recalled that Origen's speculative view that the devil may in God's good time be saved (*De princ.* 3.6.5) was the basis for one of the main indictments levelled against him by the fourth-century polemicists. The attack by Epiphanius in 374–5, and the subsequent involvement of Jerome and Rufinus in the dispute in the 390's, made the topic a relevant one, and Paulinus here takes the opportunity to emphasize his own orthodox position. For a lucid survey of the whole question, cf. Cavallera bk. 4. There is an interesting discussion of Origen's theological attitudes in H. Chadwick, *Early Christian Thought and the Classical Tradition* (Oxford 1966) ch. 4. Cf. also Quasten *Patr.* 2.37–101, esp. 87–91.
[262] Cf. Ps. 145.8.
[263] Luke 19.10.
[264] Ps. 115.12.
[265] Isa. 53.12.
[266] Rom. 11.36.

[267] Ps. 99.3.
[268] Rom. 11.35.
[269] Ps. 17.1.
[270] Cf. John 13.54 f.
[271] Cf. Acts 4.32; Matt. 7.12.

LETTER 24

[1] It is clear from the opening words, *adhuc aliquid*, that this is a postscript to another letter. That previous epistle is Letter 23. In the opening paragraph of the present letter Paulinus mentions that he ended the last one with some comments on charity and perfection (*superioris fine . . . de caritatis videlicet et perfectionis verbo*). This description applies well to Letter 23.46 f. Hence this letter, as Letter 23, probably was written in 400, and the two letters were probably sent by the same courier.

[2] Cf. Letter 23.46 f.

[3] Cf. above, n. 28 to Letter 23.

[4] 1 Cor. 13.4; Rom. 13.10.

[5] Gen. 4.7 (LXX).

[6] It is clear, as Rosweyde comments (ML 61.886), that Severus has passed his remaining farm into the custody of the Church. In his note Rosweyde quotes an interesting comment of Prosper, *De vita contemplativa* 9, which suggests that both Paulinus at Nola and Hilary at Arles countenanced ecclesiastical ownership of lands.

[7] 1 Cor. 12.4. The "queen" in the following quotation symbolises the Church with its adornment of various virtues.

[8] Ps. 44.10.

[9] Cf. Gen. 12.1, 4; Job 1.21.

[10] Ps. 67.14.

[11] Cf. Ps. 67.14; 1 Pet. 5.3.

[12] Cf. Col. 1.12, etc.

[13] Cf. Matt. 7.3.

[14] Cf. 1 Cor. 7.30.

[15] Cf. Eccli. 13.1.

[16] Ps. 87.6.

[17] Cf. Ps. 87.6.

[18] Matt. 19.21.

[19] Cf. Luke 15.8.
[20] Matt. 19.21.
[21] Cf. Matt. 5.40.
[22] Cf. 1 Tim. 6.7.
[23] Cf. Rom. 12.1.
[24] Cf. Eph. 2.20 f.
[25] Lev. 11.44.
[26] Cf. Deut. 6.5; Matt. 22.37.
[27] Ps. 53.8.
[28] Philem. 14.
[29] Ps. 141.6.
[30] The image of the athlete in depiction of the ascetic is, of course, very common in patristic writing. Ducaeus at ML 61.886 quotes passages from Clement of Alexandria and Tertullian in exemplification of this. But Ambrose, as so often, may have put the image in Paulinus' mind here; at any rate, the phraseology here recalls that of Ambrose, *De off. min.* 1.36 (ML 16.82).
[31] Cf. Gen. 32.28. The discussion of the symbolic nature of Jacob's struggle may owe something to Ambrose, *De Jacob et vita beata* 2.7 (ML 14.656). There, too, Jacob is mentioned as symbolising the unfaithful Jews.
[32] Luke 23.21 ff.
[33] I excise *non* from the text, and read: *ut . . . intellegamus posse nos esse idoneos ad congrediendum deo.*
[34] Cf. Luke 16.16.
[35] Gen. 32.25.
[36] Cf. 1 Kings 2.5. These words from the canticle of Anna symbolise the synagogue.
[37] Cf. 1 Cor. 9.25.
[38] Matt. 8.22, 19.21.
[39] Phil. 3.12.
[40] Mark 16.19.
[41] Matt. 11.28 f.
[42] Cf. 1 Tim. 2.4.
[43] Cf. Gen. 1.26. This distinction between "image" and "likeness" is often drawn by the Fathers; cf. Rosweyde's note at ML 61.866.
[44] Phil. 2.8.
[45] John 12.32; Matt. 19.21.
[46] Ps. 62.9.

[47] 1 Tim. 1.5; Rom. 13.10; Ps. 72.23.

[48] Since the emphasis of the chapter is wholly on scrutiny of self, I prefer to read *exploratione* rather than the *expoliatione* of the MSS and Hartel.

[49] Prov. 4.23.

[50] Rom. 7.24.

[51] Rom. 7.18.

[52] Ps. 50.12.

[53] Ps. 138.23 f.

[54] Ps. 138.13.

[55] Cf. John 15.5.

[56] Luke 12.49.

[57] Ps. 45.11.

[58] Matt. 6.24.

[59] Cf. Matt. 26.41; Luke 12.40.

[60] Cf. Rom. 6.13.

[61] Cf. Eph. 6.12.

[62] Rom. 6.13.

[63] 1 Cor. 7.31.

[64] Cf. Wisd. 14.11.

[65] A quotation from Virgil, *Aeneid* 7.337 f.

[66] Ps. 119.4.

[67] Matt. 10.36.

[68] This emphasis on the destructive effect of avarice echoes the warning of Ambrose, *De off. min.* 1.39 (ML 16.86).

[69] Cf. Job 1.21.

[70] Ps. 26.1, 3.

[71] I.e., St. Paul. Cf. Acts 9.15.

[72] Cf. Eph. 6.14, 17.

[73] Ps. 90.7.

[74] Cf. Eph. 6.15.

[75] The text is dubious. I read: *arrogans mihi vindico, sed omni fideli de virtute Christi promissum.*

[76] Rom. 4.17.

[77] St. Paul.

[78] Cf. 1 Cor. 9.27, where the Vulgate's *castigo* gives a metaphorical interpretation of the Greek ὑπωπιάζω, the literal sense of which is "I give a black eye to," and hence "I bruise."

[79] Phil. 3.13.

[80] Cf. Phil. 4.13.

[81] 1 Cor. 9.24.

[82] Cf. 1 Cor. 12.25.

[83] Ps. 64.12.

[84] Gal. 5.17.

[85] Prov. 27.6.

[86] There is a hiatus in the text here. I translate Sacchini's suggested reading: *unde victoria sit, ubi Christus cum spiritu* . . .

[87] Cf. Matt. 5.40.

[88] Bar. 3.36, 38.

[89] Ps. 45.11.

[90] Gen. 1.1; Exod. 3.2; Ps. 105.21 f.

[91] Cf. Matt. 15.8.

[92] Paulinus here has in mind the argument for God's existence *ex consensu gentium,* an argument popular especially with the Stoics; cf. Cicero, *De natura deorum* 2.5. The argument from design which follows next is likewise a common Stoic argument; cf. Cicero, *De natura deorum* 2.15 ff.

[93] Ps. 18.2.

[94] Rom. 1.20.

[95] I read *talia* for the *et alia* of the MSS and Hartel.

[96] Ps. 18.3.

[97] Cf. 1 Cor. 1.18.

[98] 1 Cor. 1.21.

[99] Cf. Matt. 13.44.

[100] Cf. Matt. 13.46.

[101] Ps. 103.25.

[102] Cf. 1 Cor. 4.5.

[103] Matt. 19.21.

[104] 1 John 2.6.

[105] 1 Pet. 2.22 f. Cf. also Isa. 53.9.

[106] Matt. 5.17.

[107] Matt. 5.20.

[108] Cf. Matt. 5.22.

[109] Cf. Matt. 5.28.

[110] Cf. Rom. 2.29.

[111] Cf. Col. 3.10.

[112] Cf. Rom. 13.14; 1 Cor. 11.7.

[113] 2 Cor. 5.21.

[114] 2 Cor. 7.5.

[115] Cf. Rom. 11.20.

[116] 1 Cor. 1.27; Ps. 8.3 (where the Vulgate has *ultor*, not *defensor;* but Severus, *Vita s. Martini* 7, also has *defensor* in quoting this Psalm, so it must have appeared in a pre-Vulgate version, the meaning being that the devil is *inimicus boni et defensor mali*).

[117] 2 Cor. 13.4.

[118] Rom. 1.24.

[119] Cf. Gen. 14.14 ff.

[120] On the symbolic meaning of the four kings, compare Ambrose, *De Abraham* 2.7.41 (ML 14.497). Ambrose says that the five conquered kings are the five senses, and the four conquering kings are the enticements of the body and of the world. Our senses yield to these enemies as the five kings yielded to the four. Paulinus, perhaps reproducing this from memory, appears to have confused the symbolism somewhat.

[121] T was the regular abbreviation in Greek for 300, the approximate number in Abraham's force (cf. Gen. 14.14). Paulinus may have borrowed the conceit from Ambrose, *De fide* prol. 3 (ML 16.551).

[122] Cf. Gen. 6.15. The description of the Church as ark, sailing over the billows of the world, is a favourite figure of Paulinus; cf., e.g., Letter 49.10.

[123] Ps. 16.7.

[124] Cf. Ps. 45.10, 23.8.

[125] John 16.33.

LETTER 25

[1] Though there is no superscription to this letter, it is clear from internal evidence that it was sent to the same soldier as was Letter 25* (cf. § 1 of that letter). Since Victor was Paulinus' informant about this soldier, Crispinianus, and since Victor arrived at Nola for the first time in 400, this letter cannot be dated earlier than that year. It is reasonable to assume (with Reinelt 36) that Victor told Paulinus of this former army comrade during that first visit. Hence 400 is a likely date for this letter.

[2] 1 Cor. 7.31.

[3] Matt. 10.37 f.; Luke 14.27.

[4] Prov. 10.2. The Vulgate reads: "Treasures of wickedness shall profit nothing. . . ."

[5] Cf. Soph. 1.11.

[6] Luke 6.24 f.

[7] James 4.4.

[8] Matt. 6.24.

[9] Honorius, who succeeded as emperor in the West in 395 at the age of ten, was a Christian who continued Theodosius' policy of discouraging paganism.

[10] John 1.3; Apoc. 17.14; Ps. 134.6.

[11] Eccli. 31.5; Prov. 11.27.

[12] Eccli. 31.6 (LXX).

[13] Luke 12.15.

[14] Eccli. 5.8 f.

[15] Matt. 11.12.

[16] In the fourth century, the most important part of the soldiers' pay was the donative of five solidi and a pound of silver made to each man at the accession of the emperor, and a further yearly donative of five solidi thereafter. There were also other donatives on commemorative days. All this money had to be raised by levy from the province in which each army was stationed. Cf. Jones 2.624 ff., 435 ff.

[17] Matt. 11.12.

[18] Cf. Apoc. 1.6, 20.6.

[19] Isa. 40.6 ff.

[20] Ps. 83.2.

[21] 1 Cor. 7.29 ff.

[22] 1 Cor. 7.27.

[23] Cf. Eph. 5.32.

[24] 1 Cor. 7.26.

[25] 1 Cor. 7.32.

[26] 1 Cor. 7.28.

[27] The comment is autobiographical. Paulinus and Therasia did not have a child for many years, and when a son was at last born to them, he died when eight days old (cf. Paulinus' *Carm.* 31).

[28] For *satis* of the MSS and Hartel, I read *versatus*.

[29] This exaggerated account of the miseries of the married state, previously a motif popular in Roman satire, is characteristic of some fourth-century Christian writing. It reaches perhaps its most extreme formulation in Jerome's *Adversus Jovinianum* (cf.,

e.g., 1.7 of that work), to which Augustine replied with the more balanced *De bono coniugali*.

³⁰ *comes Christi*. The *comes rei militaris* (on which, cf. n. 29 to Letter 18 [= ACW 35.249]; also Jones 3.20) was the commanding officer of the provincial army; Crispinianus is urged to abandon worldly aspirations.

³¹ The rank of *protector* indicated preferment, because on attaining it the soldier joined the elite corps of staff officers who received their commissions personally from the emperor. Cf. Jones 2.366 ff.

³² That is, to the emperor. God will be Crispinianus' protector as Crispinianus hopes to be the emperor's. In origin the office of *protector* was concerned with guarding the emperor's person; the full title was *protector divini lateris*.

LETTER 25*

¹ This letter does not appear in the earlier editions of Paulinus. On its discovery amongst the correspondence of Jerome, cf. C. P. Caspari, *Tidskr. f.d. evang. luth. Kirke* 10.2.225 ff., 10.3.379 ff. The relationship of this letter with Letter 25 is shown by the content of the letters. Letter 25, written perhaps in 400, was delivered by Victor. When the courier returned to Nola (in the following year?) without a reply (cf. § 1 of this letter), Paulinus wrote this second letter. A probable date, therefore, is 401, or shortly after.

² Lev. 19.18.

³ Prov. 16.8. I retain *iusto*, the reading of the MS, against the *iustum* of Hartel.

⁴ Matt. 16.26.

⁵ Cf. Matt. 22.21.

⁶ Matt. 6.24.

⁷ Cf. Luke 16.19 ff. Paulinus, in this discussion of Dives and Lazarus, follows closely his earlier commentary on this parable in his Letter 13.17 (= ACW 35.133) to Pammachius.

⁸ The word in Latin is *rabies;* there is a pun here on the dog's disease.

⁹ Ps. 6.6.

[10] Ps. 52.6. I read, with the Vulgate, *non invocaverunt;* Hartel has *invocaverunt.*

[11] Prov. 19.17.

[12] Prov. 14.31.

[13] Luke 16.25.

[14] Matt. 5.5.

[15] Luke 6.25.

[16] Ps. 125.5.

[17] Eccle. 7.3.

[18] Ps. 1.1.

[19] Ps. 125.6.

[20] Gal. 6.8.

LETTER 26

[1] This letter provides us with our sole information about Sebastianus; cf. Fabre *Paulin* 181 ff. It provides a glimpse into that eremitic practice in the tradition of St. Antony of which we know little in Gaul before the time of Cassian. This letter cannot be dated with any precision, but the fact that Victor had informed Paulinus about the vocation of Sebastianus (cf. § 1) means that it cannot have been written before 400 (cf. above, n. 1 to Letter 25).

[2] Acts 9.15.

[3] Ps. 54.8.

[4] Cf. 4 Kings 6.2 ff. Does the phrase "beyond a rushing stream" describe the actual retreat of Sebastianus, or is this merely a literary evocation of the haunt of Elias, who dwelt by "the torrent of Carith" (3 Kings 17.3)?

[5] Cf. 3 Kings 17.10; 4 Kings 4.8.

[6] Cf. Gen. 8.11.

[7] Ps. 67.7.

[8] Matt. 26.41.

[9] Matt. 4.4.

[10] 2 Cor. 8.14.

[11] Cf. Rom. 14.6; 1 Cor. 5.8; Ps. 135.25.

[12] Ps. 42.4.

[13] Ps. 140.10.

[14] Gal. 6.2.
[15] Rom. 8.15.

LETTER 27

[1] While there is no evidence which securely dates this letter, Fabre *Chron.* 45 argues from the pattern of the letters to Severus that this letter fits into the sequence most easily in 401 or 402. Such a dating would accord with the movements of both parties of couriers who were in Nola when this letter was composed. Posthumianus and Theridius have made their return from Gaul (cf. n. 3 to Letter 16 [= ACW 35.244]), and Sorianus will likewise have returned from Gaul. Sorianus' earlier visit to Nola was probably in 399 (cf. n. 1 to Letter 22 [= ACW 35.255 f.]).

[2] Ps. 33.2 and 102.2, 10.

[3] They are mentioned as couriers to Jovius in Letter 16.1 (= ACW 35.151).

[4] Sorianus is praised by Paulinus in Letter 22.1 (= ACW 35.197).

[5] 1 Kings 2.1.

[6] Ps. 12.5.

[7] Cf. Rom. 13.8.

[8] These couriers referred to are Posthumianus and Theridius, since they had brought the first letter now being answered. Severus must have pressed them to stay at Primuliacum, but they pleaded their prior obligation to Nola.

[9] Ps. 125.6.

[10] On Martin and Clarus, cf. n. 80 to Letter 11 (= ACW 35.233) and n. 24 to Letter 23.

[11] Ps. 22.5.

[12] Ps. 102.1.

[13] This is a most interesting passage. The *pueri* here referred to are not Severus' natural sons, nor are they members of the monastic community, since Paulinus laments the absence of their like at Nola. It would seem that these *pueri* formed a small monastic school at Primuliacum, the first of which we have evidence in Gaul.

[14] Ps. 125.1.

[15] Ps. 67.29.

LETTER 28

[1] This letter contains the information (§ 3) that Victor is now a regular courier, staying the winters in Nola and the summers in Primuliacum. Victor arrived in Nola for the first time in 400; that was the occasion of Paulinus' enthusiastic praise of him in Letter 23. In the present letter, Paulinus indicates that instead of arriving at Nola in autumn, Victor arrived at the end of winter and stayed till after Easter; hence the date of this letter is at the earliest 402. Now Letter 32, sent in 403 or 404 (cf. below, n. 1 to Letter 32) begins with the statement that Paulinus had just enclosed some verses with a letter; as § 6 of this present letter promises to enclose Paulinus' *Natalicia*, we may assume that Letters 28 and 32 were sent by the same courier.

[2] On Victor, cf. above, n. 22 to Letter 23.

[3] Gen. 3.19.

[4] Prov. 15.19.

[5] Prov. 26.13.

[6] Ps. 90.6.

[7] Ps. 90.12; Gen. 49.17.

[8] Eph. 6.15.

[9] Isa. 52.7.

[10] Eph. 2.14.

[11] Luke 12.49.

[12] Deut. 4.24.

[13] 1 Cor. 3.13.

[14] Ps. 142.10.

[15] Ps. 121.3.

[16] Ps. 47.3, 9.

[17] 1 Cor. 3.11; Ps. 60.4.

[18] John 10.7, 14.6.

[19] Ps. 47.15.

[20] Ps. 22.2.

[21] Luke 14.15.

[22] Phil. 3.20.

[23] Ps. 73.14.

[24] John 1.12; Phil. 2.9.

[25] Matt. 5.14; Ps. 86.1.

[26] Ps. 86.5; Prov. 9.1.

[27] 2 Cor. 5.1.

[28] Ps. 65.12.

[29] The courier mentioned in Letters 16.1 (= ACW 35.151) and 27.1.

[30] The agreement was that Victor should stay the winter in Nola and the summer in Primuliacum, travelling in spring and autumn.

[31] Cf. Apoc. 3.16.

[32] Cf. Prov. 10.19.

[33] Paulinus means that he had always been more attracted to the classical poets and orators. His lack of interest in historical analysis is reflected in his own discussions of historical events. Cf. my remarks on this in the Introduction in ACW 35.10 f.

[34] This work, the *Chronicle* of Severus, has survived; it is a sacred history of the world down to 400 A.D.

[35] Rufinus (c. 345–411), a regular correspondent of Paulinus, is a figure of great importance in Western Christianity because he translated Greek patristic treatises for the increasingly Greek-less West; cf. P. Courcelle, *Les lettres grecques en occident de Macrobe à Cassiodore* (Paris 1943) 130 ff. Cf. in general F. X. Murphy, *Rufinus of Aquileia, His Life and Works* (Washington, D.C. 1945); G. Bardy in DTC 14.153 ff.; J. N. D. Kelly in ACW 20 (1955) *passim*.

[36] On Melania, cf. below, n. 22 to Letter 29.

[37] These are the *Natalicia*, poems addressed to St. Felix, the patron of the monastery at Nola. Paulinus, as he states here, wrote a poem every year to celebrate the anniversary of Felix's death on January 14. Fifteen of these, one for every year between 395 and 409, have survived. I assume that Paulinus sent an anthology of these poems; Fabre (*Chron.* 43 n. 3) believes that only a single poem was sent.

[38] Ps. 49.14.

[39] This was probably Severus Sanctus Endelechius, a Roman rhetorician and poet; cf. Rosweyde at ML 61.870.

[40] This panegyric of Theodosius the Great (379–395 A.D.) has not survived; Jerome praises the work as *prudenter ornateque compositum*. For a recent assessment of Theodosius ("a pious, not to say fanatical, Christian"), cf. Jones 1.165 ff.

LETTER 29

[1] The first sentence of this letter refers back to Letter 23.46 f., and shows that Letters 23 and 29 were sent at the same time. It has already been pointed out (cf. above, n. 1 to Letter 23) that the probable date of composition is 400. This further letter seems to have been added by Paulinus to inform Severus of the visit of Melania to Nola.

[2] On cloaks of camel's hair, cf n. 4 to Letter 22 (= ACW 35.256).

[3] Cf. 4 Kings 1.8; Matt. 3.4.

[4] Ps. 131.1, 50.19, 68.11 ff.

[5] Cf. Gen. 3.7.

[6] Cf. Ezech. 16.7.

[7] Ps. 118.101.

[8] Matt. 19.24.

[9] The disciples of Christ.

[10] Cf. Luke 18.23.

[11] Cf. Matt. 7.14.

[12] Eccli. 35.21.

[13] For the use of thorns to fasten up clothing, cf. Virgil *Aeneid* 3.594; Tacitus, *Germania* 17.

[14] Cf. Luke 13.8.

[15] Cf. Job 2.8.

[16] Ps. 112.7.

[17] Cf. Prov. 16.5.

[18] Ps. 30.6, 35.10.

[19] Ps. 36.23.

[20] Ps. 142.2.

[21] Cf. Jonas 3.4–10.

[22] The elder Melania (the masculine form Melanius is used as a tribute to her virile Christianity; cf. Goldschmidt 105) was a Spanish noblewoman widowed in her early twenties. She went on pilgrimage to Egypt, and protected there with her immense prestige the monks who were enduring the Arian persecution. From there she went to Jerusalem, where she established a convent. Cf. the article by W. Ensslin in RE 15.415; Palladius, *Hist. Laus.* 46 and 54 (= ACW 34 [1965] 123 ff. and 134 ff.); F. X. Murphy,

"Melania the elder, a biographical note," *Traditio* (1947) 59 ff.; T. C. Lawler in ACW 33 (1963) 191.

²³ The passage suggests that Paulinus and Melania were relatives (so Lebrun in ML 61.15). Since Paulinus' wife Therasia was a Spaniard, the kinship may have been through her.

²⁴ Since this letter was written in 400, Melania's departure for Jerusalem was on this evidence in 375. But the phrase of Paulinus, *post quinque lustra*, is intentionally vague, and the testimony of Palladius (*Hist. Laus.* 46.5) that she was away for twenty-seven years is to be preferred. C. Butler, *The Lausiac History of Palladius* 2 (Cambridge 1904) 277, accordingly dates her departure in 373; F. X. Murphy, *art. cit.* 66, suggests 372.

²⁵ This was the *Vita s. Martini;* cf. n. 80 to Letter 11 (= ACW 35.233).

²⁶ Roman rhetorical historians usually began their biographies with mention of their hero's antecedents; cf. e.g., Tacitus, *Agricola* 4.1. As so often, Paulinus is stressing his emancipation from classical literature.

²⁷ Luke 1.5. Cf. 1 Par. 24.10.

²⁸ Luke 1.5.

²⁹ Matt. 11.10.

³⁰ Cf. Matt. 11.9.

³¹ Cf. John 1.6.

³² Cf. Matt. 1.1 ff.; Luke 3.23 ff.

³³ These differences (Matthew draws the lineage through Solomon to David, Luke through Nathan) were seized on by the Manichees; cf. J. J. O'Meara, *The Young Augustine* (London 1954) 68.

³⁴ On Antonius Marcellinus, who was consul in 341, cf. W. Ensslin in RE 14.1442. Jerome (*Chron. ann. Abr.* 2390) calls him Melania's father, but Rufinus' evidence that he was her grandfather is to be preferred.

³⁵ Her husband was Valerius Maximus, probably *praefectus urbis* under Julian in 361–3. Cf. the late Cardinal Rampolla's *Santa Melania Giuniore, senatrice romana* (Documenti contemporanei et note, Rome 1905) 111 ff.; D. Gorce, *Vie de sainte Mélanie* (SC 90, Paris 1962) 24.

³⁶ This was Valerius Publicola, born in 365 and later *praetor urbanus*. He married Caeionia Albina and was the father of the

younger Melania. His death is mourned in a later letter (45.2) of Paulinus to Augustine.

[37] Deut. 32.39.

[38] Cf. Acts 9.8.

[39] John 9.4.

[40] Heb. 12.6.

[41] Melania arranged for a tutor to supervise her son (cf. Palladius, *Hist. Laus.* 46). He was eight years old.

[42] Cf. 1 Kings 1.11.

[43] Cf. 1 Kings 2.21.

[44] Luke 1.49.

[45] Cf. Gen. 22.

[46] Cf. Exod. 12.3.

[47] For detail of the persecution waged by Valens in the east between 371 and his death in 378, cf. Jones 1.151 ff.

[48] Are these the five thousand monks of Nitria? Cf. Jones 2.930.

[49] Cf. Matt. 14.21.

[50] Cf. 3 Kings 18.4.

[51] Nola lies twenty miles east of Naples.

[52] The plural is used to denote her son Publicola and his wife Albina.

[53] Since the younger Melania had married Valerius Pinianus in 397–8, the plural may refer to the married couple. Palladius, *Hist. Laus.* 54.6 (= ACW 34.135), states that the younger Melania had a brother, but it is doubtful if he survived; cf. D. Gorce, *Vie de sainte Mélanie* (SC 90, Paris 1962) 33 ff.

[54] The Appian Way actually ran from Rome to Capua and then to Beneventum; the Via Poplilia joined Nola to this road.

[55] Cf. Luke 1.53.

[56] This passage provides interesting evidence of congregational singing at vigils. Augustine, *Conf.* 9.15, mentions that this had been introduced at Milan by Ambrose in 386 on the pattern of monastic practice in the East, where Basil had initiated it about 372. Cf. Paulinus, *Carm.* 23.111 and 27.556 (CSEL 30.198, 287); also J. Quasten, *Musik und Gesang in den Kulten der heidnischen Antike und christlichen Frühzeit* (Münster i. w. 1930) 242-5. On the early practice of vigils, cf. A. Baumstark-O. Heiming, *Nocturna Laus: Typen frühchristlicher Vigilienfeier und ihr Fortleben vor allem im römischen und monastischen Ritus* (Liturgiegeschichtliche Quellen und Forschungen 32, Münster 1957).

[57] A poetic way of describing Melania's return from Jerusalem to Rome; cf. Letter 47.1.

[58] Ps. 119.5.

[59] Ps. 136.1.

[60] Ps. 1.3.

[61] On Nicetas, bishop of Remesiana (in Dacia Mediterranea, an area thoroughly Romanised by 400), cf. the biography by A. E. Burn (Cambridge 1905). Nicetas is famed as the probable author of the *Te Deum*. Cf. G. Morin, RB (1894) 49; C. Mohrmann, *Études sur le latin des chrétiens* 1 (Rome 1961) 161 f. Paulinus, *Carm.* 17, hymns him as evangeliser of Dacia. Burn suggests that the purpose of his visit to Italy was to report on the movement of the Goths under Alaric, and on problems of Church discipline in Dacia.

[62] 2 Tim. 1.18.

LETTER 30

[1] Letters 30, 31, and 32, all written to Severus, form a cohesive group written within a brief period, for all are concerned with the new building at Primuliacum. Letter 32 (cf. below, n. 1 to that letter) can be attributed to 403 or 404, the year of the dedication of the new basilica. The present letter answers Severus' request for a portrait of Paulinus; it is clear from Letter 32.2 that this was required so that the portrait of Paulinus could adorn the new basilica. Paulinus takes up the subject in Letter 32.2, which shows that the present letter has not long preceded Letter 32. Hence the suggestion of a date of 402 or 403 (Fabre *Chron.* 40 f.) cannot be far off.

[2] Acts 26.24.

[3] The next few sentences, down to "That ancestral venom . . . remains in me," are quoted verbatim in Augustine, *Ep.* 186.40, written in 417. That was a joint letter written by Augustine and Alypius to warn Paulinus of the dangers of Pelagianism. They quoted these words of Paulinus on the descent of Adam's sin to all men in order to remind him of his earlier admirable statement of Christian orthodoxy. Cf. Fabre *Paulin* 89.

[4] Gal. 5.17.

[5] Gen. 3.6.

[6] Gen. 3.7.

[7] John 9.39.

[8] Luke 19.10.

[9] Ps. 111.4.

[10] Deut. 32.39.

[11] Luke 2.34.

[12] John 9.39.

[13] Deut. 32.39.

[14] Col. 2.14 f.

[15] Cf. Eph. 2.6.

[16] Col. 3.9; Ps. 102.5.

[17] Ps. 76.11.

[18] Eph. 4.24, 22.

[19] Cf. Ps. 72.20.

[20] *Civitas circumstantiae* is an older and more literal translation than the Vulgate's *civitas munita* of *polis perioches* (Ps. 30.22).

[21] Ps. 72.26.

[22] Ps. 72.26.

[23] Luke 2.34.

[24] 2 Cor. 4.16.

[25] 2 Cor. 12.10.

[26] 2 Cor. 3.3.

[27] I read *artificis* (Lebrun) for the *artis* of the MSS and of Hartel's edition.

LETTER 31

[1] This letter was written shortly before the dedication of the basilica at Primuliacum (cf. § 1), and after the visit of Melania to Nola (also § 1). Melania's visit was in 400 (cf. above, n. 1 to Letter 29), and the dedication was in 403 or 404 (cf. below, n. 1 to Letter 32). This letter was probably sent in 402 or 403; Fabre *Chron.* 40 confidently ascribes it to 403.

[2] Primuliacum is the modern Prémillac in the Perigord; cf. E. Babut, *Revue Historique* (1915) 146.

[3] The basilica at Fundi; cf. Letter 32.17.

[4] Cf. Letter 29.6 ff.

[5] Bishop John of Jerusalem, intimate friend of Rufinus and Melania during their years in his diocese, is chiefly remembered

as an apologist of Origen, and for his conflict with Jerome in the Origen controversy. Cf. Cavallera 1.393 ff.

[6] On Bassula, mother-in-law of Severus, cf. Letter 5.6 (= ACW 35.57).

[7] Eph. 4.13.

[8] Matt. 27.51.

[9] Matt. 27.51.

[10] Cf. Rom. 8.17.

[11] For other ancient accounts of the finding of the Holy Cross, cf. Ambrose, *De obitu Theod.* 46 (ML 16.399); Rufinus, *Hist. eccl.* 1.17 (ML 21.475); Socrates, *Hist. eccl.* 1.17 (MG 67.117); Sozomenes, *Hist. eccl.* 2.1 (MG 67.929); Theodoret, *Hist. eccl.* (MG 82.959). The information recounted here by Paulinus is reproduced, with rhetorical additions, by Severus in his *Chronicle* 2.33 f. That *Chronicle* must accordingly have been published after this letter.

[12] Punctuating: *Quid ergo? Nunc quaeritur.* . . .

[13] On Hadrian's building on Mount Calvary, cf. L.-H. Vincent, *Jerusalem, Recherches de topographie, d'archéologie, et d'histoire* 2 (Paris 1922) 1–38.

[14] These statements may have been taken from Jerome's *Ep.* 58.3 to Paulinus, for Jerome likewise refers to the statue of Jupiter (*in loco resurrectionis*) and the shrine of Adonis at Bethlehem. For the dating of that letter by Jerome in 394–6, cf. J. Labourt, *Saint Jérôme: Lettres* 3 (Paris 1953) 235. It is nowadays regarded as certain that Hadrian's policy, in establishing a shrine of Jupiter on the site of the Temple, was anti-Jewish; with Christianity the emperor was more lenient. Cf. Th. Mommsen, *Provinces of the Roman Empire* 2 (London 1909) 223 ff.

[15] Cf. Matt. 22.32.

[16] Isa. 1.3.

[17] The yearly feast of Adonis commemorated Venus' love for him and his death whilst hunting.

[18] On Helena's building at Jerusalem, cf. Eusebius, *Vita Constantini,* 25–43, 51–4. Helena set out to Palestine in 326, and built churches at Bethlehem, Golgotha, and the Mount of Olives.

[19] Acts 1.9; Eph. 4.8.

[20] Ps. 131.7. This statement about the open nature of the site of the Ascension is echoed by Paulinus' contemporaries Jerome and Severus, and by such later descriptions of the Holy Places as

Bede's *De locis sanctis* 7. Cf. the texts assembled by Rosweyde at ML 61.876.

[21] Ambrose, Rufinus, and others record a different tradition that a woman was restored to health on this occasion. On the historicity of the whole episode, cf. J. Leclercq in DACL 3.2.3131 ff.

[22] Cf. Acts 2.27.

[23] Matt. 25.34.

[24] Cf. Luke 24.37 ff.

[25] Cf. Matt. 28.19.

LETTER 32

[1] This letter was written shortly after the dedication of the basilica at Primuliacum. So, too, was Paulinus' *Carm.* 28, and if that poem is the tenth in the series of *Natalicia*, it was composed in January 404; hence Fabre *Chron.* 40 dates this letter definitely to 404. This is too confident an ascription; §§ 7 and 8 of this letter suggest that the relic of the true cross had arrived at Primuliacum only recently, and it was sent with Letter 31. The possibility cannot be dismissed that Letters 31 and 32 were sent together. So the more cautious attribution of Letter 32 to the year 403 "but not with certainty" (Goldschmidt 17) is not to be dismissed. It is possible that *Carm.* 28 comes before *Carm.* 27 in the chronological order of the *Natalicia* (cf. the discussion in Goldschmidt 15 ff.), in which case it was written in 403. Accordingly the date of Letter 32 must be left open as either 403 or 404.

[2] Presumably the *Natalicia* mentioned by Paulinus in Letter 28.6; cf. n. 37 to that letter.

[3] See Letter 30.2.

[4] In the baptistry.

[5] 2 Cor. 6.14.

[6] Ps. 109.3.

[7] Ps. 38.2.

[8] Cf. Prov. 10.19.

[9] That is, the two basilicas and the baptistry.

[10] See n. 32 to Letter 19 (= ACW 32.251).

[11] On Clarus, see Letter 23.3.

[12] *Clarus* in Latin means "bright."

[13] Paulinus here plays on the secondary meaning of *clarus*, "renowned."

[14] Tob. 4.16.

[15] Ps. 16.4, 128.3.

[16] St. Felix.

[17] On the basilicas, cf. H. Belting, *Die Basilica der SS. Martiri in Cimitile* (Wiesbaden 1961); Goldschmidt, *op. cit.*

[18] For the modern literature on this mosaic, cf. Goldschmidt 97.

[19] Cf. Ps. 1.2.

[20] This custom of orientation of churches was adopted by Western Christendom from the East, and was the regular practice at least until the fifth century; cf. J. Leclercq, DACL 12.2.2666 s.v. "orientation." Cf. also F. J. Dölger, *Sol salutis* (2nd ed. Münster i. W. 1925) 320–336, and *Antike und Christentum* 2 (1930) 41–56.

[21] This would be a large monument, a *cella memoriae*, for which the apsidal shape would be apposite; cf. Goldschmidt 111.

[22] The three doors symbolise the Trinity.

[23] Paul was bishop of Nola, the predecessor of Paulinus. It is often assumed, on the basis of Augustine, *De civ. Dei* 1.10, that Paulinus had already become bishop before the barbarian invasion of 410. In fact, the comment of Augustine shows only that Paulinus was bishop at the time of composition of the *De civ. Dei* (about 413). Cf. below, n. 1 to Letter 49.

[24] In § 13 above.

[25] On the *secretarium*, or sacristy where the sacred hosts and vessels were kept, cf. Possidius, *Vita Augustini* 24: . . . *secretario, unde altari necessaria inferuntur.* Earlier in this letter the bishop is said to celebrate Mass there; cf. Goldschmidt 109.

[26] Fundi (Fondi) was almost halfway to Rome from Naples. It is likely that Paulinus owned this property when governor of Campania in 381 (so Fabre *Paulin* 26).

[27] On the remarkable symbolism of this picture, cf. Goldschmidt 97 f., with the literature listed there. The *Dies Irae* of Thomas of Celano comes at once to mind (*Inter oves locum praesta/ne ab haedis me sequestra/statuens in parte dextra*), and that poem was probably inspired by a representation similar to this; cf. F. J. Raby, *Christian Latin Poetry* (2nd ed. Oxford 1953) 443.

[28] What were believed to be the bodies of Saints Andrew and

Luke had been translated in 357 from Patras to Constantinople, from where relics were sent to many western churches. Nazarius, Gervasius, and Protasius were all, according to tradition, first-century martyrs buried at Milan. Relics were sent to Paulinus when Ambrose discovered their tombs; cf. Paulinus, *Carm.* 27.436; Augustine, *De civ. Dei* 22.8.

[29] Further elucidation of §§ 10–17 can be found in Goldschmidt's commentary, 93 ff.

[30] Ps. 67.20, 71.18.

[31] Ps. 113.8.

[32] Cf. 2 Cor. 3.18; 1 Cor. 13.12 f.

[33] Cf. John 14.2.

[34] Cf. Matt. 8.5; Luke 7.2. Paulinus is guilty of a lapse of memory; it was the servant of the centurion who was healed.

[35] Ps. 14.5.

[36] Matt. 9.13.

[37] Eph. 5.14.

[38] Cf. Matt. 25.40.

[39] Matt. 26.11.

[40] Luke 16.9. Cf. n. 100 to Letter 13 (= ACW 35.240 f.).

[41] Luke 16.9.

[42] 2 Cor. 8.14.

[43] Cf. 1 Cor. 9.11.

[44] Cf. Gen. 11.4 ff.

[45] Cf. Eph. 2.20.

[46] Ps. 60.4.

[47] Ps. 126.1.

[48] 2 Cor. 5.1.

[49] 1 Cor. 13.12.

[50] Cf. Exod. 26.30.

[51] Exod. 13.21; Ps. 139.8, 66.3.

[52] Ps. 41.5.

[53] Ps. 117.23.

[54] Apoc. 21.6.

[55] Ps. 80.7.

[56] I have rendered as "waste our efforts" the phrase *laterem lavare*, "to wash the colour out of bricks." The proverb is used by Terence, *Phormio* 186.

[57] Cf. Ps. 80.7.

[58] Cf. 1 Cor. 3.10; 1 Pet. 2.5.

[59] Cf. Wisd. 3.6.

[60] 3 Kings 6.7.

[61] Cf. 1 Esdr. 4.21 ff.

[62] 1 John 4.4; Rom. 16.20.

[63] Jer. 50.23.

[64] Cf. Matt. 21.12.

[65] Prov. 14.4. The Vulgate reads: ". . . , the crib is empty (*vacuum*)."

[66] Matt. 21.13.

[67] At Bethsaida. Cf. John 5.2.

[68] Ps. 102.3.

[69] Cf. John 5.8.

[70] Ps. 106.9; 2 Cor. 5.1; Ps. 117.15.

[71] 1 Thess. 4.16.

LETTER 33

[1] On Alethius, cf. the Introduction in ACW 35.7. According to the superscription of three manuscripts, Alethius was the brother of Florentius, bishop of Cahors (on whom, see Letter 42). Gregory of Tours, *Hist. franc.* 2.13, lists Alethius himself as *episcopus Cadurcensis;* hence the surmise that Alethius succeeded his brother in that see.—This letter has no content which permits exact dating. Victor had been the bearer of the letter from Alethius to which this was the reply, and § 1 of this letter shows clearly that he did not bring that letter on his first visit to Nola in 400. This reply, then, is after 400, but no further precision is possible.

[2] 2 Cor. 2.14.

[3] Cf. Matt. 12.34 f.

[4] Cf. Luke 11.5.

[5] The accepted text, *ipse tibi auctor iniuriae tuae eris diutius esurire,* is dubious. I propose and translate: *ipse tibi auctor iniuriae tuae eris, si diutius esurieris.*

[6] Cf. John 7.38.

[7] Cf. Exod. 15.25.

[8] Cf. Exod. 17.6.

[9] The rest of the letter has not survived. There is insufficient evidence to establish, as Fabre *Paulin* 186 seeks to do, that only a

few words have been lost. Nor do I see any basis for Fabre's suggestion that Paulinus is using formal language to brush off an unwelcome correspondent. On the contrary, he asks for further letters, and the tone in which he stresses their common affection for Victor is most friendly.

LETTER 34

[1] This is not strictly speaking a letter but a sermon. It appears in five manuscripts in a part of Letter 13 to Pammachius which had been attached in error to Letter 33. The superscription of one manuscript intimates that the sermon was sent to Alethius. This is a likely speculation in view of the request made by Alethius (cf. Letter 33) for an example of Paulinus' sacred eloquence. The date of composition here may, of course, be earlier than that of Letter 33, but this document would have been sent with that letter.

[2] The *gazophylacium* was sometimes a storeroom for alms (cf. Augustine, *In psalm.* 63), sometimes a chest (cf. Tertullian, *Apol.* 39). Here (§ 2) it is a table (*mensa*). Cf. Rosweyde's collection of texts at ML 61.893.

[3] Prov. 17.5.

[4] Prov. 19.7.

[5] Cf. Matt. 13.45.

[6] Gal. 2.10.

[7] 1 Tim. 6.7.

[8] 1 Cor 4.7.

[9] 1 Cor. 9.17.

[10] Cf. Matt. 25.14 ff.

[11] The corrupt reading of the manuscripts, *quam sterili fide odiosam reminiscant. Quare . . .* , can be simply amended to: *quam sterili fide otiosam rem inique antiquare.* The words *mensa* and *fides* are both used punningly. *Mensa Domini* means the alms table and simultaneously the bank of the Lord, and *fides* means credit as well as faith. These double meanings cannot be reproduced in English.

[12] Matt. 25.21; Luke 19.22.

[13] Matt. 25.29; Luke 19.26.

[14] Cf Matt. 12.42 ff.; Luke 21.2 ff.

[15] Cf. Matt. 25.35.
[16] Cf. Matt. 25.34.
[17] Cf. Matt. 19.17.
[18] Cf. Ps. 15.2.
[19] 1 Tim. 2.4.
[20] Cf. John 15.15.
[21] Cf. Matt. 11.12.
[22] Ps. 40.2.
[23] Cf. Luke 16.22 ff.
[24] John 12.35 f.
[25] Matt. 25.23; Luke 19.17.
[26] 1 Tim. 3.15.
[27] Ps. 67.6. I retain *iudicem,* "judge," from the MSS and the Vulgate against Hartel's *vindicem,* "avenger."
[28] Ps. 10.6.
[29] Rom. 13.10.
[30] Cf. 1 Cor. 10.33.
[31] Ps. 40.2.
[32] Cf. Matt. 13.8.
[33] Cf. 1 Pet. 5.8.
[34] Prov. 14.12. Cf. Prov. 16.25.
[35] Ps. 16.12.
[36] Cf. Gen. 3.18.
[37] A reminiscence of Horace, *Odes* 2.1.8.
[38] Cf. Eccli. 38.1.
[39] Matt. 24.46.

LETTER 35

[1] This and Letter 36 to Amandus are the earliest of the extant letters of Paulinus, and were sent to Bordeaux from Spain. The early date can be inferred from the content. First, these letters refer to the death of Paulinus' brother as a recent occurrence; the date of that death was probably 389 (cf. n. 3 below). Secondly, though Paulinus has by now been baptised (cf. n. 4 below), he has not finally embarked on his monastic vocation. This is clear not only from the tone of these letters, but also from Paulinus' *Carm.* 21.414 ff. Now Letters 1 and 2 were written in 395 (cf. n. 1 to Letter 1 [= ACW 35.211]); Letters 9 and 10

were written earlier than that year (cf. n. 1 to Letter 9 [= ACW 35.227]); and since these letters are earlier still, they must have been sent by 393 or earlier. It may in fact be hazarded that they were written about 390. On the addressee, Delphinus, bishop of Bordeaux, cf. the Introduction in ACW 35.4.

[2] Eccle. 3.1.

[3] It is reasonable to assume that this is the brother whose violent death precipitated Paulinus' departure to Spain in 389; cf. n. 14 to Letter 5 (= ACW 35.220).

[4] Delphinus had baptised Paulinus and his brother; cf. n. 28 to Letter 2 (= ACW 35.215).

[5] Cf. Luke 15.13.

[6] Luke 15.18.

[7] Cf. 2 Macc. 7.1.

LETTER 36

[1] On Amandus, cf. the Introduction in ACW 35.4. On the dating of this letter, cf. above, n. 1 to Letter 35; the phrase in § 2 of this letter, *ex recenti dolore fraternae divulsionis*, is a powerful argument for putting the date of composition back to 389/390.

[2] Matt. 12.35; Luke 6.45.

[3] Cf. Matt. 13.32.

[4] Cf. Matt. 13.46.

[5] Cf. Luke 24.32.

[6] Cf. Col. 4.6.

[7] Ps. 134.6.

[8] Deut. 32.22.

[9] Cf. Ps. 38.5.

[10] Cf. Ps. 101.25: *ne revoces me in dimidio dierum meorum.* The context here in Paulinus shows clearly that some verb of removing is required, and accordingly I have amended the *revolvamur* of the MSS and Hartel to *revellamur*.

[11] Cf. Ps. 72.10.

[12] 1 Cor. 14.20.

[13] Cf. Eccli. 22.13.

[14] Cf. Matt. 5.25.

[15] John 16.8.

[16] Cf. Matt. 5.25.

[17] Cf. Matt. 5.26 and 25.24 ff.
[18] 1 Tim. 4.8.
[19] Cf. Matt. 24.51.
[20] Cf. James 2.17.
[21] Cf. Eccli. 22.13.
[22] Deut. 28.44.
[23] Ps. 10.6.
[24] Matt. 22.13.
[25] Rom. 5.1.
[26] Cf. John 14.27.
[27] 1 Cor. 6.17.
[28] Eph. 2.14.
[29] Cf. 1 John 5.8.
[30] Cf. John 14.23.
[31] Matt. 25.21.

LETTER 37

[1] On Victricius, bishop of Rouen, cf. the Introduction in ACW 35.7, and also Letter 18 (= ACW 35.167–77). This second letter to Victricius is of interest for its reference to attacks on that bishop's orthodoxy. A decree of Innocent I, dated February 15, 404 (text in ML 20.469–81), which vindicates Victricius, is of service in dating this letter. The content of the letter clearly indicates that it was sent about the time of the decree, in 403/4. The *fratri*, "brother," in the superscription from a priest to a bishop (contrast the *patri*, "father," in Letter 18) would be unusual if the salutation could be definitely ascribed to Paulinus and not to a later scribe.

[2] Prov. 25.25.
[3] Candidianus is a courier not mentioned in the other letters.
[4] Cf. Ps. 16.4.
[5] Cf. Ps. 54.7, 17.34.
[6] Ps. 18.6.
[7] Ps. 18.11.
[8] Cf. Exod. 15.23 ff. The tree which Moses cast into the waters of Mara is "the wood of divine mystery" because it prefigures the cross of Christ. Cf. Tertullian, *Adv. Jud.* 13: *hoc enim lig-*

num tunc in sacramento erat, quo Moyses aquam amaram indulcavit, et nos ligno passionis Christi aquam baptismatis potantes, fide quae est in Christum reviximus.

[9] Isa. 6.5.

[10] Cf. Matt. 25.36.

[11] Matt. 9.12.

[12] Rom. 8.3.

[13] Col. 2.14; Eph. 2.16.

[14] Ps. 34.2 f.

[15] Ps. 12.5.

[16] Ps. 77.57.

[17] Ps. 67.2, 11.6, 53.7; 1 Tim. 1.15.

[18] Cf. Luke 17.10.

[19] Cf. 1 Cor. 9.18; 2 Thess. 3.8.

[20] Ps. 26.12.

[21] Matt. 5.15.

[22] Apoc. 2.1, 1.16.

[23] Cf. Eph. 6.16; Ps. 90.7.

[24] Cf. Ps. 63.4.

[25] Ps. 63.9.

[26] Cf. Ps. 26.1.

[27] Cf. 2 Tim. 1.11.

[28] 1 Cor. 2.1 f.

[29] Apoc. 1.4.

[30] Cf. Exod. 5 ff.; Matt. 18.19.

[31] John 1.3.

[32] John 1.14.

[33] Since Paulinus does not emphasise the dangers of Apollinarianism elsewhere, not even in his list of dangerous heresies in Letter 21, it is clear that he delineates its character here because Victricius has been accused of it; cf. Fabre *Paulin* 58. For the works of Apollinaris, the fourth-century bishop of Laodicea who initiated the first important heresy concerning the person of Christ, cf. H. Lietzmann, *Apollinaris von Laodicea und seine Schule* (Tübingen 1904). On Apollinaris and Apollinarianism, cf. A. Grillmeier, *Christ in Christian Tradition* (London 1965) ch. 3; H. de Riedmatten, *Studia Patristica* (1957) 208–34; R. Aigrain in DHGE 3.962 ff.; Quasten *Patr.* 3.377–83.

[34] Cf. 2 Cor. 4.17; 2 Tim. 4.8.

[35] Cf. 2 Cor. 12.9 f.

[36] 2 Cor. 6.6 ff.
[37] Phil. 1.12.
[38] Phil. 3.20.
[39] 1 Cor. 4.20.

LETTER 38

[1] On Aper, cf. the Introduction in ACW 35.9. An old friend of Paulinus, as the joking against Aper's personal appearance in this letter shows (cf. § 8), Aper had been an eminent advocate and a provincial governor before being converted to the monastic life. Cf. Lagrange 2.224; Fabre *Paulin* 190. It is uncertain whether this Aper is the same as the person of that name in the *Dialogues* of Sulpicius Severus (3.1.7; 3.5.7). Of the three letters addressed by Paulinus to Aper (38, 39, 44), Letter 38 is undoubtedly the earliest. Paulinus shows throughout that he has recently heard of Aper's retirement from secular life. Though Fabre (*Chron.* 75 ff.) attaches a tentative dating of 399/400 to this letter, this is no more than a plausible suggestion, and a firm date is impossible.

[2] Ps. 121.1.
[3] Cf. Gen. 3.19, 18.27; Eccli. 10.9.
[4] Ps. 121.2.
[5] Cf. Gen. 18.27.
[6] Ps. 127.2; Matt. 16.17.
[7] Phil. 2.10 f.
[8] Bar. 3.36.
[9] Rom. 1.3.
[10] Cf. 1 Cor. 14.20.
[11] Cf. 2 Cor. 13.3; 1 Cor. 7.40.
[12] 1 Cor. 2.1.
[13] Cf. Phil. 3.8.
[14] 1 Cor. 2.2.
[15] Cf. Col. 2.3.
[16] 1 Cor. 1.20.
[17] Cf. 1 Cor. 4.7.
[18] Cf. Matt. 11.25.
[19] John 15.18 f.
[20] John 13.16. Cf. John 15.20.
[21] Matt. 10.25.

²² Ps. 138.21 f.
²³ Matt. 5.12.
²⁴ Ps. 37.21.
²⁵ 1 Cor. 4.13, 9.
²⁶ Apoc. 1.8.
²⁷ Ps. 67.36.
²⁸ Cf. Gen. 4.8, 9.22, 12.10, 22.9, 27.25, 37.28; Exod. 2.3.
²⁹ Cf. 2 Par. 24.21.
³⁰ Cf. Acts 27.14 ff.
³¹ Cf. Isa. 53.4.
³² Ps. 50.6; Rom. 3.4.
³³ 2 Cor. 2.14. Paulinus here has *triumphat in nobis;* the Vulgate reading is *triumphat nos.*
³⁴ Phil. 2.7 f.
³⁵ John 16.33.
³⁶ 2 Par. 20.15.
³⁷ Exod. 14.14.
³⁸ Ps. 48.7.
³⁹ Isa. 42.14.
⁴⁰ Eccli. 28.28.
⁴¹ John 12.31.
⁴² Ps. 34.13 f.
⁴³ 2 Tim. 2.15; 2 Cor. 9.7.
⁴⁴ Ps. 49.17.
⁴⁵ Cf. Prov. 9.7.
⁴⁶ In ancient literary theory, oratory and literature were closely connected, oratory being the spoken and literature the written form of eloquence.
⁴⁷ Cf. 1 Cor. 1.21 ff.
⁴⁸ Gal. 6.14, 2.20; Rom. 6.4.
⁴⁹ Wisd. 5.4 f.
⁵⁰ Ps. 36.2, 143.4.
⁵¹ Cf. John 14.6.
⁵² Ps. 16.11.
⁵³ Ps. 145.7 f.
⁵⁴ Ps. 18.8.
⁵⁵ Wisd. 7.27; Eccli. 24.10.
⁵⁶ Cf. Matt. 3.7.
⁵⁷ Cf. 1 Tim. 2.4.
⁵⁸ The manuscripts and editions read: . . . *hanc beatissimam*

*inmutationem mentis ac vitae tuae non existiment errorem stulti-
tiae tuae, sed sapientiae dei esse virtutem intelligant.* But clearly
veritatem is the word to balance *errorem*, and I accordingly read
veritatem for *virtutem*.

⁵⁹ Luke 1.51 ff.

⁶⁰ This is the evidence for Aper's former exalted station. The
title *iudex* in the late fourth century meant that Aper was a provincial governor. Cf. Jones 1.499 ff.; H. Mattingly, *Roman Imperial Civilisation* (London 1957) 129.

⁶¹ Ps. 68.32.

⁶² Isa. 1.3.

⁶³ Ps. 54.7.

⁶⁴ Ps. 41.5.

⁶⁵ The name Aper means "boar" in Latin, and throughout this
section Paulinus plays on that meaning of the word.

⁶⁶ Cf. Ps. 79.14.

⁶⁷ Cf. Gen. 10.9. For Nemrod as the symbol of Satanic power,
cf. Letter 9.4 and n. 31 thereto (= ACW 35.85 and 229).

⁶⁸ Such retirement from city life was often the prelude to a
full conversion to monasticism. Cf., e.g., the description of Augustine's retirement in Possidius, *Vita Augustini* 3, and the other
passages quoted by Rosweyde at ML 61.894.

⁶⁹ Cf. 2 Thess. 3.9.

⁷⁰ 1 Cor. 15.49.

⁷¹ Cf. Luke 16.12.

⁷² Ps. 31.9.

⁷³ Rom. 6.19.

LETTER 39

¹ On Amanda, wife of Aper, and the part she played in encour-
aging Aper's monastic vocation, cf. the Introduction in ACW
35.9 and Letter 44 below. Whether the present letter was sent
before or after Letter 44 is controverted. The traditional view, to
which I incline, is that Letter 39 is the earlier; but Fabre (*Chron.*
76) demonstrates that the arguments for this order are insecure.
On the other hand, his reasons for preferring the reverse order,
based as they are on the correspondence between the references
to Paulinus' garden in Letters 44.6 and 39.4, are similarly dubious.

Accordingly his suggested dating of this letter to 401/2 has little to support it, though he is justified in assuming that it was sent within the decade 397–406.

[2] This phrase reveals that there was a regularly ordered exchange of letters each year between Aper and Paulinus; this alone suggests a date after 397 for this letter.

[3] Cf. Matt. 13.8. This sentence suggests that Aper was at an early stage in his monastic vocation. He and Amanda had renounced their marital rights, but their new life was just beginning. The promise of fruit a hundredfold "from the children of your virginity" (de prole virginea) implies that Aper, like Paulinus, hoped to found a monastic community to which others would be attracted.

[4] Cf. Gen. 1.26.

[5] Wisd. 8.1; Eccli. 7.16.

[6] Cf. Prov. 6.8, 30.25; Eccli. 11.3.

[7] Cf. Luke 13.6 ff.; John 4.35.

[8] Cf. Matt. 13.25.

[9] I punctuate: . . . et animarum discrimina variis terrarum expressit ingeniis. Ne sterilis sit caveamus. . . .

[10] Matt. 25.21.

[11] Aper had presumably likened his soul to a restricted garden. Paulinus' reference to "a half-cooked beet" echoes the Septuagint version of Isa. 51.20. Interpreters of this passage suggest that it connotes vacillation between duty and inclination. But Jerome shows that the Hebrew had been misinterpreted; cf. the note at ML 61.894.

[12] Cf. Matt. 5.13.

[13] Cf. Joel 1.4.

[14] I read: in via hac quam ingredi iussit ac praestituit.

[15] Ps. 31.8 f.

[16] John 15.1.

[17] I.e., Gethsemani. But there is nothing to connect this field with the site of the Resurrection.

[18] Joel 1.4.

[19] This division of the four principal emotions goes back to Stoic theories of psychology. The Stoics, however, posit desire (libido) and not hope as one of the four; cf., e.g., Cicero De finibus 3.35. Augustine, De civ. Dei 14.3, follows the Stoics in this classification. It is Ambrose who substitutes hope for desire

as a chief feeling, and he is followed in this by St. Thomas Aquinas (*ST* 1a2ae 25.4) who includes desire as a subdivision of hope.

LETTER 40

[1] This Amandus, as is clear from § 3, is not Paulinus' former confessor and regular correspondent, but an otherwise unknown friend of Sanctus, who knew Paulinus in their secular lives in Aquitania (cf. n. 9 below). The only information about Sanctus himself comes from this and the next letter, which is a postscript to this one and was sent with it. The date of the letters cannot be closely determined, though certain general indications suggest they were sent a number of years after the establishment of the monastery at Nola. First, Paulinus informs us that a long interval has elapsed since he had earlier written to Sanctus (§ 3). Secondly, Paulinus talks of his increasingly aged appearance (§ 6), though the same passage suggests that he has not advanced far in the life of the spirit. Thirdly, there is a reference to "a holy and most learned man" who has both read and travelled widely. This is surely Rufinus, whose presence in Italy is attested here (§ 6), which suggests a date after 397. Finally, in Letter 41.1 we read that the letters of Paulinus are already being collected for publication, and this argues for the lapse of a few years since the establishment of his monastery. We may surmise a date of 398 or later for these two letters, but no further precision is possible. Cf. Fabre *Paulin* 175.

[2] Eccle. 3.17.

[3] Exod. 3.14.

[4] Cf. Matt. 6.17.

[5] Cf. Hab. 3.17.

[6] 1 Tim. 1.5.

[7] Ps. 62.6.

[8] Eccle. 3.17.

[9] Paulinus' friendship with Sanctus thus goes back to the years before his conversion. We may assume that his friend was also an Aquitanian, or at any rate a Gaul. Note that in § 6 Paulinus speaks of Rufinus (on the identification of the "holy and most learned man" as Rufinus, cf. n. 1 above) as a person wholly un-

known to his friend. This could hardly have been the case if Sanctus had been an Italian.

[10] Ps. 36.2.
[11] Cant. 8.6.
[12] Ps. 88.49.
[13] Rom. 8.35.
[14] Ps. 20.4.
[15] Cf. Cant. 4.11.
[16] Prov. 18.19.
[17] Isa. 5.20.
[18] Ps. 32.1.
[19] Acts 8.23; Ps. 13.3.
[20] Ps. 50.19.
[21] Ezech. 36.26.
[22] Ps. 94.6.
[23] Cf. Jer. 9.1.
[24] Cf. Ps. 6.7.
[25] Ps. 37.5, 39.13.
[26] Ps. 37.6, 31.3.
[27] Ps. 68.28, 16.11, 120.1.
[28] Ps. 102.3; Rom. 7.24.
[29] 1 Cor. 15.45.
[30] Rom. 6.19.
[31] Wisd. 8.1.
[32] Eccle. 3.17, 3.3 f.
[33] 2 Cor. 6.2.
[34] Rom. 13.12.
[35] Ps. 10.3.
[36] Deut. 32.39.
[37] 1 Kings 2.6.
[38] Ps. 138.18 f.
[39] Ps. 74.8 f.
[40] Cf. Matt. 6.24.
[41] Ps. 125.5.
[42] Ps. 101.4.
[43] Ps. 102.5.
[44] Eph. 4.24.
[45] Ps. 101.7.
[46] The reading of the MSS, *ut spiritali alacritate volucres et in alta virtutum arduo fine perfecti*, is retained by Hartel. But Ros-

weyde's *pervecti* for *perfecti* is attractive in this representation of the soul by a bird. Rosweyde also suggests *ardua penna* for *arduo fine*, but an easier change is to *ardua fide*. I have translated *ardua fide pervecti*.

[47] Ps. 101.8.

[48] This will have been Rufinus (cf. n. 1 above), on whom cf. the Introduction in ACW 35.6. Cf. also n. 35 to Letter 28, and Letters 46 and 47.

[49] These attributes of the pelican are noted in other patristic commentaries on Psalm 101. For example, Augustine (ML 36. 1298) remarks: *nascitur in solitudinibus, maxime Nili fluminis in Aegypto*. And Eusebius of Caesarea in his commentary (MG 23.1255) gives full details of how the bird mounts its attacks on snakes.

[50] The observation that the *nycticorax* was not a raven but an owl is accepted by D'Arcy Thompson, *A Glossary of Greek Birds* (London 1936) 207. Both Jerome and Isidore render this Greek word in Latin as *noctua*, "night owl."

[51] Ps. 101.7.

[52] Ps. 90.13.

[53] I read, with the Codex Monacensis 26303 s. XIII and Parisinus nouv. acq. 1443 (= Cluniac. 25) s. IX–X, *pugnemus*, a word not in the other MSS here.

[54] Cf. Eph. 6.12.

[55] Ps. 101.7.

[56] I read and translate *defaecatae* (as in the Codex Monacensis and the ML text).

[57] Ps. 138.12.

[58] Ps. 101.8.

[59] Ps. 140.10.

[60] Ps. 83.4.

[61] Matt. 10.29.

[62] Phil. 2.8.

[63] Cf. Prov. 8.2 f.

[64] John 12.32.

[65] Ps. 54.7, 11.7; Phil. 3.14.

[66] Ps. 112.5; Eph. 4.8 ff.

[67] Rom. 10.15.

[68] Ps. 101.8.

[69] Matt. 24.17.

[70] Luke 9.62.
[71] Cf. Prov. 1.17, 7.23.
[72] Paulinus describes in his *Carm.* 1 how he himself participated in such bird-snaring in his earlier days in Aquitania.
[73] Ps. 10.2, 6.9.
[74] John 1.9.
[75] Ps. 48.13.
[76] Cant. 1.3.
[77] 2 Cor. 2.15.
[78] Cf. Wisd. 2.7; Ps. 115.13.
[79] Eccli. 49.1.
[80] 1 Cor. 12.11.
[81] 2 Cor. 2.14; Cant. 1.2.
[82] Phil. 3.20.
[83] Col. 3.1 f.
[84] 2 Cor. 10.3.
[85] Eph. 6.12.
[86] Rom. 13.12.
[87] Ps. 17.30.
[88] 2 Cor. 12.9.
[89] Ps. 90.5 ff.
[90] Ps. 123.7 f.
[91] Acts 4.12.
[92] Cf. Ps. 106.8, 105.47.
[93] Ps. 99.3.
[94] 1 Cor. 4.7.
[95] 1 Cor. 1.31.
[96] Matt. 19.17; John 1.16.
[97] Ps. 64.11.
[98] Cf. Isa. 1.18.
[99] Eccli. 2.7.
[100] John 14.6.
[101] Prov. 4.23.
[102] Matt. 19.21.
[103] Ps. 61.12.
[104] Matt. 10.39.
[105] Ps. 6.6.
[106] Cf. Apoc. 20.14, 21.8.
[107] 1 Cor. 15.52.
[108] Rom. 7.24.

[109] Ps. 23.8, 106.16, 71.4, 9.15.
[110] Ps. 127.5, 141.6.

LETTER 41

[1] This letter has been generally regarded as a postscript to Letter 40. In § 1, the expression *sancte pater* is probably one of Paulinus' punning salutations, for nowhere else does the adjective *sanctus* appear alone in such greetings (so Fabre *Chron.* 83 n. 6). Moreover, this letter was written to more than one addressee (cf. § 3), as was Letter 40. Again, the manuscript tradition suggests that Letters 40 and 41 were considered to be connected (cf. Hartel viii f., xx), just as the order of letters suggests that Letters 23 and 24 are connected.

[2] This remark provides interesting evidence of how the letters of Paulinus were being collected for publication even in his lifetime, and without his taking the initiative.

[3] This gift of a hymnary is particularly significant because of its probably Gallic provenance. The earliest known composer of Christian hymns in Latin was Hilary of Poitiers. Cf. A. J. Mason, "The First Latin Christian Poet," JTS 5 (1904) 413 ff.

[4] Or "holy brother"; cf. n. 1 above.

[5] Cf. Matt. 25.10. Perhaps one of the hymns in the hymnary was a versification of the parable of the ten virgins.

[6] The reference is to Onan; cf. Gen. 38.9.

[7] This symbolic interpretation of the wise and foolish virgins is traditional in the Fathers. It is as early as Origen (cf. his *In Matt. comment. ser.* 63 [MG 13.700]). But there is no mention of it in Hilary's commentary on Matthew.

[8] Jer. 9.21.

[9] Eccli. 28.28.

[10] Ps. 118.37.

[11] The text is corrupt. Rosweyde's *disquatiant*, adopted by Hartel, is dubious in form and impossible in sense. A verb like *desiderent* is required, and I have translated accordingly.

[12] Paulinus discussed the three ways of life in Letter 18.5 (= ACW 35.171 f.). Though Paulinus insists that virginity is the highest state and most pleasing to God, and though on occasion he harps on the miseries of the married state (cf. Letter 25 and

n. 29 thereto), he hymns the praises of Christian marriage in his *Carm.* 25. Cf. the Introduction in ACW 35.25.

[13] I Cor. 3.19.

[14] Rom. 8.7.

[15] Ps. 140.5; Eccle. 10.1.

[16] Cant. 1.2.

[17] This is a reference to the Virgin Birth.

[18] Cf. Prov. 10.19.

LETTER 42

[1] The newly consecrated bishop of Cahors (cf. Duchesne 2.44) is the recipient of this letter, which has no indications whatsoever by which it can be dated. Reinelt 37 suggests that it was sent with Letter 33 to the bishop's brother Alethius. But there is no evidence for this suggestion, and in any case Letter 33 can itself not be precisely dated (cf. n. 1 to that letter).

[2] Eccli. 9.15.

[3] Ps. 125.3, 20.4, 11.7.

[4] Ps. 112.2; cf. Ps. 103.31.

[5] Matt. 12.34.

[6] Cf. Matt. 4.6.

[7] Cf. Ps. 33.9.

[8] Cf. John 10.15.

[9] Cf. Isa. 53.7; John 1.29.

[10] Bar. 3.38.

[11] Cf. Num. 17.1 ff.

[12] Ps. 22.4.

[13] Cf. Isa. 7.14.

[14] 2 Cor. 8.9; Rom. 10.12; Eph. 1.23; Ps. 64.6; 1 Tim. 2.5; Phil. 2.11.

[15] Cf. Matt. 4.19.

[16] Cf. 1 Cor. 3.9.

[17] Cf. Matt. 25.40.

[18] Cf. Matt. 7.15.

[19] Cf. Ps. 118.80.

[20] Ps. 27.3.

[21] Rom. 10.10.

[22] 1 Cor. 15.49.

²³ Cf. 1 Cor. 10.4.
²⁴ Cf. Eph. 1.22, 4.15, 5.23; Col. 1.18.
²⁵ Cf. 1 Cor. 3.11.
²⁶ Cf. Apoc. 1.8.
²⁷ Cf. Exod. 17.6.
²⁸ Cf. Matt. 7.24; Luke 6.48.
²⁹ Cf. John 19.34.
³⁰ Prov. 10.19.
³¹ Cf. Job 42.7 f.

LETTER 43

¹ On Desiderius, another Aquitanian and close friend of Sulpicius Severus, cf. the Introduction in ACW 35.9. The sole evidence for dating this letter lies in the analysis of Victor's journeys.
It is tempting to invoke the similarities to the details of Letter 28,
where likewise Victor is said to have stayed a long time in Nola
because of illness, and not to have left till the summer (so Reinelt
32). But Fabre *Chron.* 51 ff. catalogues the differences. In that
earlier letter Paulinus was ill, whereas here it is Victor. In Letter
28, Victor arrives at Nola at the end of winter, whereas here it is
before winter. So this letter is not contemporaneous with Letter
28. If it is justifiable to assume that the barbarian invasions of
Gaul in 407 (cf. Jerome, *Ep.* 23; Jones 1.185) made the journey
from Italy to Gaul impossible from that year on, the only likely
date for this letter, in the context of Victor's journeys, is 406. For
further detail, cf. Fabre *Chron.* 53 ff.
² Paulinus here, as so often elsewhere, puns on his correspondent's name: *desiderantissimo Desiderio desideriorum meorum.*
³ On Victor, cf. Letter 23 and n. 22 thereto.
⁴ Paulinus journeyed annually to Rome on pilgrimage to the
shrines of Saints Peter and Paul. In earlier years he went only
for the period of their feastday on June 29; cf. Letter 17. In
later years he made the journey earlier; in Letter 45, probably
written in 408 (cf. n. 1 to that letter), he tells of going after
Easter and returning to Nola in mid-May.
⁵ The arrangement made by an earlier pact (Letter 28.3) that
Victor would winter in Nola and spend the summer at Primuliacum has clearly lapsed.

[6] Cf. James 3.11.

[7] The query of Desiderius perhaps referred to the meaning of the blessings of individual patriarchs. Paulinus later put the question to Rufinus, and received the *Benedictions* by way of reply (cf. Letter 46).

[8] Wisd. 1.4.

[9] I.e., Jacob. Cf. Gen. 49.

[10] Eph. 1.23; Col. 1.19; Apoc. 1.8.

[11] Cf. Matt. 5.8.

[12] Cf. Matt. 21.19.

[13] Mark 11.13. Origen, in his *Commentary on Matthew* 16.29 (MG 13.1469), had already remarked on this difference.

[14] 1 Cor. 9.9.

[15] Cf. Matt. 3.12; Luke 3.17; Matt. 13.30.

[16] John 1.11. Origen (MG 13.1460) likewise describes the fig tree in its barrenness as a type of the synagogue.

[17] Cf. Matt. 27.34; Ps. 68.22.

[18] Cf. Matt. 27.29.

[19] Cf. Ps. 68.22.

[20] Cf. John 15.1.

[21] Ps. 68.23; Deut. 32.33.

[22] Cf. Isa. 5.7.

[23] Rom. 9.29.

[24] 1 John 2.18.

[25] Cf. Luke 13.7 ff.

[26] Cf. Luke 12.40.

[27] Eph. 4.26.

[28] Ps. 43.22.

[29] The echoes of Origen (MG 13.1464 ff.) are strong in this citation of the cursing of the fig tree to emphasise the need for the soul to bear fruit for God.

LETTER 44

[1] On Aper and Amanda, cf. the initial notes to Letters 38 and 39. As explained in n. 1 to Letter 39, Letter 44 cannot be given a firm date. It could not have been written before 396, because it incorporates verbatim some comments made by Augustine in a letter received by Paulinus in that year (cf. n. 1 to Letter 7

[= ACW 35.224 f.] and n. 2 below). The barbarian invasion of Gaul in 407 (see n. 1 to Letter 43) makes it unlikely that any letters were sent from Italy to Gaul after that date. Within these limits of 396 and 407, the letter has been variously attributed to 397 (Reinelt), 400/401 (Fabre), and 406 (Lebrun). Fabre puts forward the parallel content of Letters 29.3 and 44.7 as an argument that both were composed within a short time of each other, but this is a dubious claim.

2 Amusingly enough, after this depreciating assessment of his own literary abilities, Paulinus in §§ 2 and 3 incorporates into his letter without acknowledgment sections of Augustine's *Ep.* 27. Augustine in his letter had praised the roles of both Paulinus and Therasia; these comments are now directed to Aper and Amanda.

3 Cf. Deut. 32.13; 1 Cor. 10.4.

4 Cf. 1 Cor. 3.12.

5 Cf. Ps. 1.3.

6 Ps. 11.7.

7 Cf. Ps. 50.14.

8 Ps. 68.30.

9 Cf. Eccli. 13.12, 31.12 ff.

10 Cf. Prov. 19.17; Luke 14.14.

11 Ps. 64.11, 51.10, 91.13.

12 Ps. 118.162.

13 The whole of this section, from "that letter of goodly hope," is taken verbatim from Augustine, *Ep.* 27.3.

14 Ps. 136.9.

15 Cf. Ps. 91.13. Here again Augustine's words (*Ep.* 27.2) are reproduced.

16 Cf. n. 122 to Letter 24.

17 Cf. Matt. 8.26.

18 Ps. 83.4.

19 Matt. 8.20.

20 Cf. Gen. 2.23. The praise of Amanda here is taken over from Augustine.

21 Cf. Eph. 5.23 ff.

22 Ps. 71.18; Eph. 2.14 f.

23 Cf. Ps. 22.3.

24 Cf. 2 Cor. 5.16.

25 Ps. 76.11, 65.6.

26 Cf. Luke 1.28. This section of the letter reveals Paulinus'

attitude toward a wife who did not join her husband in his monastic vocation. Aper and Amanda had several children (§ 6: *numerosae animae*), and because of their family responsibilities they retained their property. Paulinus wholly approved of this, and he regarded Amanda's administration of their possessions as a wholly Christian vocation, since it had the aim of fostering Aper's spiritual welfare.

[27] Cf. Matt. 7.24.
[28] Ps. 60.4.
[29] 1 Tim. 4.8.
[30] Ps. 83.11.
[31] Cf. 2 Tim. 2.4.
[32] Cf. Gen. 2.18.
[33] Prov. 31.19, 17, 27, 14.
[34] Matt. 22.21.
[35] Rom. 13.7; Prov. 31.20.
[36] Prov. 31.11 f.
[37] Ps. 126.5.
[38] Prov. 31.23.
[39] Cf. Prov. 31.21: "All her domestics are clothed in double garments."
[40] Cf. Prov. 31.22.
[41] Cf. Prov. 12.4.
[42] Cf. 1 Cor. 11.3.
[43] Cf. Matt. 24.18.
[44] Prov. 31.31, 23.
[45] Ps. 125.7.
[46] Ps. 113.14.
[47] Cf. Eccli. 3.11.
[48] Ps. 127.3, 90.7, 127.3.
[49] Cf. Ps. 102.5.
[50] Cf. 4 Kings 6.2.
[51] Cf. Lev. 10.1 ff.
[52] Cf. Lev. 10.6.
[53] Luke 12.49.
[54] Cf. Luke 24.32.
[55] Cf. Dan. 3.50 f.
[56] Cf. Matt. 18.20.
[57] Cf. Luke 16.3.
[58] Cf. Ps. 106.35.

[59] Cf. Exod. 17.6.

[60] Cf. Judges 6.37. The fleece of Gideon is "mystical" because God's sprinkling it with dew was regarded by the Fathers as a prefiguration of the miracle of Mary's conception of Christ by the Holy Spirit. Cf. n. 25 to Letter 19 (= ACW 35.251).

[61] Cf. Cant. 4.16.

[62] Cf. Luke 13.6 ff.

[63] Cf. Heb. 7.25.

[64] Rom. 4.17.

[65] Ps. 64.13.

[66] Paulinus has developed the image of the bag of dung representing humility in Letter 29.3.

[67] Ps. 112.7.

LETTER 45

[1] Although Paulinus and Augustine corresponded regularly (cf. § 1 of this letter: *saepe alias per munera epistularum tuarum*), this third surviving letter from Paulinus was written more than a decade after Letters 4 and 7, which were composed in 395/6. Two factors help to date this letter. First, Augustine's reply to it (*Ep.* 95) was brought to Italy by Possidius, bishop of Calama. The purpose of Possidius' visit to Rome was to remonstrate about the violence used against his flock following the fresh legislation suppressing pagan cults. The law in question, promulgated at Rome in 407, was applied in Africa in June 408 (cf. Goldbacher in CSEL 58.27). If Augustine's reply was carried to Nola late in that year, Paulinus' letter was presumably written earlier in 408. The second feature which assists dating is in Paulinus' letter. He writes that he journeyed to Rome after Easter (§ 1) and returned to Nola before May 14th (§ 8). Since the double journey of almost three hundred miles took almost a fortnight, and since Paulinus seems to have been in Rome for several days before hearing of Quintus' presence (§ 1), this must have been in a year in which Easter fell early. In 408 Easter Sunday was on March 29th. This letter can, therefore, be securely dated, with Reinelt and Fabre, to May 15, 408.

[2] Ps. 118.105.

[3] Cf. Apoc. 3.18.

[4] Augustine in a later letter (*Ep.* 149, written in 414) calls him *compresbyter.*

[5] Cf. above, n. 4 to Letter 43.

[6] Cf. Gen. 8.21.

[7] About ninety miles from Rome, and sixty from Nola.

[8] Cf. 2 Cor. 13.3.

[9] Ps. 55.11, 90.5.

[10] On Melania and her son Valerius Publicola, cf. Letter 29 and nn. 22 and 36 to that letter. Paulinus had already lamented Publicola's death in an earlier letter to Augustine now lost (cf. the reference in § 3 of this letter). Publicola must, therefore, have died in early 407 or even in 406.

[11] Publicola died in his early forties; he had "attained a high degree of education and character, made a good marriage, and became great by worldly standards" (Palladius, *Hist. Laus.* 54.3 [= ACW 34.134]).

[12] Cf. Matt. 11.29.

[13] Ps. 36.37; Matt. 5.4; Ps. 114.9.

[14] Rom. 12.16; Ps. 36.26.

[15] Ps. 111.2, 46.10.

[16] Paulinus thinks not only of Publicola's mother, but also of Publicola's daughter, the younger Melania, and her husband. They had already in 408 renounced their marital rights and were living a devout Christian life. Cf. D. Gorce, *Vie de sainte Mélanie* (SC 90, Paris 1962) 40 ff.

[17] Ps. 111.2.

[18] Cf. Rom. 11.16.

[19] Cf. Isa. 6.5.

[20] This is the characteristic orientation of the letters of Paulinus. Though in this epistle he tries to answer Augustine's speculative question, he more regularly addresses himself to the practical issues of how to live his life by the canons of Scripture.

[21] Cf. Col. 3.16.

[22] Cf. Ps. 45.5.

[23] Cant. 8.6.

[24] Col. 2.20.

[25] Cf. Col. 3.5.

[26] Cf. 1 Thess. 4.3.

[27] Cf. 2 Cor. 5.15.

[28] Cf. 2 Cor. 1.22.

[29] Ps. 38.8.

[30] Cf. Phil. 3.21.

[31] Cf. 1 Thess. 4.16.

[32] John 17.24.

[33] Ps. 83.5.

[34] Cf. 1 Cor. 15.35 ff. For a survey of early Christian expositions of the resurrection of the dead, cf. A. Michel, "L'enseignement de la tradition," DTC 13.2520 ff.

[35] Cf. 2 Cor. 12.4.

[36] Ps. 64.14.

[37] Ps. 36.11.

[38] Cf. Apoc. 5.6 ff.

[39] Isa. 6.3. The whole sentence echoes the conclusion of the Preface of the Mass. The prayer was already firmly established in the Eastern liturgy earlier in the fourth century; cf., e.g., Cyril of Jerusalem, *Myst. cat.* 5.5 f. On the development of the Preface, cf. J. A. Jungmann, *The Mass of the Roman Rite* 2 (New York 1955) 115 ff.

[40] Augustine in his reply stated that he was impressed with Paulinus' insistence that we should concentrate our efforts on the Christian life in this world; so he devoted only a brief section (*Ep.* 95.7 f.) to the question of life in heaven.

[41] 1 Cor. 13.1.

[42] Cf. 1 Cor. 12.10, 28.

[43] Cf. James 3.5.

[44] Since Paulinus read the letter from Augustine at Formiae on the way back from Rome (cf. § 1 above), Quintus must have called at Nola on his return journey to Hippo in order to collect Paulinus' reply.

LETTER 46

[1] This letter and the next, both addressed to Rufinus, are not in the manuscript collections of Paulinus' letters, but precede the *Benedictions* of Rufinus in two Vienna manuscripts (cf. Simonetti's edition in CCL 20). But the suggestion (e.g., in Reinelt 45 ff.) that the ascription of the two letters to Paulinus is not

soundly based has little validity; cf. the comments in Fabre *Chron.* 88 ff.

The difficulty of dating the letters is considerable. The *Benedictions* were written at Pinetum in Lent (Rufinus himself states this in the Preface to the second book), but the year is not specified. Rufinus returned to Italy from Jerusalem in 397 and retired to Aquileia between 398 and about 407, when he returned southwards. The *Benedictions* were, then, composed either in 398 or almost a decade later. This letter of Paulinus could therefore have been written in 397/8 or about 406/7. Fabre rejects the earlier dating, because he assumes that Paulinus' request to Rufinus was prompted by an enquiry from Desiderius (cf. Letter 43.3 and n. 7 thereto) sent after 400. Fabre's assumption is plausible but not certain. More cogent is the argument in the following note in favour of the later date.

² The reading, *vos in aestu sollicitudinis et incerto morarum Romam pati indicastis*, has been queried as dubious Latin (e.g., in Fabre *Chron.* 94), but there is a similar usage in Letter 8.3: . . . *quisquis Romam sponte miser patitur.* . . . This passage can, therefore, be taken as good evidence that Rufinus and his companions (*vos*) were at Rome when this letter was written. The phrase *in aestu sollicitudinis* is more apposite to the critical period shortly before the investment of Rome by Alaric in 408 than to a date ten years earlier; and the plural *vos* (contrast *tu* and *tuus* elsewhere in the letter) may well refer to the younger Melania and Pinian who later accompanied Rufinus to Sicily. The letter was brought from Rufinus to Paulinus by "the servant of the sons we share." These *filii* could well be Pinian and Melania. Cf. further n. 1 to Letter 47.

³ The use of *vos* and *vestrae* indicates that Rufinus' companions are included in the invitation to Nola.

⁴ Rosweyde (ML 61.897) suggests that Paulinus is trying to translate the *Recognitions*, a work allegedly addressed to the Apostle James at Jerusalem by Clement of Rome. Rufinus himself translated this spurious work (cf. ML 1.1207 ff.). Cf. F. X. Murphy, *Rufinus of Aquileia, His Life and Works* (Washington, D.C. 1945) 112 f.; Quasten *Patr.* 1.61 ff.

⁵ Cf. Matt. 15.27.

⁶ The whole of this passage is of the greatest interest for the insight it provides into Paulinus' knowledge of Greek, and this

in turn helps to determine the provenance of the direct influences on his thought. As has been demonstrated in the Introduction in ACW 35.20, Paulinus certainly learnt Greek at school in Aquitania. But this passage shows how rusty his knowledge of it had become, suggesting that he had not systematically read the language for years. The direct influences on his writings must accordingly be sought amongst the Latin interpreters of the Greek Fathers, and Ambrose is especially important here.

⁷ Gen. 49.

⁸ Cf. Luke 11.5 ff.

⁹ Gen. 49.11. Rufinus, *De ben. patr.* 1.2 ff., explains that the reading of the Septuagint, τῇ ἕλικι, was misunderstood in the pre-Vulgate translation followed by Paulinus, which rendered *ad cilicium*, "to the goat-hair covering." Jerome rightly rendered *ad vitem*, "to the vine."

¹⁰ Rufinus, *De ben. patr.* 1.8, suggests that Christ is the vine, Gentile Christians are "his foal," and the Jews who are converted to Christ are the foal of the ass, which itself represents the Jewish people.

LETTER 47

¹ The beginning of this letter shows that Rufinus had been in Rome according to Paulinus' latest intelligence, but that he was expected to depart at any time. Later in § 1 Paulinus reveals that his friend is making for the East (*remeaturus ad orientem*). This is a further indication that Letters 46 and 47 are to be dated after Rufinus' return from Aquileia; and § 2 suggests that the present letter was written only a few months after Letter 46. Rufinus died in Sicily in 411; though the date of his departure from Rome is uncertain, it is probable that he quitted the capital with the younger Melania when Alaric's threat to Rome was intensified in 408. This letter may be most probably dated to that year. Fabre *Chron.* 95 suggests 408 or 409.

² *ad sanctum Petrum.* Paulinus may be using the phrase as a personification of Christian Rome. But more probably Rufinus, as a distinguished cleric, was a guest of Pope Innocent I.

³ Rom. 8.28.

⁴ Ps. 106.9.

[5] Paulinus used this expression earlier for Rome in Letter 29.13.

[6] Rom. 1.28.

[7] Cf. Luke 11.5.

[8] Cf. above, n. 10 to Letter 46.

[9] This is probably a reference to Desiderius. Cf. Letter 43.3 and n. 7 thereto.

[10] Referring to Paulinus' disposal of his riches and his espousal of the monastic life.

LETTER 48

[1] This fragment of a letter is found in Gregory of Tours, *Hist. franc.* 2.13, where it is ascribed *tout court* to "Paulinus." It is, therefore, uncertain whether Paulinus of Nola wrote it. The only close evidence for dating is the listing of Amandus amongst the Gallic bishops; Amandus became bishop of Bordeaux between 401 and 404, so this letter must have been written in 401 or later (cf. n. 4 below). This is confirmed by mention of Alethius as bishop of Cahors; Alethius was still a priest when Letter 33 was sent, but that letter, though after 400, cannot be closely dated (cf. n. 6 below).

[2] On Exuperius, cf. Duchesne 1.307. Pope Innocent I wrote to him in 405, and Jerome (cf. his *Ep.* 125.20) was also acquainted with him.

[3] Simplicius was bishop before the Council of Turin, that is, by 400 A.D. (so Duchesne 1.205).

[4] This is the confessor and regular correspondent of Paulinus. He succeeded Delphinus in the see of Bordeaux. Paulinus' last extant letters addressed to Delphinus (Letters 19, 20, 21) can be confidently ascribed to late 400 or early 401 (cf. n. 1 to Letter 20 [= ACW 35.252]), and Delphinus had died by 404 (cf. Paulinus' *Carm.* 19.154; this is the eleventh in the series of *Natalicia* and was written in January 405). Amandus must have been consecrated bishop between 401 and 404.

[5] Nothing further is known of Diogenianus, Dynamius, or Venerandus. Cf. Duchesne 2.42, 68, 34.

[6] On Alethius, cf. Letter 33 and n. 1 thereto.

[7] Pegasius is not otherwise known (so Duchesne 2.87).

LETTER 49

[1] This letter is preserved in but a single manuscript, which is, however, the earliest of the codices of Paulinus' letters. The superscription "Macario Paulinus" is written in by a second hand. If the name of the addressee was indeed Macarius, he may have been the Christian official (*praefectorum vicarius*) who prevailed on Rufinus to translate the *De principiis* of Origen, and also the man to whom Paulinus addressed a lost *Consolatio* (cf. Augustine, *Ep.* 259.1). The sole indication of the date of this letter is that Paulinus was bishop of Nola when he wrote it (§ 14: *pastor exigui gregis*). Since Paulinus was not greeted by Augustine as bishop in 408 (cf. Augustine's *Ep.* 95; for the date, cf. above, n. 1 to Letter 45) but is so termed in Augustine's *De civ. Dei* 1.10 and *Ep.* 149 (in about 413 and 414/6 respectively; cf. Goldbacher in CSEL 58.40), he must have become bishop within the period 409–413, and this letter must be after 409.

[2] Tob. 12.7.

[3] John 5.17.

[4] Cf. Acts 1.3.

[5] Or, perhaps, "not waiting for the usual sailing-season." One wonders if this anxiety to replenish the imperial granaries during winter was occasioned by the investment of Rome by Alaric in the successive campaign seasons of 408, 409, and 410.

[6] Or, perhaps, "The Sandbanks" (*ad pulvinos*).

[7] Merchantships towed their boats astern, from where they could be hoisted up. Cf. Acts 27.37; also C. Torr, *Ancient Ships* (Cambridge 1895) 103.

[8] I cannot translate the *renovatis ancoris* of the editions. The MS has *renotatis*. I propose *renatis* or *renatatis*, and translate accordingly.

[9] Ancient merchantships had several anchors; cf., e.g., Acts 27.39.

[10] A reminiscence of Virgil, *Aeneid* 3.193.

[11] Ps. 41.4.

[12] Paulinus' description of the removal of the mast suggests that Juvenal, *Sat.* 12.53 f., was in his mind. This satire celebrates the glad day on which Juvenal's friend reached safety after shipwreck, so that the reminiscence is apposite.

[13] The *artemo* was "something between a foremast and a bow-sprit with a spritsail on a spritsail yard" (C. Torr, *op. cit.* 88).

[14] Cf. Rom. 6.6. The whole of this description evokes the passage in Acts 27 where Paul is visited by an angel and gives strength to the centurion and soldiers guarding him on the ship. In Acts, too, the crew launches the boat on the pretext of dropping anchor; there, too, the tackle is thrown overboard; and there is the same play on the words *incidere* and *excidere* in the Latin version of Acts 27.32 as in § 2 of this letter.

[15] Cf. Apoc. 1.14.

[16] The phrase literally means "at the poles." Steering on merchantships was by two projecting poles; hence the phrase is appropriate for denoting the rudder.

[17] I.e., St. Felix or Christ Himself.

[18] John 17.22 f.

[19] Matt. 28.20.

[20] Cf. Mark 16.19.

[21] Matt. 22.32; Mark 12.27.

[22] John 6.41; Ps. 135.25.

[23] 1 Tim. 2.4.

[24] Wisd. 1.13.

[25] Matt. 9.13.

[26] Cf. Matt. 22.16; Mark 12.14; Ps. 74.8.

[27] Cf. Ps. 10.5.

[28] Ps. 33.7.

[29] Ps. 68.2 f., 16.

[30] Ps. 78.8.

[31] Ps. 68.3, 16.

[32] Ps. 24.16, 101.7 f.

[33] Ps. 29.11, 33.8.

[34] Cf. Ps. 106.29.

[35] Ps. 105.9, 106.29.

[36] Ps. 106.24.

[37] Ps. 80.17.

[38] Cf. Matt. 5.3 ff.

[39] Phil. 2.8.

[40] Cf. Matt. 26.41.

[41] Ps. 12.4.

[42] Ps. 12.5.

[43] Matt. 26.41.

[44] Matt. 26.45.

[45] John 16.33.

[46] Eph. 2.14.

[47] Ps. 71.18; Rom. 4.17.

[48] Cf. Gen. 7.14 ff.

[49] The emperors Claudius and Trajan had built artificial harbours at Ostia, fifteen miles from Rome, and around them the separate township of Portus gradually arose. Cf. R. Meiggs, *Roman Ostia* (Oxford 1960), ch. 8. In the Claudian harbour stood a famous lighthouse modelled on the Alexandrian *pharos;* cf. Suetonius, *Claudius* 20.3.

[50] Cf. n. 88 below.

[51] In classical mythology (cf. Hyginus, *Fab.* 14; Cicero, *Aratus* 126) the Argo after its expedition in search of the Golden Fleece became a constellation.

[52] Aesculapius, or Asclepius, the god of healing whose shrine was at Epidaurus, was conveyed to Rome in the form of a snake by sea in 293 B.C. The Sibylline books had commanded that a plague be averted by this means. Paulinus represents the snake here as a manifestation of Satan.

[53] Cf. Gen. 6.14 ff.; Jon. 1.3; Acts 27.2 ff. Paulinus punningly connects the ship in which Paul of Tarsus was wrecked with that in which Jonas was making for Tharsis. In fact Josephus, *Jewish Antiquities* 1.6.1, wrongly identified Tharsis with Tarsus. On Tharsis, cf. P. Antin, *S. Jérôme, Sur Jonas* (SC 43, Paris 1956) 58 n. 4.

[54] In Jon. 1.7 the ship's company cast lots to discover why God afflicted them.

[55] Cf. Acts 27.24.

[56] I propose and translate *tussiens singultibus* for the *iussis singultibus* of the MS and Hartel.

[57] The Fathers often depict Jonas as the symbol of Christ, and his three days in the whale as prefiguring the three days in the sepulchre. Cf. Jerome, *In Ionam prol.:* . . . *qui typus est Salvatoris et tribus diebus ac noctibus in ventre ceti moratus praefiguravit Domini resurrectionem.* . . .

[58] Acts 9.15.

[59] The waters here are the waters of baptism.

[60] I propose and translate here: *et portus salutis ecclesia, et*

teste Graecia nomen est Roma virtutis. Rhome in Greek means strength.

[61] Ps. 112.5, 146.10 f. Where the older Latin version used here by Paulinus has *tabernaculis*, "tents," the Vulgate has *tibiis*, "legs." The difference may have arisen from the similarity in Greek of σκηναῖς and κνήμαις.

[62] Ps. 146.3.

[63] It should be remembered that Paulinus was writing to a friend who is both a Christian and a prominent Roman administrator.

[64] "Sardinian idiot" in the previous sentence is a free rendering of *mastruca Sardorum*, which literally means "a Sardinian sheepskin."

[65] Cf. 4 Kings 2.8, etc. (The Septuagint rendered the Hebrew word for mantle with μηλωτή, "sheepskin"); Matt. 3.4; Mark 1.6.

[66] I read *quanto eorum . . . quanto eorum . . . quanto eorum* for the *quantorum . . . quantorum . . . quantorum* of previous editors.

[67] Cf. Gen. 32.30; Num. 12.8; John 13.23.

[68] Cf. Gen. 17.5, 32.28; Mark 3.16; Acts 13.9.

[69] Eph. 6.12.

[70] Ps. 129.6.

[71] Rom. 11.29, 3.20.

[72] Cf. Rom. 4.5, 9.

[73] Cf. Matt. 3.9.

[74] 2 Cor. 6.2.

[75] Ps. 50.19.

[76] Cf. 2 Cor. 6.16.

[77] Ps. 50.19.

[78] Eph. 5.2.

[79] Cf. 1 Cor. 14.20.

[80] Cf. John 5.24. For Hartel's *per quem (fluctus) vitae* I read *per quem vita e(st)*.

[81] 2 Cor. 2.15.

[82] Exod. 23.15, 34.18.

[83] Paulinus was now bishop at Nola; cf. n. 1 above.

[84] Ps. 131.7.

[85] For Hartel's *hortus (orantis) magistri,* I read *hortus traditi*. The balance of the sentence demands such a participle.

[86] The *procurator* of a distant estate had at the time of the bar-

barian invasions often uncontrolled power. He sometimes leagued with pirates, and even mortgaged his master's property. Cf. S. Dill, *Roman Society in the Last Century of the Western Empire* (2nd ed. London 1899) 268.

[87] Perhaps this is the Rufus Praetextatus Postumianus who was *praefectus urbis* twice. Cf. Jones 2.558; W. Ensslin in RE 22. 1.890 f.

[88] Earlier, in § 8, Paulinus stated that the ship ran aground in Lucania, thus specifying the province; here he more specifically details the site as the southwestern promontory of Italy.

[89] I retain *piraticam* with the MS.

[90] Cf. Exod. 13.15.

LETTER 50

[1] As has been shown above in n. 1 to Letter 45, Paulinus' Letter 45 to Augustine and Augustine's answering *Ep.* 95 can be dated to 408. The next letters that passed between Paulinus and Augustine are lost. Paulinus raised (perhaps in 409) "a second question" about the resurrection of the body; an answer was sent by Augustine during the winter (possibly the winter of 409/410; cf. § 14 of the present letter). After the loss of other letters from Augustine (cf. n. 66 below), Paulinus sent the present letter. The date was 410 at the earliest. Augustine at once replied, but the letter again failed to reach Nola. So Paulinus again wrote, and Augustine answered with his *Ep.* 149 (§ 2: . . . *quas ipse continuo rescripsi, sicut his tuis recentioribus comperi, non sunt redditae Venerationi tuae*). Since *Ep.* 149 of Augustine cannot be later than 416 (cf. Goldbacher in CSEL 58.39 f.), Paulinus' Letter 50 cannot have been written after 415. Within the period 410–415, Fabre *Chron.* 74 inclines to 413; the loss of a number of letters certainly makes a date later than 410 likely.

[2] Cf. Ps. 118.18.

[3] Ps. 15.3 f.

[4] Cf. Rom. 9.7.

[5] Cf. Phil. 3.19.

[6] Rom. 7.6; Gal. 6.15.

[7] Apoc. 21.4 f.

[8] Matt. 9.13.

[9] Cf. Rom. 2.23.
[10] Matt. 3.9; Luke 3.8.
[11] Cf. Luke 18.11.
[12] Cf. Ps. 52.6.
[13] Ps. 52.6; cf. Ps. 50.19.
[14] 1 Pet. 5.5. Cf. Prov. 3.34.
[15] Isa. 66.2.
[16] Rom. 10.3.
[17] Cf. Rom. 4.2 f.
[18] Rom. 1.17.
[19] Rom. 8.4.
[20] Phil. 3.20.
[21] Rom. 2.28 f.
[22] Ps. 15.3.
[23] Ps. 102.7.
[24] Cf. John 9.16; Matt. 12.24.
[25] Ps. 15.4.
[26] Ps. 15.4.
[27] Cf. Acts 2.37.
[28] Cf. John 8.12; Mal. 4.2.
[29] Matt. 23.32.
[30] John 14.6.
[31] Ps. 16.14. Regarding the variant readings cited by Paulinus, note that the Septuagint version may read either υἱῶν, "sons," or ὑειῶν, "swine." Augustine commented on this verse in his *Ep.* 149.5 to Paulinus. In his *Enarr. in ps.* 16.14 (= ACW 29.165), Augustine says "the two readings are due to the ambiguity of the Greek original."
[32] Ps. 58.8.
[33] Ps. 58.12.
[34] Luke 23.34.
[35] Cf. Gen. 22.17.
[36] Cf. Rom. 10.4.
[37] Cf. Apoc. 7.4 ff.
[38] Apoc. 14.4.
[39] Ps. 67.22.
[40] Isa. 1.5 f.
[41] Ps. 67.24.
[42] Cf. Matt. 15.26.
[43] Cf. Matt. 24.51; Tit. 1.16.

[44] Eph. 4.11 f.
[45] Cf. Acts 11.28, 21.11.
[46] 1 Tim. 2.1.
[47] Rom. 11.28.
[48] 1 Tim. 2.4.
[49] Ps. 138.21 f.
[50] Ps. 138.17.
[51] Cf. Ezech. 14.14 ff.
[52] Col. 2.18 f.
[53] Matt. 15.14.
[54] Jer. 2.13.
[55] Col. 2.21 ff.
[56] 2 Tim. 3.5.
[57] Rom. 14.23.
[58] Cf. Rom. 8.7.
[59] Ps. 93.11.
[60] 2 Cor. 11.15.
[61] 1 Cor. 9.27.
[62] 1 Thess. 4.4.
[63] Rom. 12.1.
[64] I assume, with Rosweyde and Fabre, that *exhiemarem* (retained by Hartel) cannot be right, and I render *exhiemares*. The error may have arisen from a scribe's misunderstanding of Augustine's *Ep.* 149.2: *epistulae quam tuae caritati apud Carthaginem de corporum resurrectione rescripseram*, where it is the writer who is at Carthage. Cf. the full discussion in Fabre *Chron.* 72 n. 5.

[65] This comment is a clear indication that Augustine kept copies of his letters with a view to their publication. Paulinus did not do this; cf. the Introduction in ACW 35.2 f.

[66] This indicates that a number of Augustine's letters have gone astray, doubtless because of the hazards in Italy following the barbarian invasions.

[67] Cf. John 20.14; Luke 24.16, 37.
[68] Cf. Luke 24.30 f.
[69] John 20.17.
[70] Luke 24.5.
[71] Luke 2.34 f.
[72] Ps. 104.18.
[73] Cf. Gen. 37.28, 39.20.
[74] John 19.26.

[75] *framea vel gladius.* The word *framea* could also mean "sword," the meaning of *gladius;* Paulinus may here be quoting alternative renderings of the Greek.

[76] Ps. 7.10.

[77] 1 Cor. 4.5.

[78] Eph. 6.17.

[79] Heb. 4.12.

[80] Ps. 104.19.

[81] Luke 12.49.

[82] Matt. 10.34.

[83] Cf. Ps. 66.2.

LETTER 51

[1] On Eucher (Eucherius) and Galla, cf. the Introduction in ACW 35.9; also A. C. Cooper-Marsdin, *The History of the Islands of the Lerins* (Cambridge 1913). Eucher's writings are collected in ML 50.685 ff.; cf. C. Wotke's edition in CSEL 31 (Vienna 1894). After entering monastic life at Lérins, Eucher about 434 became bishop of Lyon.

This is the latest of the extant letters of Paulinus. It was written when Eucher had been at Lérins for at least a year; he retired there shortly after 420 (cf. Reinelt 54; Fabre *Chron.* 88: "vers 422"). Honoratus was still a priest when the letter was sent (§ 1: *compresbyter*), and as he became bishop of Arles in 426, the letter was composed before or during that year. Hence the dating of 423/6 proposed by Reinelt and approved by Fabre can be accepted.

[2] The life of Honoratus, founder of Lérins in 410 and subsequently bishop of Arles, is recounted in the *sermo* of Hilary of Arles in ML 50.1249 ff.; cf. the edition by S. Cavallin (Lund 1952).

[3] In § 2 of this letter Paulinus mentions that Eucher also had sent members of his community to Nola.

[4] These two islands (now Ste. Marguérite and St. Honorat, off Cannes) are together known as Lérins. On this monastic settlement, in which amongst others Hilary of Arles, Patrick, and Caesarius were monks, cf. H. Leclercq in DACL 8.2596 ff.

[5] The reading of the MSS, *brevi interiecta maris rupe,* though

accepted by editors, is impossible. I propose and translate: *brevi interiecto maris euripo* (cf. the description in Cooper-Marsdin, *op. cit.*: "The narrow channel of the Frioul divides them").

[6] 1 Cor. 4.20.
[7] Cf. Phil. 1.8.
[8] Ps. 127.4 f.
[9] Ps. 125.5.
[10] Ps. 22.6.

INDEXES

I. OLD AND NEW TESTAMENT

2. AUTHORS

3. GENERAL INDEX

Aaron, 107; sons of, 241

Abdias, 114

Abel, 187

Abia, 106 f.

Abraham, bosom of, 2, 81, 167, 271; perfect in the Law, 52; father of Jews, 276 f., 281; sees Christ, 44; Christ in, 187; hospitality of, 43 f.; offers Isaac, 111 f.; condemns Dives, 83; his victory over kings, 72

Absalom, 22

ad temones, 261

Adam, 15, 28, 188, 205, 311; sinned through being deceived, 47; temporary punishment of, 47; image, not likeness, of God, 58; made naked, 101 f.; infected human race, 120; old and new, 138

Adonis, 128, 328

Aesculapius, 360

Africa, 265

Agabus, 282

agriculture, imagery from, 2, 196 ff.

Alaric, 326, 355 f., 358

Albi, 257

Albina, *see* Caeionia

Alethius, bishop of Cahors, 160, 257, 332, 347, 357

alien fire, meaning of, 241

alms table, 162

Alypius, 326

Amanda, wife of Aper, 196, 234, 340, 349 f.; attends to secular business, 237 ff., 350 f.

Amandus, confessor of Paulinus, letter to, 174 ff., 335; becomes bishop, 257, 352

Amandus, companion of Sanctus, 202 ff., 342

Ambrose, St., sends relics to Paulinus, 151, 331; introduces singing at vigils, 325; his influence on Paulinus' letters, 356

ancestry indicating merit, 107

Andrew, St., relic of, 150, 330 f.

angels, pure spirit, 250; speech of, 251; after Resurrection, 288; in Col. 2.18, 284; aid Valgius, 261; wicked, tempters of women, 28, 307

anger, dangers of, 232

Angoulême, 257

Anna, and Melania, 110; and synagogue, 313

Antony, St., 319

Aper, letter to, 184 ff.; 196 ff., 234 ff., 338, 349 f.; outstanding intellectual, 192; attorney and judge, 193 f., 338, 340; his renunciation of the world, 186, 237 ff.; priesthood of, 194

Apocalypse, 261

Apollinarianism, 182, 337

Apollinaris, 181 f.

apostles, witnesses of Christ, 133; feet of, washed by Christ, 6

Appian Way, 114, 325

Aquileia, 355 f.

Aquitania, 342, 345

Argo, 360

Argonauts, 267

Arian persecution, 113, 323

ark, type of Church, 32, 72, 268, 316

Arles, 365

artemo, meaning of, 359

Ascension, site of, 129 f., 328 f.

Assyrian king (Nabuchodonosor), 22

athlete, image of, 313